HOUSE

A MEMOIR

Michael Ruhlman
HOUSE

A MEMOIR

VIKING

VIKING

Published by the Penguin Group

Penguin Group (USA) Inc., 375 Hudson Street, New York, New York 10014, U.S.A.

Penguin Group (Canada), 10 Alcorn Avenue, Toronto, Ontario, Canada M4V 3B2
(a division of Pearson Penguin Canada Inc.)

Penguin Books Ltd, 80 Strand, London WC2R 0RL, England

Penguin Ireland, 25 St. Stephen's Green, Dublin 2, Ireland (a division of Penguin Books Ltd)

Penguin Books Australia Ltd, 250 Camberwell Road, Camberwell, Victoria 3124, Australia
(a division of Pearson Australia Group Pty Ltd)

Penguin Books India Pvt Ltd, 11 Community Centre, Panchsheel Park, New Delhi–110 017, India

Penguin Group (NZ), Cnr Airborne and Rosedale Roads, Albany, Auckland 1310, New Zealand
(a division of Pearson New Zealand Ltd)

Penguin Books (South Africa) (Pty) Ltd, 24 Sturdee Avenue, Rosebank, Johannesburg 2196,
South Africa

Penguin Books Ltd, Registered Offices: 80 Strand, London WC2R 0RL, England

First published in 2005 by Viking Penguin, a member of Penguin Group (USA) Inc.

10 9 8 7 6 5 4 3 2 1

Copyright © Michael Ruhlman, 2005
All rights reserved

LIBRARY OF CONGRESS CATALOGING-IN-PUBLICATION DATA
Ruhlman, Michael, 1963–
    House : a memoir / Michael Ruhlman.
        p.   cm.
    ISBN 0-670-03383-9
        1. Dwellings—Remodeling—Ohio—Cleveland—Anecdotes.   2. Ruhlman, Michael,
    1963—Anecdotes.   I. Title.
    TH4816.R84 2005
    643—dc22   2004055499

This book is printed on acid-free paper. ♾

Printed in the United States of America

Designed by Nancy Resnick

For Reynolds Price

Contents

HOUSE

A MEMOIR

1

Possession

It was our house now—I had the key in my pocket. I steered into the empty driveway for the first time; until this moment Donna and I had been visitors, and we felt as welcome as a threat. But all that was over. They were gone at last. The old brick house on the shady street was empty.

I'd seen the owner and two of her sons nearly my dad's age out front by the truck, speaking intently, maybe still arguing about the furniture, I couldn't tell. Perhaps—this was my biggest fear and the reason for spying—they were having second thoughts about leaving at all. But the last possessions were in the truck, I guessed: bags, a few last boxes, a crate of motorcycle parts. A small mountain range of refuse lay on that strip of lawn between sidewalk and street called a "tree lawn" here in leafy old suburban Cleveland Heights—unwanted and broken furniture, old lamps, half a splintered Ping-Pong table, boxes of moldering books spotted with mouse turds, and bags and bags of who-knows-what that called to mind a playwright's dictum that no problem is insolvable given a large enough plastic bag. Decades' worth of the crap a big old house can hold out of sight with ease.

Poignant scents of summer's end blew through the windows of my idling car, gold grass and drying leaves, a perfect mid-September day. I peered uneasily at the three of them there, in the front yard of the house they'd all lived in, for a time, at least, and she for most of her adult life, preparing to leave it for the last time.

Throughout the negotiating and the purchase of this house, Steve, our real estate agent, always implied that the owner continually threatened to take the house off the market, just like that. The deal always had a feeling of precariousness to it, the sense of an imminent collapse. It made Steve nervous as well. The house had been on the market for nine months with scarcely an offer. No one would touch it; it needed too much work. We knew this, knew how long the house had been on the market and had made a bid that was about 60 percent of the initial asking price. It was on the low end, but not disrespectfully low given the extraordinary amount of renovation and repair we suspected it needed. To do everything we wanted was probably more than we could afford, so a low offer was all we could make at that point.

Steve seemed desperate to be done with it, period; he'd been walking uninterested people through the crumbling monster since January. His just-below-the-surface desperation and the septuagenarian owner's wrenching decision to give up a home of forty years for considerably less cash than she thought it worth hung over negotiations like a swampy miasma, hovered there still—papers signed and money transferred—as I watched the troika in the front yard and wondered if they would ever leave, would we ever have this done?

One of the sons turned in my direction, spotting me through the leaves, and I drove off. When I returned at noon, as agreed, the third owner of a century-old suburban house was gone.

I'm not sure I believed it, was still suspicious. I could well imagine the difficulty of leaving a house you'd lived in for that long. So much life played out within a house, this one a big old brick box erected on the edge of the Victorian era, this house must embody it all, carry the memories of all that life, of all the lives lived there—couldn't have been easy to leave, and who wouldn't resent strangers offering so little for it, I suppose.

But perhaps more than the simple nostalgic forces at work was the paralyzing apprehension at giving up a house, this large physical object; suddenly you're vulnerable to the world, your protective shell abandoned, with nothing but the uncertainty of your final years somewhere else ahead of you.

Then again, who that age would desire to stay in a house so run-down that nine months of house hunters marching through it had resulted in two other offers besides ours. The neglect was on view to every potential buyer: the water stains on the ceiling whose plaster buckled precariously, holes in windowpanes covered with clear packing tape, mortar crumbling out between the exterior brickwork. Decay spread over four entire floors—up the high sides of the house, the gables, the front porch, and the separate brick garage with its leaky roof. After a while I guess a homeowner just gets tired. Maintenance slips. You patch rather than repair. Then you stop patching. Ignore anything that's not pressing. And while you grow old, the house continues to be a house. Houses and boats, they're like living things in that they require continual work and care; that's their food—ignore this fact at your own risk. If it wasn't actively dripping on the carpet, a leak didn't really need to be fixed, did it? And yet the Second Law of Thermodynamics applied especially to houses; all systems tend toward entropy, and continuous energy is required to maintain order. Stop putting energy into a house, it will fall apart.

It wasn't just the general dilapidation and neglect that lent a dark cast to this house, though, nor the hundred years of soot blown four miles east of Cleveland's industrial center to these verdant heights. Something more pervasive seemed to be at work here, causing the fights Donna and I almost invariably fell into upon leaving the place. They were nothing to speak of, just general pissiness toward each other, but their pointlessness made them all the more unnerving.

"You put the dictionary in the car?" I asked Donna, driving home from the house yesterday before we hoped to take possession, irritable, as if I had something sticky on my hands. In an effort to help the owner clear the house of objects she couldn't lift, we'd begun to carry boxes of books out to the tree lawn to be discarded. To *help* the owner. Donna found the unabridged dictionary, a gargantuan book published in 1950, *Webster's New Twentieth Century Dictionary of the English Language, Unabridged, Based Upon the Broad Foundations Laid Down by Noah Webster.*

"It's a shame to throw this away," Donna said to me. "She told us to take it. She was going to throw it out. She's going to throw out all those books."

"We were also just asked to leave. It wasn't exactly a friendly environment in there."

"Steve said she needed help. She asked us to come. We did nothing wrong."

"So why does it *feel* wrong?" I continued.

"You're the writer. I wanted it for you. You want to take it back and throw it on the tree lawn? Go ahead." Donna, my wife of more than ten years, my love, was angry but I couldn't figure out why, and this annoyed me as it did her.

"I'm not going back there," I said.

Why did we go at all? It was Wednesday, September 12, the day before the possession date, and Steve was on the phone telling us the owner wasn't ready for the walk-through. In fact, he said nervously, she didn't know if she could be out of the house at all by tomorrow. This, of course, made us anxious. "She's got no one helping her," Steve had told me.

"Obviously," I said to Donna now, pulling into our drive. "That was not a good idea."

"Then why did we do it?" she said angrily. "We shouldn't have to be doing this."

I wanted to shower, wanted a clean start to that morning. We were trying to *help*. I had no desire for those ratty old couches. All I'd said was, "Leave them here. We'll carry them out to the yard." My God, they made it sound as if we were trying to steal their furniture. The old books, same thing. I'm not going to sell them at a profit. We'd come because Steve said we could help, and anything—anything at all—we could do to ensure this transition we wanted to do, because no one knew if it was going to happen. We wanted it to be over.

"At least the dining room table and buffet were still there," Donna had said sarcastically. "I guess we should be pleasantly surprised."

We'd actually gone up in our offer, but after we'd found how much internal electrical and plumbing work the house needed, we'd entered into further negotiations. We were told that a lot of the furniture in the house wasn't needed. The owner couldn't use it, but her leaving it would help us a great deal. We'd come up in our offer provided that certain pieces of furniture were part of the purchase agreement. In addition to the dining table and buffet, there were several other items that would go a long way toward making Donna feel better about increasing our offer—especially in light of the new info on disintegrating pipes and rotting rafter tails. But the additional pieces agreed upon verbally were no longer in the house, a fact that started the arguing between Donna and Steve, whom she held responsible.

She actually got so mad at Steve, who was our old neighbor, that he hung up on her. The guy representing us hung up on her. That's how bad it got; by the end the agent supposed to be looking out for our best interests wasn't speaking to us. That was the tone of this deal.

Taking a long view of events, none of it mattered all that much, but emotions run high in a house purchase, nerves are exposed, and a bitterness escalated beyond the value of what we were bitter about. It was as if things were actually possessed by bad energy—the dictionary, for instance. I didn't want the thing, but there it was in the back of my car like a dead pet, not mine. I didn't know if it was the seller or Steve or the house itself that was doing it, the feeling it gave you. Our six-year-old daughter loathed the place, hated to be in it, as if she, like the Zen horse master, could see more purely what it was than we, in the throes of houselust, were able to. It was incomprehensible in her eyes that we would want to leave our wonderful, familiar little house for a big old run-down creepy one. I couldn't tell her how beautiful it might be, because she didn't have that in her experience. But I wondered if it were she who saw the true character of the place.

I told myself that all the ill-will that had accrued around this house purchase was an inherent buyer-seller antagonism built into the purchase of anything so substantial, costly, monumental, nostalgic, and that once the previous owners were gone, they'd take their karma with them and life would return to normal, that a breeze would clear the miasma, and the good and exciting stuff, the renovation of what had once been a grand old house, could begin.

I'd not yet been able to walk through the house freely, to imagine at leisure what it would look like when all the 1960s carpeting got hauled out (the floors would surely be hardwood, but what kind of shape would they be in?), when the wallpaper was removed and the smooth plaster became a blank canvas. I wanted to survey the sprawling third floor and imagine fully its restoration for our two young children; to imagine the handsome staircase, Gothic windows at a landing midway up, composed entirely of two-inch leaded squares, each window with a stained-glass shield-shaped crest in the center; the front hall with its fine raised paneling and the heavy mahogany pocket doors to the study and dining room. Truly it was a grand old house. I wanted to be able to take a tape measure and plan out the space for the new kitchen once the current dining room and kitchen walls were removed. And now that the previous owner had gone—*finally*—I could scarcely wait. I saw that nothing remained but a mountain of refuse on the tree lawn indicating the major clean-out of an old house.

My car's wheels crunched to a halt in the gravel drive. It was my driveway now. I could park here, I almost didn't believe it. I left the car, fishing in my pocket for the back-door key; there was no remaining key for the front, lost years ago, the owner had told us. The back door was painted a vivid red, of all colors (the second- and third-story shingles and trim were otherwise a yellow and brown); it was chipped and gashed and generally beat to hell, like most of the rest of the house. I jiggled the handle, almost didn't need a key the latch was so loose. I gripped the knob and pushed the key into our new home.

I froze for one moment, then yanked the key out as I heard footfalls pounding through the house, two sets from the sound of it, and in a hurry. I was directly beneath the spot where both main and back staircases did a U-turn. I could feel the vibration. My shins pricked and my stomach turned—it *had* been too easy, I knew something strange was going to happen. I ran to the front of the house to discover who it was trying to race out of here. *What the hell was going on?*

When I reached the yard, I saw no one, not a person, not a car in sight anywhere. I walked up the porch steps. I cupped my face to the glass in the door. I saw no movement within. I tried the handle, but the door was locked fast. I peered in all the windows. The house appeared to be empty. I returned to the back door and entered via the breakfast room, passed through the narrow kitchen and out a swinging door into the dining room, where the table and buffet remained. I stood quietly in the center of the main downstairs hallway, trying to quiet my breathing. The house was stone silent.

I began in the basement, stepping into each damp, brick-walled chamber in a layout identical to that of the first floor. I walked up the unfamiliar back staircase to the third floor. Instead of experiencing the anticipated pleasure of imagining the changes that were about to transform this neglected house, I crept through it, yanking open closet doors, expecting to confront someone. I descended to the second floor and checked each of the four bedrooms, each of their closets, a hallway closet, and the two bathrooms. Down to the first, again into each room.

Nothing, no one. I didn't stay longer.

When I arrived home, Donna was feeding lunch to J., age two, and A., six, was in her preferred spot for ruminating, beneath the dining room table. Donna looked at me with anticipation: *Did they finally leave? Is it actually ours?*

"They're gone."

Donna exhaled, and a brightness I hadn't seen all week shone from her; her blue eyes, brown hair still streaked blond from summer's sun seemed to lighten. She gave me a hug and a kiss. "Well, how is it? How does it look?"

I considered not telling her about the footsteps I'd heard, because I knew she wouldn't take it seriously, but I always told her everything, and so I told her this.

I should make it clear right away that I don't believe in ghosts. A surprising number of people do, I've since realized. I have an imagination, but my convictions and beliefs are based on evidence. I don't believe in something for which there is no evidence. And yet those footsteps had been actual. Hadn't I heard and felt them so distinctly that I immediately *ran* around to the front of the house to catch the people? But the house was locked and, I'd made certain, empty.

Donna actually looked grave. "So are you telling me the house is . . . *haunted*?"

"I'm just telling you what happened."

"We've bought a . . . *haunted house*?" She paused, laughed. "Are you serious?" She shook her head to answer for me and then carried on with business, which was keeping us organized and the kids looked after on this unusual day. "I talked to Danny at Allen Locks. He'll be up there later today. And you're meeting the architect at three. Right?"

"Right."

"Now will you have a talk with your daughter?"

I glanced into the dining room. A. on her back, with her feet pressed against the underside of the table. The female sex tends to be quite a bit more emotionally complex than the male, and my daughter added an intensity to this quality that both Donna and I found surprising in a six-year-old.

I squatted and said, "Sweetheart, what's the matter?"

"Mom says we're moving into that old house."

"You knew that. We've been talking about it."

"But I hate that house!" she cried.

"Why?"

"It's hideous!" she said desperately.

"It's old, not hideous, and we're going to fix it up."

"What about the old woman?"

"She sold us the house, and now she's gone. And it's not going to look anything like it does now. It's going to be beautiful. You're going to have a room that looks out onto beautiful trees, not a used-car lot."

"I don't want a new room."

"You're going to have a new room, I'm afraid, and I hope you like it."

"But that house is scary."

"Why is it scary?"

"It makes strange noises."

This gave me a jolt, but I said, "All houses make strange noises, especially old ones."

She seemed to be giving in, I thought. Then she said, "OK. But I want to stay here."

"Sweetheart. We've sold this house to buy the new one." She didn't seem to understand. I continued. "When we got back from Maine, remember we had a meeting with some people? Remember the man with rectangular glasses and the woman he was with, Jeremy and Michelle? They bought this house. That's what we were meeting about that day. They're going to live here."

A. has a defined chin, like her mom's, but her cheeks are still big and round and plump, as they were when she was a toddler. They flushed, and she ran up stairs and threw herself onto the bed in her cherished room.

2

Houselust

On the Fourth of July, 2001, two and a half months prior to our taking possession of the new house, I sat on our back deck, coffee mug in hand. I glanced up from the morning *New York Times* when it occurred to me that one of our cars was not in the driveway where I'd left it the night before. I stood up aggressively, as if that would set things right. When it didn't, I went inside and told Donna that our car had been stolen. She strode onto the deck, and she, too, stared at the spot where the car ought to have been.

We looked at each other without speaking: the keys.

A set of keys had been missing for days, and we'd assumed J. had thrown them behind some bureau or in the bottomless toy chest in the dining room. They'd turn up. Evidently J. had not touched the keys. They'd gone missing while the house was being painted, surly college kids tramping through to remove storm windows; the car had vanished the day after painting was completed. Also on that day, we had submitted our bid on a fine house in superb condition on Demington Road, a lovely street—we'd gritted our teeth and offered $340,000, $40,000 more than we could realistically afford—and it had been bettered substantially by a couple relocating from a big city and desperate to buy. (How could we offer $40,000 more than we could afford? What is it about houses? What were we thinking? Jesus!) The price the other couple paid was foolhardy, but it was still a blow. After that day's two defeats—stolen car, lost house—we had admitted it aloud to each other.

"OK, there it is," I said to Donna. "This is not the year. Given all that's going on—my work, our finances, and now we've got to deal with this car—we're not going to buy a house this year, and we certainly aren't going to buy a *project.*" This had been our hope, not to buy someone else's carpeting and design choices, but to buy cheap and do a lot of work to make it our own.

Donna nodded acceptance. She sat on our front steps with a consoling glass of wine at noon, having moments earlier lost the Demington house and all her visions of a domestic future in that lovely place. She looked so depressed I thought she was going to cry. The day was overcast and sultry. We didn't speak much, and there wasn't much to do other than have the house locks changed. Rain had threatened all day and, with a bit of cosmic nastiness, had held off till nine-fifteen, just before fireworks, drenching our crestfallen kids. That day was really how and when it started. I should have known then that Donna would be out Monday, her determination redoubled, to have a look at what would become our house—one she'd already *seen,* months earlier, and had at the time no intention of returning to.

Maybe it was just chance that our old-neighbor-turned-real-estate-agent called Donna and said, "Come on, it's *you,* guys—just have a look. You saw it before, but it's been on the market for a half year. The family is eager to sell. They're entertaining all offers."

Donna actually took the two flights up to my office to ask my permission to see it, "to just have a look," she said. This was a genius diplomatic maneuver in marriage politics: We had agreed definitively on the Fourth of July and had reiterated over the course of the weekend that we would stop pursuing houses; by saying, as I did, "Well, of course, you can do whatever you want"—what was I going to say? that I forbade it?—I was allowing not this one look but anything that might follow from it. By asking my permission, she had drawn me into the role of colluder—if a disastrous cascade of events was to follow, then I was a partner in those events. Had she not asked me and had the cascade followed, it would be her doing alone, and I could always resent her for going back on what we together had definitively agreed was the plan.

She waited till that evening to mention it. "It needs a lot of work," she said.

"What does?" I gave more attention to cutting the grilled chicken breast from the bone and keeping all black specks off it, or neither J. nor A. would touch it, to tossing the green beans and squeezing lemon over them, to removing from the oven the baked potatoes that I'd pre-mashed with butter and salt.

"The house," she said.

Our table, a hand-carved German antique that Donna cherished, was too big for our kitchen, so not only was synchronized dinner service an effort, but just getting it to the right spot on the table required dancelike maneuvers, A. at the kitchen-sink end, J. in a plastic booster seat backed up against the far counter. I seated myself, and all of us, J. included, lifted our glasses to one another, and I said my silent prayer of gratitude that we were all together and healthy amid such bounty. As ever, dinner was practically over before I'd had two bites, the kids having eaten almost none of their food and already begging for dessert. Between "one more bite of chicken" or "no dessert till you eat at least three beans," Donna, wicked in her smoothness, brought it up again.

"I can see why they reduced the asking price," she said.

"I'm sorry, what?"

"The work it needs. The house. I can see why no one's made an offer, why they've reduced the asking price."

"To what?" I said, feeling at last the comfort of perfectly grilled chicken and cold white wine on a summer night at home. "One piece of chicken, J.," I said, bending to retrieve his fork and set it on his world-atlas place mat. He grinned at Dad the sucker.

"Thank you, Daddy."

"You're welcome."

"Three twenty-five."

"How about that," I said. Three hundred twenty-five thousand was what we'd agreed was our highest-possible offer for the Demington house, which was in excellent, move-in condition. No matter what we'd offered in a moment of panic and want, $325,000 *plus* major renovation wasn't in the picture for us, and I continued to enjoy my summer meal. Also, as we'd already agreed, this was not the year for us.

Donna said, and here she did not actually whisper, but her tone implied one, "Steve told me they'd entertain, as he put it, '*anything north of two hundred.*'" I tried not to stutter in my actions, but this was a major price reduction from when she'd first seen it, and all the looking she'd done in the intervening six months had made vividly clear to her what a great neighborhood the house was in.

I didn't even pause, just carried on with the steaming baked potato and lemony salty beans and grunted with closed mouth. But the hook had been deftly placed. As if giving her rod a jerk to set it, she dropped all pretense and the restraint she'd struggled to maintain to say in a powerful, quiet voice, "*Michael, think of it.*"

I was already halfway through the math in my head. How much could we get for this house—$150,000 at least, and probably ten or twenty thousand more? How much then to borrow, how much renovation did it need? *Think of it*—was it possible, on that beautiful street? My God, the houses started at $400,000 there—a figure that meant something in Cleveland; our friends in suburban D.C. turn green when they see what $300,000 buys in this city. Splendid big old houses, sprawling lawns with gigantic oaks, space. A greedy sweat began to bead at my temples. On a beautiful street populated mainly by middle-aged physicians and financial guys and counsels for the city's big companies. The kids there went to private school and in summer took tennis lessons and swam at the country club. Just like that, in two or three minutes tops, I was blinded by houselust, by fantasy and self-deception.

We currently lived in a decidedly lower-rent part of Cleveland Heights, very nice, respectable, between two university professors, but on the edge, with a used-car lot and traffic-clogged Mayfield Road just beyond our backyard fence, the actual boundary between Cleveland Heights and East Cleveland, the latter among the most unfortunate areas of the city. Technically East Cleveland was a suburb, but I don't know anyone who thought of it as one; it was more accurately thought of as the kind of place where your stolen car wound up, as ours did, recovered by the police only when its driver, stoned on reefer and malt liquor, smashed it into a stop sign. I went to check it out in the baking fall heat in the ash heaps of the deep Flats, a desolate stretch of downtown Cleveland where they hauled such cars. Front end caved in, airbags deployed, trash on the floors, a cigar box filled with ashes and roaches, and, strangely, a bunch of photographs of a child's birthday party, a girl named Ashandra, according to the cake; all this was of no interest to anyone, and, as the car was deemed totaled by the insurance agent, of no interest to me either. I retrieved some of Donna's photo equipment—a light box, a light stand, a reflector—which remained in the trunk with someone's dirty T-shirt, and never saw the car again.

My daughter's window overlooked the car lot out to Mayfield and across to East Cleveland. That was her view. The new house, while only a few blocks away, would take us out of view of Mayfield and used cars, in itself a luxury, but it would also place us well above our station; we certainly had done nothing to deserve a shot at this kind of life, and yet . . . could it be? I might no longer worry about my kids playing out front on our tiny lawn while ominous rusted Chryslers rolled past, vibrating with bass notes of indecipherable songs, menacing drivers in no hurry, staring out at you. I might never again have to cringe when guests were over for dinner and I directed them to the second-floor bathroom—"Top of the stairs. Just follow the trail of bath toys and ignore the wet towels, please." Most of these Cleveland Heights homes had been built with a single bathroom on the second floor.

We could do it. I hadn't even seen the house, knew only the street, and I was already submitting purchase offers. I probably didn't even need to go there to make up my mind. Wasn't it already made up? During that careless dinner, distracted by children's voices, our new course had somehow locked irrevocably into place.

We arrived at the house the following morning, and the moment I stepped through the front door and short foyer, over the tiled floor with marble steps, into the front hall, my heart picked up its pace.

We would walk slowly through all four levels of the structure, from the hot, hot attic to the basement, regarding each room. But I knew everything from the moment I passed through the spacious vestibule and into the main hall. It was grand, this hall. I could see past the outdated décor, the worn carpeting, the heavy use. The entrance hall was about twenty feet long and eight feet wide, with the living room on one end and the dining room on the other in standard, if spacious, Colonial style and, in between, the central front room of the house, a study with triptych bay window, floor-to-ceiling shelves, and a massive pocket door that probably hadn't slid closed in ages. The staircase was five feet wide, with eight steps up to a broad landing featuring three Gothic window frames and leaded glass. The staircase here reversed direction. This allowed for a cozy space beneath the second half of the stairway in the main hall, a kind of alcove facing the front door, marked off by the staircase banister on one side, a paneled wall on the other, and more paneling overhead, rising on the underside of the staircase. A small window here looked out into the backyard, above a bench of heavy mahogany whose seat lifted up for storage space below. The alcove and stairs were framed by an elegant curved arch. Architects proclaim their ambitions for a house with the design of the entryway and the main staircase. This one was magnificent.

I didn't need to see more. I knew that its structural soundness was now the only thing that mattered. Unless the posts and timbers were rotted or devoured by carpenter ants, we could make this house great. I knew it.

"Well, guys," Steve said, "what did you think?"

We stood in the street beside our cars. Steve was a little shorter than average, carried a few extra pounds, but still looked like he could handle himself respectably on a basketball court. He had scrappy, quick, schoolyard movements. He wore fine slacks and a Hawaiian shirt. I knew he was basically honest—he looked you in the eye, his smile and laugh were natural—I mainly trusted him, though I knew he wanted to make a deal, too. He and his wife Julie, a talented pediatric anesthesiologist, had been our neighbors before they themselves had moved to grander digs. They were bright, easy people whom we considered friends.

"We like it," I said. "Donna tells me they're entertaining 'any offer north of two hundred.'"

Steve stuck his chin way out, but then said, "Yeah."

"But?"

He shrugged. "It's not going to be easy. Make an offer. It's her house, but it's too big for her, and none of her kids want to buy it. Everyone's frustrated. The house has been on the market a long time. They want to be aggressive about selling it."

"What offers have been made?"

"There have been two verbal offers," Steve explained. "One was three-twenty, shortly after it went on the market. There were a lot of contingencies, and it didn't work out. In April a couple from out of town saw it once and offered two seventy-five. They turned it down, convinced they could get more. Now it's July, the market's flat. You could get a great deal."

"You know the family," I said.

Steve nodded, said he'd known some of them growing up. "One of the kids is on death row," he added.

"Really," I said. "What for?"

"Drug-related murder. I hear it was pretty sick."

"Really." I turned and regarded the house again. "Why have there been no offers since April if there's a deal to be had?"

"No one wants to do any work. Everyone wants to move right in. Families are busy—moms and dads work; who has time to renovate a house?"

"You were a contractor, Steve. What are we looking at in terms of renovation?"

"You haven't seen the sheets of violations—big as a telephone book. I'll bring a set by this afternoon. Buyer has to take all violations on." Steve grinned and held out a palm. "That's in your favor if you're willing to do the work. Like I said, buyers today expect to move right in—no one has time for work."

"How much work?"

Steve knew we'd have to stretch. He paused a moment, looked thoughtfully up at the great oaks spread out above us, squinted, rubbed his chin.

"Electric's a big problem. It'll cost five thousand just to get it up to code, minimum. Plumbing, I don't know what kind of shape it's in, but you've seen the condition of the house—it hasn't been well taken care of. Another ten at least for plumbing repair, if you're not doing anything major. There's a lot of galvanized in there. You know you want a new kitchen—you can do it for thirty, if you're frugal and don't get greedy for designer appliances. Bath renovations, figure another twenty. Should probably put in central air if you're planning to use the third floor—I did our house for ten. Then there's general fixing up, redoing floors and walls, taking care of structural violations. Off the top of my head, just to fix it up, bring it up to code, make it nice but nothing fancy, plan on a hundred grand easy."

I trusted Steve and his guess—it sounded right to me. A hundred grand was a lot of money, but the house needed a lot of work. We could do it for a hundred, but we could certainly do less, especially if we did the painting and basic carpentry ourselves, but let's say a hundred. Donna was grinning flat out at me. She couldn't wait to get away from Steve to talk to me alone. We could go as high as $240,000 if we had to, and not have someone else's house but have the house we wanted—new kitchen, new baths, refinish the imposing front hall—all this for what we'd offered last week for a lesser structure on a lesser street.

When we were in our car, Donna looked at me, ready to laugh or cry. "Michael?" she said. I made a bug-eyed face in return. I couldn't believe it either.

What followed that little morning outing was a series of highly serious meetings between me and Donna on our back deck, mapping out a financial plan. We were very methodical about it, our enthusiasm taking on grave and somber overtones. How much did we guess we'd need to spend, how much could we offer for the house—let's be realistic now, no, *really*—how much could we get for the house we were in, and what kind of mortgage were we looking at? Not one of these critical questions was answerable, and as each unanswerable affected or was affected by another unanswerable, it's hard to say what the point of our discussions really was. Amazingly, we managed to answer each and every question, but all they meant was that we wanted to make this work pretty much no matter what. All the figures and lists and percentages on the legal pad amounted to an expression of determination, an emotion, want.

True houselust can grow only under specific conditions. It's not something one lives with and manages continually, like diabetes. It lies dormant in its victims, expressing itself as an admiration for certain kinds of domestic architecture, a windy appreciation of fine carpentry or a certain style of interior design. In order for inert houselust to bloom into the virus characterized by wanton craving, an overmastering desire for an enormous object, a hunger that supersedes all reason, one must be at a specific stage in life, a transition point. This is the catalyst.

We were at such a point. A year earlier we'd been living on Martha's Vineyard so I could work on a book based there, and we had fallen for the island and the people on it to the extent that we decided to try to live there. We'd learned of a historic restoration project that had been abandoned by its instigator: a traditional Cape Cod house from the Federal period had been dismantled piece by numbered piece, placed in an enormous shipping container, and floated over to the island. It lay locked and abandoned at a storage facility. Its preservationist owners, having found a better project they couldn't turn down, only wanted their money back, so the house, or rather the materials for the house sweating in the big metal box, were relatively inexpensive. The sticking point was finding a little bit of land on a highly desirable island at a time when the economy was still bloated from the technology bubble. Real estate was laughably inflated. One couldn't have dreamed up conditions for a worse time to buy property there; we certainly couldn't afford that nor, by the way, the labor skilled in historic restoration that the project deserved.

We returned to our house in Cleveland Heights, where I completed the Vineyard book, and after many imaginative and determined attempts to wangle some sort of creative financial arrangement, we admitted that the House-in-a-Box operation had been a pipe dream.

But the process had opened the possibility of living in the East somewhere, if not on the Vineyard, then perhaps on the coast. What about the romantic coast of Maine, now that we were thinking this way? Why, we could live anywhere. I had roots in Cleveland, but Donna didn't. She'd separated from her New York roots, the real estate of her life now comprising one house, one husband, and two children—one of which could be sold and the rest of which were portable.

It was nice to think about, but I was writing a book and hunkered down. I could work from anywhere, even Cleveland Heights, and since we did already have a house here, and since it was a family-friendly, eminently affordable city, I did nothing to change our place. Inertia took over, then gathered weight as I began another book about a surgical team at the Cleveland Clinic, a medical behemoth ten minutes from our house. With the coming of spring, Donna, sensing that we were not going anywhere, began to look at houses here. "You mind if I just run out real quick and check this out?" she'd ask on a Sunday morning when she saw a new "For Sale by Owner" listing in the paper. Nothing was serious unless we were both involved in it, so I chalked these trips up to curiosity more than anything. By this point, talk of finding a permanent house was becoming more than mere talk, but I was only about 50 percent committed to helping Donna look. We'd begun to figure how much we could offer for a house—something to decide on *before* you find the house you want, and we had. It was after one of these little Sunday excursions that Donna returned to say that I had to see a house on Demington, the house we made an offer on. Once we made our first offer, that was the moment. It was as if the houselust egg had been fertilized.

House watching was a pastime here in Cleveland Heights. Spring and summer, on foot or two wheels, touring the neighborhoods was a pleasure because of the houses. I'm sure this is true of most suburbs created before the Depression that are still alive, born during a time when most things were handmade, every house distinct, the materials excellent, the streets curved, the trees now old and tall. Early photographs of Cleveland Heights are not appealing because they show grand houses rising out of a barren landscape. But put in some tall trees and a canopy of leaves and the place becomes warm, inviting, lush, even mysterious. The imagination comes alive.

The houses here had been created largely in the first three decades of the century—spacious Tudors, humble but elegant Colonials, Gothic Revivals, Italianates, Queen Annes, Beaux Arts, quintessential bungalows, Prairie, Victorian—virtually every style of residential architecture from those decades was represented here, neighboring one another, along with a few nineteenth-century farmhouses. On a twenty-minute bike ride, you might see a sizable swath of residential architectural history, homes built with the materials that were mainly taken for granted when they were used—first-growth timber, blocks of quarried sandstone that had been hand carved. Even the bricks had a patina and warmth that distinguished them. The operative fact was that the structures built during or before the 1920s had a textural richness in their details—the mullions, the eaves, the gables—and had an integrity in their materials, none of which existed anymore. That kind of construction is unlikely to return. But these houses, they enrich the city and the people who live here by their durable presence every day in every season.

One of the main pleasures of looking at these houses—and it's something we do without realizing it or being reflective about it—what makes house watching fun is that you imagine yourself living there. Those are the ones you adore. Donna and I used to ride through the neighborhoods before we were parents, and I would imagine a life for us in this house and in that one. I worked as an editor at a local magazine but had ambitions to be a novelist, and in these houses I *was* a novelist and life was sophisticated and grand. I was F. Scott Fitzgerald writing *The Great Gatsby*. These rides to look at houses was a satisfying activity on a summer evening or a Sunday afternoon, a bit of healthy dreaming and fresh air.

Reviewing a book about the Manhattan row house, longtime city resident Judith Thurman describes the urban experience of houselust and the imagination, which scarcely differs from my own suburban variety; perhaps the desire is even more powerful in Manhattan, given the age of the city and the domestic discomfort and inconvenience that all but the wealthy endure in order to live there.

"I roamed the brownstone blocks of lower Manhattan and Brooklyn Heights," writes Thurman, "often at dusk, just as the lights came on and before the shades were drawn, peeping into the parlor windows of old houses inhabited by rich bohemians, and lusting for a saffron-yellow library with floor-to-ceiling bookshelves and a sliding ladder; a gilt pier glass with chipped gesso above an Eastlake mantel; French doors opening to a little balcony or a cobbled patio. . . . Fashions in and prices of New York real estate are, as one knows, eminently labile, but the habit of yearning for a poetic old house is so ingrained in some of us—me in particular—that I sometimes forget I have one."

Yearning for what she already has, she concludes, "I know that one should resist the impulse to anthropomorphize, but town houses have a presence and a civility missing from more monolithic forms of residential real estate, particularly high-rise apartment buildings. Those 'human' qualities are obviously a function of scale, age, and the imprint of hand labor, though perhaps not merely. The mien of old houses—their solidarity and defiance as survivors—makes them seem animate. . . . [A] house may guard the mystery of its inner life, but its face invites us to imagine that it has one" (*The New Yorker*, December 1, 2003).

When I drove down the street for the first time with Donna to go look at this latest house, curved around the bend in the road to behold it, so clearly old, the thrill began. And when I stepped through the vestibule into the main hallway, with its paneled walls and high ceiling, the possibility of merging my fantasized life with real life exploded into full-blown houselust. We were drawn to this old house by the very qualities that made it seem animate to us—its age, its hand-wrought details—a poetic house built at the turn of the century. Even its scale relative to the street and the houses around it, the space between them, was luxurious. Donna and I felt drawn to it by the imagined pleasures of becoming a part of its inner life. This response was completely sentimental and superficial. We both had an extraordinary capacity to imagine a perfect and rich life within a grand, turn-of-the-century residence.

This one was it, this was the kind of house, an old house from the edge of the Victorian era that we had once imagined ourselves living in as we cycled through the neighborhood. Incredible though the situation was, the house of our dreams was within our reach. Here fantasy and reality might merge.

3

The Suburban Home

W hy on earth had we purchased this mother of a project in the first place? I would continue after the day of possession to bolt awake, middle of the night, in a panic. *We don't have this kind of money—what was I thinking? My God, I've set us on an irrevocable course toward financial ruin.* But in daylight I was simply tense, edgy, and excited. A new house, a new phase of life. We'd make it work somehow. We'd engaged in the American compulsion to upgrade our dwelling place, to live in a house we dreamed of and could *almost* afford, completely ignoring the facts:

- The home we already owned, several blocks away, was fine (indeed, cherished by our daughter).
- Our financial state would always be precarious because of my work; it's critical to save money when we happen to have it.
- We might move anyway after I finished the next book, who could say? I never knew where I was going next, and Donna had never been completely sold on Cleveland.
- I couldn't afford a major upheaval now, when I was in mid-book.

- We didn't have the time to devote to a renovation while working and taking care of our two-year-old, who could be expected to get into the power tools and saw blades and paint thinners and piles of rotten wood with rusty nails sticking up, the normal landscape of a live-in renovation.
- There was always next year. If we still felt the need, OK, but not this year—what's the rush?

The situation was all too plain when viewed as a pros-and-cons list on my legal pad. And yet the visceral need to buy the house that we could consider permanent gathered and accelerated within me at first like a boulder down a hill and then like an avalanche. The purchase of a huge, needy house we could not afford felt absolutely unstoppable. All creepiness, bad karma, and noisy ghosts aside, it was an excellent structure on a lovely street in a suburb of the city where I was born and raised. I loved my hometown, and I was eager to establish our lives in a place and a house where we meant to stay. I loved the *idea* of home generally and felt good about joining in one of humankind's more durable impulses, establishing permanent home place.

And while I would argue that this is a desire so common as to be a genetic component of our species, it was contradicted by our country's demographics—America was populated almost exclusively by immigrants—and by our actions—Americans left their homes for somewhere else with increasing frequency, about once every four years on average. According to the 2000 census, there were 262 million of us over the age of five. Of those people, 120 million—almost half—had moved to a new residence since 1995. According to U-Haul, a company that rejoices in our wanderlust, 20 percent of the population moves in any given year. And yet our culture simultaneously adores the idea of "home," and does so with a fervor that suggests it arises out of more than superficial sentimentality. Newspapers devote a weekly section to house and home. Coffee-table books on homes and decorating abound, as do magazines devoted to the subject. Currently, a whole television network devoted to house and home programming runs around the clock.

We are a country of itinerants in love with the idea of home, the truth and sentimentality of it intertwining so tightly they are almost indistinguishable from one another. What did house and home mean anymore to us generally in this country? Is a yearning for home some prehistoric vestige, one that initially created tight communities for efficient food gathering and mutual safety, something we're born with that we no longer require? Why do we idealize it? Why do we do it, long for a home of our own, yearn to make it? What is the source of and reason for this longing, which runs counter to the American spirit and myth? America is about renewal and reinvention, the open road, flight. And yet our true longing might be for permanent home, a hunger more primitive and deeply rooted than the American wanderlust imperative.

These opposing thrusts make us a confused culture on some levels, and I wondered, were we depleting ourselves by moving around so often, by raising our families in a series of changing homes and unconnected places?

And what of the house itself? The lives of people and families weave themselves into the very architecture. How does the structure of a house shape the life of a family? And what is the place of a house in the evolution of a marriage, a cultural construct I'd always denigrated but now cherished more than I'd imagined possible? I'd found my perfect lifelong companion and had the good sense to know what that meant. Did any of this have to do with why Donna and I had stretched ourselves to buy this thing?

What exactly did a house mean? How and why did a house compel us to act this way?

For me and Donna, the specific house meant we'd be vagabonds no longer. Part of our rationale for this questionable impulse was that we intended to stay, do the majority of our work here, and watch our kids' transformation from this spot, from within this brick behemoth with the funky karma. It was an old one with character, with "soul," as they say, on a street lined with gorgeous old homes built on either side of World War I but well before the Depression, after which time decent house construction took a permanent nosedive. We had looked only at old houses in old neighborhoods. The new houses in the new develop-

ments way outside the city felt cold and without character to us, discon-
nected from any kind of community at all. The only center out there
was a highway access ramp. And more than our simply connecting with
a community was the possibility of being grounded in time. This might
be part of why we found new houses "soulless," as it were. They had yet
to develop a past and so felt less substantial. When we moved into a
grand structure, as we were about to do, might we connect with what
came before us in that space? We would inevitably become a part of the
legacy of the house. And, by extension, a legacy of the land in which the
house was anchored and of the community sharing that land.

The house we'd bought was a structure we wouldn't tire of. A large
brick box with shingles covering the triangles of all four gables—two
main side gables as well as a gabled bay in front and a narrow gable in
back extending out of the rear corner of the house. A deep front porch
anchored the left side of the house, huge blocks of sandstone around its
foundation, carved sandstone lintels and sills at all windows. Its design
and details and natural materials could forever engage the eyes as it supported the lives within it, on a street worth staying on. The structure
itself shapes your life, shapes a family and a marriage, its intellect and
spirit, doesn't it? Worth the gamble anyway. We wanted this house.

Moreover, I sensed there was something important to be learned
from returning to the city where I'd been born and raised, to live and
raise a family of my own here. It was something fewer and fewer Americans did anymore, live in the place where they grew up.

In 1987 I returned to live with my father in my childhood home shortly
before my twenty-fourth birthday, toxic from eighteen months in Manhattan, where I'd been a copyboy in the newsroom of the *New York Times.*
A few of the ground-floor windows of my father's house didn't lock, so
in order to sleep, I lined the tops of these windows with delicate glass-
ware. That I would need to do such a thing was less a reflection of
the comfortable white-collar, middle-class neighborhood in Shaker
Heights, Ohio, than of the lingering impact of the place I'd left, a city
where you might find, say, a Hispanic man in your closet. (He'd been rip-

ping off my apartment when I surprised him; after I got him out, he knocked to ask if we could talk—I assumed to discuss his trousers, which he'd left on my bedroom floor. I told him I thought talk was an impossibility at that point. No one to whom I told this story in New York found it remarkable.)

That my paranoia carried over from where it was useful (Manhattan) to where it was pathologic (leafy old suburbia) indicates to me how powerfully home is built in to our psyche. I wasn't actually preventing a burglar with those perched wineglasses (there was none); rather, those wineglasses secured the home in my mind, the idea of home, which had been violated by my urban experience.

I came and went from my boyhood home during the next four years but ultimately returned, with Donna (born in Queens, New York), to live in the city where I grew up. Perhaps a prehistoric homing instinct exists in men, different from but no less powerful than women's so-called nesting instinct. The mythology of Odysseus, his place in our culture as an archetypal figure, one might argue, should not focus solely on his being a journeyer, quester, warrior-king but rather on his role as the ultimate homebody, a seeker of home, a figure, a myth embodying the yearning for home that is a fundamental aspect of humanity. "Yet, it is true, each day," he says to the nymph Kalypso, who keeps him on her island for her own pleasure, "I long for home, long for the sight of home."

That I've become a suburban homebody would have appalled my twenty-one-year-old self, a man at last, heading recklessly into the world, full of promise and eager for adventure. It is the irony of fate that routine, something I once so resented in my father's life (a Cleveland adman, a suburban commuter who today boards the same train at the same stop he first boarded it in 1965, age twenty-seven), is what I cherish in my own.

I had now begun to do my work in my father's house, a free and vacant space five days a week, for reasons of efficiency and quiet, given the loud facts of children. It felt strange at first, sitting to write in my childhood bedroom (generic by that time, no camp pennants or baseball trophies) at the desk my parents had bought for me before my entry into the sixth grade, still scarred by some incense I'd left burning there as a teenager.

When I took my midday break for exercise, I jogged past my elementary school each day. Halfway there, I crossed a bit of sidewalk, a cracked sandstone slab that still collected water on wet days as it always did throughout my school days, the exact sidewalk stone where my classmate Debbie Shaw had kissed my second-grader cheek for no reason. I was in love with Debbie Shaw, so that kiss marked a moment of private glory I could not help but recall each day on that run. It was as if the sidewalk slab were actually charged with some kind of memory electricity that buzzed me when I hit it.

Each step of that mile-and-a-half route I had made thousands of times, in countless versions of myself, and each step of that daily jog connected me with all those versions, good and bad—returning home with a shameful report card; returning home after midnight, a drunken teenager burning with love for a girl named Kathy who lived a ways beyond the school; returning home as an apprentice writer to work on a novel that would never be published but that would secure an agent, and still again to carry on with the books about cooking, then again with a book about a surgical team. And now this one, a book about house and home and what it might mean to live in the same place where you grow up.

The structures, the physical objects of our days, shape our thoughts more substantially than we often realize. A really comfortable chair makes reading better, of course, but more significant than the overt and recognized impact of structures is the fact that inanimate objects can be so influential as to seem almost animate, as if some force works through them.

This, too, became clear to me while running. I'd gone two blocks past the Debbie Shaw sidewalk slab when it occurred to me that for the first time I hadn't thought of her. The following day the same thing. On the third consecutive day of not thinking of her, I turned around, went back to the spot. The cracked slab where rain had gathered throughout my youth was gone, replaced by poured concrete. Debbie Shaw recedes almost out of sight. I never think of her anymore, because the object, the stone that connected me to her, is gone.

I loved to run along those streets because they were filled with houses that lit up in my imagination. Here they are not the grand structures along the park boulevards, the mansions Shaker Heights is known for, nor the ones in the old neighborhoods of Cleveland Heights where Donna and I once rode, fantasizing. The houses I loved to look at were the middle-class Colonials that truly embodied suburban culture and the life I'd known here. Some are shingled, some are brick, some are stucco, some are in a Tudor style; no two are the same, I believe, and yet in a way they are all exactly the same—four-bedroom, two-and-a-half-bath, single-family dwellings with a front lawn, a small backyard, and a detached garage, almost all of them built between 1920 and 1929. They are squeezed in tightly, some sharing a driveway, as my father's does. They are the suburban houses of a neighborhood laid out and built along a streetcar line, which here is still referred to by a name that recalls its turn-of-the-century roots, the Rapid Transit. These houses, in my imagination, are filled with industrious couples and busy families. I adored the middle-class houses and my notion of middle-class suburban life: workers like my father taking the Rapid downtown in the morning and returning at night, the routine of the week—cutting the lawn in the summer and shoveling snow in winter—the spaciousness and ease of the neighborhood, the start of baseball signaling the verdant spring, football the crisp and vivid fall, the suburban cocktail parties, the barbecues, the festive Christmas gatherings of hyperactive kids of all ages and the tipsy adults. The suburbs weren't bad.

And yet to pronounce one's love of suburbia is not the coolest thing you can do or a surefire way to make a lot of friends at a party where you don't know anyone. Why is this so? The suburbs are where most people in the country live by choice. And yet commentators continue to describe life in the suburbs as suffocating, homogenized, and vacuous.

I'm a suburban boy, raised in the suburb of a much-denigrated midwestern city during its nadir (the 1970s), now returned to it. I've never not liked suburbs—the older ones, I mean, with old houses and old trees, cracked sidewalks and irregular street patterns—and so I've always been perplexed that they should be so consistently bad-mouthed. Conformity, mediocrity, consumerism, self-homogenization happen in the

suburbs, but they also happen everywhere else. Mediocrity and conformity and a reliance on consumer goods to fill the void of an insubstantial life are caused by our own choices, not a residential setup . . .
aren't they? Donna and I were about to make a permanent decision. In
order to purchase this brick house in the suburbs of Cleveland, we were
committing to this place. We weren't going anywhere from now on.
Were we dooming ourselves?

Put aside for the moment the antisuburban zealots and disdainful
urbanites, the cement dwellers who pride themselves on living side by
side with the homeless. Those commentators work from stereotype and
emotion. To defend the American suburb I need only point to the facts.

The cultural forces at work, making suburban houses desirable,
began with the changing city in the mid-nineteenth century, not in
1950s America. Regents Park in London, completed in 1832, is considered
to be the first suburb. In America, New Jersey's Llewelyn Park, completed 1869, promised romantic dwellings in a country setting, isolating
the primary perceived benefit of the suburb. In that year Frederick Law
Olmsted and Calvert Vaux designed Riverside, a community nine miles
south of Chicago, as a "romantic landscape" featuring curved streets,
plenty of open areas—as in their design of Central Park a decade earlier,
the same qualities that distinguished the neighborhood Donna and I
would be joining, in fact—and lots on which no one was permitted to
build a house costing less than $3,000.

As cities began to team with culture and commerce, industry and
action, they got dirty and crowded. They were perceived as unwhole-
some, wicked, corrupting, not a place for women and children. People
were both attracted to and repulsed by the city, and thus was created the
desire for a house with the pleasures of the country but with easy access
to the city. Developers of Llewelyn Park advertised their dwellings as
"country homes for city people."

Some literature on the suburbs suggests that the burbs were not the
cages of conformity they often seem and that we are repeatedly told
they are, but rather the opposite: Suburbs were wild. Not like an animal

but rather like a fire no one person or group could contain. And also like a fire, they inevitably burn themselves out. Historians, in fact, are already documenting the death of the suburb; indeed, the true suburb has been dead for twenty years or so.

Certainly, fine old suburbs still live and breathe today, but they are in their twilight years and not to be replaced. My commuter father, who this morning closed the back door of his house, deposited a bag of garbage in the can in the detached garage, and strode to the train stop, did so as a bygone icon, the suburban commuter. When he retires at the end of the year, he won't be replaced. The person who next inhabits his house is more likely to work at an office complex built at the intersection of two highways miles from Public Square in downtown Cleveland; he or she will likely spend a good amount of time working from home.

The building of good houses in a well-designed neighborhood, the people living in those houses, the life of suburbia—it was a good thing, not the cliché that our literature told us it was, and this sense that it was good came not only from my own nostalgia and carefree childhood (made possible in part by the suburban form) but also from an intuition that it was subversively good, that it was in fact revolutionary, born of a radical change in values among an entire population, and nobody recognized this, and now it's lost, gone to sprawl.

I took some pride in adoring something most people were either openly contemptuous of or simply didn't talk about. With the exception of D. J. Waldie's excellent and artful *Holy Land. A Suburban Memoir,* suburbs have almost always been derided in contemporary culture, most visibly in movies. The suburb was a lovely-looking vista of trees and grass, surrounding houses that festered within, breeding a killing boredom like a cancer (*The Ice Storm*), or sickos (*Blue Velvet*), or perversions of social, racial, and sexual prejudices (*Far from Heaven*), making marriages bitter and brittle (*Ordinary People*). One of the best and most respected American novels of the post–World War II era, *Revolutionary Road* by Richard Yates, casts the suburb as a main character and is ruthless in the clarity with which it presents the mediocrity of suburban married life in the 1950s. At worst the suburb was passively corrupt and at best a place for the lives of nobodies.

But the truth is this: Most of us can't avoid the mediocrity of everyday life no matter where we live. Human nature tends toward corruption, which is easy, rather than toward integrity, which is difficult.

Historians of suburbia almost invariably quote the writer Lewis Mumford, who argued that "the building of houses constitutes the major architectural work of any civilization." Mumford was a wickedly clever commentator on suburbia in his massive book *The City in History: Its History, Its Transformations and Its Prospects,* published in 1961, when he was sixty-six years old. He's ruthless in his contempt for suburbia and so good a writer he's convincing even to me; I can only shake my head and grin when I read, for instance, his conviction that "the ultimate effect of the suburban escape in our time is, ironically, a low grade uniform environment from which escape is impossible," or that the suburbs were in fact a prison, "a sort of green ghetto dedicated to the elite," creating conditions of life that result in boredom and "a bland ritual of competitive spending."

He is the key figure in one of suburbia's most interesting and distinguishing features: the intense intellectual disdain for the suburbs that began the moment the middle classes entered the picture in the 1920s.

Anyone who reads about the subject will find two separate branches of suburban commentary: one on suburbia's physical development and another on the intellectual response to that development; that is, on the real estate itself—the suburban lot, the four-bedroom Colonial with a well-tended lawn among a sea of them—and on the *idea* of the suburb, which gives a lot of people the creeps, even though few really pause to think what it is or where it came from.

Most people tend to think about and even write about suburbia as being, for instance, a recent phenomenon that flowered in the 1950s. In fact the suburb is a centuries-old domestic arrangement whose *death* begins in the fifties.

The first suburbs, or "suburbes," in the sixteenth and seventeenth centuries were in fact wretched places where the fringe members of society gathered—"shantytowns," according to Robert Fishman in his book about the suburbs, called *Bourgeois Utopias.* Most people wanted to live in cities for protection, community, and efficiency of living at a time when living was not so easy as it is now. The classes lived interspersed. The late eighteenth century was of course a revolutionary time, an "age of improvement" that saw creation of new and powerful forces such as the novel, the steam engine, the Constitution—a list that includes, Fishman says, suburbia.

John Nash was the first to put all the principles of the suburb into place in Regents Park, an imitation of aristocratic luxury, minus the landownership. The small plots of land there were owned by various families, to be enjoyed by all. He created, in effect, houses in a park.

America assimilated these qualities in Llewelyn Park and in Riverside, then elsewhere, but development was relatively slow in the hundred-year-old country and would remain so until transportation provided the spark for explosive growth in its next major phase: the streetcar suburb, the suburb's best incarnation, the place that created the houses where I grew up and the house where I was about to move. Both houses had been built near a streetcar line.

"In the history of the middle-class residential suburb," writes Fishman, "the late-nineteenth-century railroad suburb represents the classic form, the era in which suburbia most closely approached the bourgeois monument and the bourgeois utopia. It exemplified the central meaning and contradiction of suburbia: a natural world of greenery and family life that appeared to be wholly separate from the great city yet was in fact wholly dependent on it."

In the first decade of the twentieth century, streetcar suburbs were looked at neither with contempt nor as exclusionary, which they surely were. Among the first traits of the suburb was that it could be defined in part by what it excluded. Not only dirt and soot but also the working class. "It was not a utopia for everyone," Fishman notes, "still less a democratic vision. If the railroad suburb was the classic embodiment of the bourgeois dream of property, family life, and union with nature, it was built on a foundation of fear as well as hope."

And yet, even in the 1920s, the end of the streetcar-suburb era, homeownership for most people remained out of reach. It was an escape from city living that most people only dreamed of. But with each successive decade, the suburb became less exclusive, needed to include more people, because the country was growing and more people needed good housing.

"The history of suburbia is at the heart of twentieth-century American history," write Rosalyn Baxandall and Elizabeth Ewen in *Picture Window: How the Suburbs Happened*. They studied Long Island—birthplace of Levittown and of what we often think of when we hear the word "suburb"—interviewed various residents and explored the literature. Long Island suburbs developed as they had everywhere else: Palatial country estates of the tycoons of America's powerful economy were transformed when easy transportation routes from the city opened up (a train first moved through an East River tunnel in 1910). In ten more years, the automobile was everywhere, and Long Island could no longer be considered rural.

At the same time, the middle class swelled right along with the economy, creating mass demand for cars, cosmetics, entertainment, and, importantly, appliances. Electricity became standard, providing modern conveniences such as washing machines and vacuum cleaners and refrigerators as a matter of course, appliances that gave people more time. The suburbs were advertised in the twenties as obvious objects of desire, the authors write. Yet such housing was expensive, remaining just beyond the reach of the stolid middle class, part of what made them so desirable. To live in the suburbs was a status symbol.

The suburban boom of the twenties ended with the Depression and a resulting housing bust, and that, combined with the economic difficulties facing most families, further distanced the middle class from the suburbs. House construction remained dormant for half a generation, till the end of World War II, when Edward Filene, the department-store magnate, a writer and social commentator, had an idea: "make houses like Fords," a command taken up with revolutionary gusto by the building firm of Levitt and Sons.

American builders put up 1.25 million houses in 1950; simple single-family dwellings clustered in suburbs designed, critics such as Mumford contended, to accommodate not adults but rather their children. It was more fuel for intellectual snobbery. "This was not merely a child-centered environment," writes Mumford. "It was based on a childish view of the world, in which reality was sacrificed to the pleasure-principle."

Perhaps the most notable successor to Mumford, certainly the most entertaining commentator on the "fiasco of suburbanism," is the novelist, journalist, and town crier James Howard Kunstler, in his book called *The Geography of Nowhere: The Rise and Decline of America's Man-Made Landscape.* That book and a subsequent book called *Home from Nowhere* are sustained rants about the trashing of our places in postwar America and about suburban culture, which he calls toxic.

In *Geography of Nowhere,* he runs through the history of suburbia's rise as do the more academic critics, though his account is edged with his personality.

"By 1915, the romantic suburb of the type pioneered by Llewellyn Park and Riverside was a fixture on the fringe of most American cities and had attained its high-water mark as *the* accepted version of the Good Life. In places like Shaker Heights, Ohio, and Brookline, Massachusetts, . . . the fortunate could enjoy the dream of an achieved Arcadia completely insulated from the industrial economy that made it possible." But: "It was an artificial way of life in an inorganic community that pretended above all other virtues to be 'natural.' . . . It was nice while it lasted, but it didn't last long in its classic form.

"The small-town life that Americans long for when they are depressed by their city apartments or their suburban bunkers," he asserts, "is really a conceptual substitute for the idea of community. But a community is not something you *have,* like a pizza. Nor is it something you can buy, as visitors to Disneyland and Williamsburg discover. It is a living organism based on a web of interdependencies—which is to say, a local economy. It expresses itself physically as *connectedness,* as buildings actively relating to one another, and to whatever public space exists, be it the street, or the courthouse square, or the village green. . . . That notion of community began to vanish in America after World War II. We have paid a lot of lip service to the idea, and indulged in a lot of easy nostalgia about it, but our small towns have never been worse off than they are now. . . .

"During this epoch of stupendous wealth and power, we have managed to ruin our greatest cities, throw away our small towns, and impose over the countryside a joyless junk habitat which we can no longer afford to support. . . . [W]ith nothing left but private life in our private homes and private cars, we wonder what happened to the spirit of community."

Without community, Kunstler says, we won't build proper homes. And unless we build proper places in which to live, we won't have much of a civilization in the future. Good houses are important.

"There is a reason that human beings long for a sense of permanence," Kunstler concludes. "This longing is not limited to children, for it touches the profoundest aspects of our existence: that life is short, fraught with uncertainty, and sometimes tragic. We know not where we come from, still less where we are going, and to keep from going crazy while we are here, we want to feel that we truly belong to a specific part of the world."

Criticism focused *on* the suburb, however, is usually not in fact a criticism *of* the suburb; its real target is the middle-class mentality and describes an intellectual disdain for the tastes of the masses. Attacking suburbia has been a convenient way to explain all kinds of societal problems, notes Kenneth Jackson in *Crabgrass Frontier*. The culture at large, many have noted, has even spun once neutral descriptions of suburban culture into terms of derogation—"housewife," "homely," "homemaker"—or has personified entire lives with a cliché such as the Soccer Mom.

Jackson calls suburbia "the quintessential physical achievement of the United States; it is perhaps more representative of its culture than big cars, tall buildings, or professional football. Suburbia symbolizes the fullest, most unadulterated embodiment of contemporary culture; it is a manifestation of such fundamental characteristics of American society as conspicuous consumption, a reliance upon the private automobile, upward mobility, the separation of the family into nuclear units, the widening division between work and leisure, and a tendency toward racial and economic exclusiveness."

And Baxendall and Ewen, writing just a few years ago, conclude, "Even though most Americans now live in suburbs, snobbery toward suburbia and its inhabitants continues. Yet suburbia was a commercial response to a long-standing social need: housing for a third of the nation. People moved to the suburbs because it was their best financial option. Some found it isolating; others found it rich in possibilities. None found it to be a changeless never-never land. From the beginning, it has been riven by conflict, and so it continues to be."

That mirrored my understanding of the suburbs, that life there *might* be a richly textured world of struggle and love and loss, the small triumphs, tragedies, and great possibilities that compose most people's lives. By the 1970s, the decade that marks the end of the suburb, more Americans lived in a suburb than anywhere else.

Having been born into the end of the suburban era, perhaps I'm writing in a sentimental effort to preserve in memory what was all but dead by the time I left it in 1981. The suburbia that formed the terrain of my childhood was shadowy in summer from the maples that flourish here, its winters filled with storms and chest-high snows. We never thought about personal safety because we didn't have to, didn't lock our house during the day when all were gone. From age five I walked nearly a mile to school with my five-year-old pal Kley, and home again, our parents scarcely giving it a thought, apparently.

While suburbia was not to be replaced and new residences that went up became a facet of sprawl (endless exurbias connected only by the interstate, their houses connected by the Internet), many suburbs would remain thriving places because the *houses* built there decades ago were so fine and durable. The houses preserved what was best. The fact of the houses themselves, the structures, was what made these places last, even though the families in them didn't, even though Americans continued to move from place to place. The design of the houses was classical in nature, and so their appearance continued to be appealing. Solid construction of beautiful houses ensured that people would take care of them. Donna and I were among those people, and, unlike most home buyers today, according to our local real estate agents, we sought a house that needed a hell of a lot of work, were eager to accept the risks involved.

4

Inspector Archer

"Nine, ten, eleven, twelve—ooooo-kay. This is a prepurchase general home inspection conducted by Archer Home Inspections. We're members of the American Society of Home Inspectors. Today is Monday July thirtieth, 2001, the time is 4:05 P.M. Our clients are Donna and Mike Ruhlman. Donna requested the inspection—she's here, Mike's here. I'm Jeff Aaron, your inspector, and I appreciate your using my company, Donna. Thanks a lot."

The inspector was an Ichabod Crane figure with a narrow face and a long neck that seemed to bow out slightly at the protuberant thyroid cartilage. He had a prominent nose, narrow like his face but thickly featured and with a high, wide bridge on which rested a pair of sensible, plastic-rimmed glasses. His expertise fascinated me, and as he spoke, I imagined in him a kind of Holmes of homes, Inspector Archer, a fine name for domicile gumshoe. His skin was fair, and his hair, which had a jagged look and gave the impression of having been cut by razor, was short and light brown, with a few streaks of gray. His six-foot frame was lean—not skinny or thin but rather sinewy and efficient. He was dressed for a trek on rugged mountain terrain: heavy wool socks rising a few inches out of hiking boots, khaki shorts, and a sturdy, well-worn linen shirt. He carried a black bag, like the kind family physicians once carried, filled with the tools of his trade, and he held in his right hand two cassette recorders, both running.

"It's important for me to answer your questions," Inspector Archer said in his nasal, somewhat nerdy voice. "Don't hesitate to stop me and ask. I'll answer anything I can. If I don't know something, I'll tell you. I'm restricted to visual, nondestructive testing. I can't open walls, tear up carpeting, or disassemble the heating system. I can't see through *things,* so there is the potential for concealed or latent defect. I'm not involved in real estate sales, I don't make contractor referrals, I won't offer to do repairs, I'm not here to offer you guarantees or warranties or insurance. I provide information. Ummmmm."

Here he stopped, pursed his lips, touched them with his finger, squinted, and slowly rotated his torso enough to glance at the house from where he stood in the grass.

"Was the house built a little before World War I?"

"We think it was built in 1909," Donna said, repeating what we'd been told.

"Mm-*hmmm!*" said the inspector. "That sounds about right. I noticed a large brick in back made by the Cleveland Block Company, dated 1909, a common street paving stone of the time. The house was not likely built the same year as the brick, but perhaps a year after, when extra pavers might have been acquired more cheaply by builders. Speculation. Certainly the Flemish style of the brickwork—you'll notice how a row of long bricks is followed on top by bricks placed end forward—was popular at the time, and you'll notice also the thick yellow sand and gravel dominant in the mortar; this is sand dredged from Lake Erie, which builders would have used to mix with cement at the time. Portland cement was in widespread use by 1905, however, and that doesn't look like portland cement, so you may want to be skeptical of the construction date."

The structure we stood before was definitely old. It looked old; the soot on brick and mortar gave it a uniform drabness. A central bay began on the first story with windows to a library or study; above this, shingles rose to a central third-floor gable, two windows at each story. Beams extended out from the corners of the rooftop, Craftsman in style.

Gables formed both east and west sides of the house, shingles making a triangle of each side. Craftsman rafter tails extended out from these roofs. The rest of the front and sides were of brick. A front porch ran the western third of the house, to the left of the gabled bay. Columns with ornate, plumelike capitals, almost Middle Eastern in appearance, supported the porch roof and were connected to one another by pointed arches. Large sandstone blocks made a low rail around the porch, the steps up the porch were likewise sandstone slabs, and the porch floor had been covered with blue-and-green striped Astroturf. Each first- and second-story window included a substantial sandstone lintel and sill. The house sat on a foundation of sandstone blocks. The details of the lintels and sills, the rafter tails, and the ornate columns suggested that the structure had been built not only before the Depression but likely before World War I, when such materials, like locally quarried sandstone, were commonplace. Archer's comments supported this.

"The exact age isn't crucial," Archer continued. "What I'm getting at is, homes have *usual* and *expected* conditions of wear. What I will do during the inspection is distinguish between what would be normal for a home around ninety years old and what would be accelerated or excessive deterioration, permanent damage from neglect or abuse." His grave demeanor became suddenly light, the nasal quality of his voice intensified. "I'm not here to nitpick. I'll skip chipped paint and loose doorknobs." He paused, the Adam's apple bobbed once along his swan's neck, and he grew serious again. "I'm here to look for major deficiencies in the structure and its mechanical systems."

Again a pause, but longer now, not for emphasis but to allow for questions, which more intelligent home buyers might be expected to have. I instead stood in wonder.

"Mm-hmm, oooo-*kay!*" he said, and this noise was like a birdcall, one he uttered at virtually every transition and one, were he to hear it from a potential mate, that would no doubt draw him near. The inspector couldn't accurately be described as effeminate—muscles rippled in his slender forearms, his fingers were lean and taut, muscle and veins gave his knees and calves a chiseled effect—but his wrists and waist were quite slender, his movements precise to the point of delicacy.

Inspector Archer turned to cast a sweeping glance from the house to the street, and, raising the tape recorders to chest level, he said, "I advise you to call the engineering or city-services department at City Hall for more information on the house. They will inform you of any sewer or drainage problems at this address. I'm not aware of any problems, but it never hurts to call. Information on file is a public record.

"Cleveland Heights does a point-of-sale inspection. You'll find that what I do is different. The city has its own priorities, its own *agenda*. What Cleveland Heights calls a violation or a defect—that carries *the weight of law* and needs to be corrected. I offer information only; it will be unbiased and without opinion."

Perhaps it was me, but I sensed in his tone a light mockery of the city, of perhaps what was considered law, and it must have been at this point, at this inference of mine, that I began to see him as outside the law.

"Did the, uh, owner . . . *disclose* any problems with the house?" he asked.

Donna said, "No. There's a leaky basement wall, that was all."

He nodded. "I don't expect the basement of a home this age in this climate to be completely dry. I noticed some negative grade along the eastern side of the house—could this be the wall the owner mentioned?"

"I believe so," Donna said.

"It would be rare to go into the basement and see no signs of moisture."

We nodded.

"Do you have any questions for me, before I march along here?" I remained dumbstruck by this private inspector and had nothing to ask. Donna had no questions. "Mm-hmm, oooo-*kay!*" he said, with almost a squeak of pleasure, and he moved into the inspection, tape rolling for our reference.

We had made an offer on the house of $245,000, and it had been accepted. Today was our last opportunity to be sensible; we could slip out of the contract if we wanted. I was certain Archer would find grounds for us to cancel the deal—a disastrous plumbing situation, a major structural flaw in the foundation—something that would allow us—force us, rather—to walk. I prayed he wouldn't. We badly wanted this house, as the emotional bargaining process had shown.

Steve had arrived the afternoon of our first offer in his customary attire of fine beige slacks and Hawaiian shirt, Cross pen at the ready for writing up a new counteroffer. Hearing that our offer of $220,000 had been turned down, I said, "So that 'north of two hundred' was just a line."

Steve held up both hands and looked away. "I was repeating what I was told."

However peeved I was, I trusted Steve. Donna, I realized later, was not silent from disappointment that our offer had been refused; she was rigid with anger, having recognized at this moment that Steve's representing seller and buyer was a bad situation. Steve was doing nothing illegal or unethical. He had presented us with a Disclosure of Dual Agency agreement, as required by Ohio law; we understood it and signed it. But the situation was inherently fraught with conflict. How could he possibly work to get *us* the best deal possible and the sellers the best possible deal? He was simply working to make a deal happen at all. Donna, looking cool in a blue cotton dress and bare feet, remained outwardly reserved. She'd set up J. before a cutting board with tiny carrots, a hot dog, chips and juice, sounds from "The Creeper" episode of the original *Scooby-Doo, Where Are You?* lilting in from the kitchen (this particular episode allowed Donna twenty minutes of unbroken concentration, a luxury she didn't enjoy wasting).

"Be honest, Steve," Donna said suddenly. "Do the right thing."

Steve's mouth hung open at the implication.

"Did she bother to make a counteroffer?" I asked.

"Two seventy-five."

"We're not bargaining, Steve," Donna said plaintively. "That isn't close. We'll go as high as two-thirty—no more. But she's got to include some of that furniture you mentioned. The bed set, the chest of drawers, the three end tables, the dining room set. You said she was willing to do that, that she didn't need furniture, she didn't want it, that it was more trouble to remove. That is what *you said.*" In my mind, as I did my fifty daily lengths at our fine community pool, I was already offering two-fifty if it came to that, and they could have the furniture—if the house was structurally sound, the location alone was more than worth it. (I was still entertaining houselust fantasies of living like the fifty-five-year-old chief counsel of a major corporation, as opposed to the late-thirties, self-employed writer walking a continuous financial tightrope.) Thus I never said another word in the bargaining department.

Donna's New York City upbringing came in handy here—I shut up. She had earned her position as lead negotiator.

Steve took a sip of his ice water, condensation dripping onto his slacks. He brushed at the spot daintily, removed the gold Cross pen from his pocket, and wrote in large, awkward block lettering the new offer.

"What about the furniture?"

"Donna, unless you want me to list each individual piece you want right here, you've got to work that out with Tim," Steve said, referring to the owner's son. "Do you know the exact pieces you want?"

"The dining room set," she said.

Steve sighed but wrote that down. Then he looked at her, waiting. "Anything *else*?" he said.

"What we talked about, you know."

"You have to be specific—which pieces by name and what room they're in."

We signed the new offer to buy without listing them, figuring there was still more negotiating to do, and Steve left, clearly without optimism. He'd have to sit down with the seller, announce our ungrateful, unappreciative, stingy counter.

I had to be out of town the following day for a few days in Los Angeles. I returned to the hotel at midnight and listened to Donna's irate messages.

"Steve is screwing us," she told me the following afternoon when we at last had time to talk. "We're going to show up there and the dining room table will be gone, just watch."

"Donna, calm down."

"Steve is working for them. He is not working on our behalf. And," she said, "he was rude to me."

"Rude?"

"Yes, told me to calm down, and then he hung up on me."

"Did you need to calm down?"

"No, I was speaking in this exact voice—he made me feel I was acting out of control. He is supposed to be representing us, and he hung up on me; I think that describes exactly the kind of relationship we have. Zero. We're acting alone here."

"Let me try to call him."

"Michael, how can you not be upset? I don't like this, and I don't trust Steve."

"How are the kids?" I asked.

A long pause followed, as anger receded into the background at the thought of them. "They're *great*," Donna said, sounding like a different person. "J. is so cute. My toes are pink with nail polish, skin and all. He was so proud. Michael, they're just great. I miss you. They miss you. A. especially. This morning when she woke up, her first words were, 'Two more days.' And then she had J. jumping on the bed chanting it."

Two more days was too long. I ached for my children, a dull, throbbing ache all day that now, when I was alone at this Los Angeles hotel, became a generalized resentment of hotel rooms and travel, the sturdy bedspread made of nothing natural, the faux furniture, the fluorescent bathroom with TV and telephone.

Shortly after I returned home, I broke my own negotiating rule (let Donna do it) and agreed to $245,000. Donna was pissed. How could I do that? In her mind I'd thrown away ten grand. I'd by now become paranoid about the deal's falling through. But, given the hundred grand we expected to put into renovation, I'd upped by five thousand our final offer on the previous house, which we'd had no business making, a commitment made from pure emotion, as I had done again.

Here is where the situation stood when we met Inspector Archer, Private Eye, who would scrutinize the structure for major defects. We had found him through Steve, who offered us two cards, saying he had no preferences.

Inspections are a relatively new development in residential real estate transactions. As recently as the late 1960s and early 1970s, home buyers required no appraisal of how well their future house was built, how well it had been maintained, nor of what they could expect in the way of major repairs over the next several years. Of course there hadn't been a need when the houses were new. Part of the reason for the new need for home inspection, particularly in the suburbs immediately surrounding Cleveland and other older suburbs throughout the country, was that most houses had grown so old that major parts of them were beginning to wear out; ninety winters of ice and shifting earth had taken their toll on these hand-built dwellings. But also, no doubt, there were simply more inspectors. As an increase in lawyers will increase the perceived need for lawyers, an increased number of home inspectors, calling on agents like our friend Steve, will increase the perceived need for inspections. But ultimately, in our case, it was a fear of spending a substantial amount of money, more by far than we were worth, for an unknown quantity that moved us to hire an inspector for $160 for the first hour and half that amount for every subsequent hour.

The convention of the home inspection had begun casually—purchasers asked their contractors to have a look at the house and give their opinion. Soon that request became so common that contractors were forced to charge a nominal fee, simply to put off the "tire kickers." In the 1960s a Cleveland contractor named Jack Bergson stopped contracting and hung out his "Private House Inspector" shingle, to become a forefather of inspectors in this part of the country. Now the American Society of Home Inspectors has its own Web site (ashi.com), where I would learn that four-fifths of home buyers now requested an inspection and also made the purchase contingent on it, as we had.

I, like most, was happy to pay for it; I thought of it simply as part of the process of house buying, a small price to pay to learn of a structural flaw, a bad roof, or a plumbing fiasco.

Inspector Archer first scrutinized the roof, then noted several rotting rafter tails and some damage to the brick and mortar where gutters had clogged and water had eroded them away the way a river cuts a channel through rock.

"Are you sure?" Donna asked. "We were told emphatically that the gutters were cleaned once a year."

"I can't comment on an owner's definition of cleaning or the quality of it," Archer said, striding around to the western side of the house, with us trailing him. "I can only show you brick and mortar deterioration below each gutter downspout. Make what you will of that information."

He stopped, craned his neck. The side of the house was sheer and tall, with two windows on each floor on either side of the chimney, which rose about three feet above the peak of the gable through which it emerged. "The chimney has no cap," Archer said. "A chimney cap can prevent debris and rodent nests. You'll also notice some dark spots, mainly in the vertical joints of the brickwork. A good mason will take the time to match the color of the new mortar to the existing mortar."

"Are you saying we need that tuck-pointed?"

"I'm pointing out where mortar is missing. Eventually more mortar will fall away, so yes, eventually that chimney will need some work. Will it fall apart this year if nothing is done? Not likely."

Donna wrote "L.R. chimney tuck-pointing" beneath "rafter tails" on a legal pad she carried.

The backyard was a small, odd shape, more or less rectangular but with the back-door neighbor's garage jutting into it. The garage was separated from the yard by a wood fence. On the next-door neighbor's side, there was a rusted chain-link fence, a high one, six feet, and on top of this, barbed-wire holders, now missing most of the barbed wire. I hadn't noticed it till today—the neighbors had put up a fence topped with barbed wire. What on earth was this for? A pretty serious embrace of the "good fences make good neighbors" adage.

In the center of the back of the house was a large square bay, supported by a giant wood corbel, which contained part of each staircase and was distinguished by the three Gothic leaded-glass windows. Below the overhang of this bay was a small patio of poured cement, encircled by a low brick wall and more sandstone slabs just to the right of the back door. Archer noted a structural crack in this knee-high patio wall. The crack descended in a steplike pattern along the mortar joints and was the result of sagging earth, Archer said, not unexpected in a ninety-year-old house; if we didn't fill the crack on the top of the wall, winter water would get in there, freeze, and break it apart.

"Should we get the entire wall repaired, or are you saying we should fill in the top crack?" I asked.

"Repairing something completely is generally a better solution than a temporary repair," he said, and this seemed to make him uncomfortable.

"I'm asking what you think we should do?"

"You're asking for an opinion. I provide information."

"If it were your house?" Donna said, a little annoyed at the need to lever information out of him.

"That's a difficult hypothetical. If it was all I had to do, yes, I'd repair that section of wall. If I had other issues—rotting rafter tails such as these—I'd get to those first. Is this wall structurally important? No, it's an accessory."

The back door was adjacent to a section of the house that stood out from the house, three narrow stories with a gable peak and chimney. This contained a breakfast room, a second-floor bedroom, and a narrow attic room. While it wasn't symmetrical with the gabled bay in front, it did in a way balance that front and add additional space and aesthetic appeal extending beyond the rectangular main body of the house.

The east side of the house, the driveway side, required more tuck-pointing, and the negative grade concerned him. He'd noted this earlier, but here he showed us how, given that the house had been built on a not insubstantial decline, water would roll from our neighbor's property across our rutted gravel drive, hit our house, and soak down around the foundation, where no doubt we would soon discover "mold and a form of mold called mildew," as he put it, flaky paint and puddle stains on the cracked concrete floor but, we hoped, no structural deterioration. "You can grade this out to prevent excessive water trapped against your foundation. You should grade about one vertical inch per horizontal foot; that should suffice. You should try to grade out eight to ten feet from the foundation."

"The basement windows are already at ground level—we can't raise the grade above those sills," Donna said.

"What you could do is install semicircular wells around the windows and build up the ground around those. Also, you might consider a cre- ating a swale along this side of the house.

"A swale," Donna said.

"A long, low area dug out here along this side of the house—water could be directed away from the building to the swale, from the swale toward the street." Donna nodded, wrote down the word "swale," and Archer said, "A landscaper would know what you're talking about if you ask for a drainage swale here."

He stepped close to a basement window and looked up. He stood beneath the driveway-side eave where the back gable met the main side gable. "Looks like the gutter here has been overflowing. You see here on the ground where the mulch has been washed away and there were splatters of mud a foot high on the foundation? I'm seeing some indica- tions of excess water around the house. What's going on up there is this: That gutter overflowed so continually that water eroded mortar out from between the bricks, and somebody did a shabby-looking repair simply by smearing mortar all over the bricks."

He looked down for a moment and then back up at the oval gray cement patch covering all the brick and mortar beneath the gutter; rather than take the time to mix proper mortar and trowel it into the joints between the bricks, someone had just pressed a big splotch of cement, about two feet in diameter, all over those nice old bricks. It was ugly, and the sight seemed to make Archer sad. "It will probably be hard to get that cleaned off and made presentable," he said. Even the ensuing "Ooo-kay" sounded a little flat.

"The overhead wires here at the east—the one with the round shape is cable, the telephone wire has a flat shape. The three wires twisted into one cable at the back, that's called triplex wiring, that's the electric util- ity. It's big enough to bring a hundred amps, two-twenty volts up to the house, a normal amount of power. Above the electric meter here, this conduit that brings power down to the meter is loose." He shook it. "That needs to be fastened to the house. This meter base—the old round style needs to be fastened to the house. These are commonly rated at sixty amps, which would limit your electrical service to that. Old houses this big were often built with sixty-amp service, but a new house this big would likely have two-hundred-amp service, maybe more. This real small wire here appears to be a phone wire—shouldn't carry any high voltage, shouldn't be a shock hazard. That black wire running the edge of the house is cable." He paused and turned to us, as if making a request. "*Workmen tend to do what's easiest for them.* You can ask them to fish wire through the wall to avoid that kind of clutter." He turned back to the house, then turned 180 degrees and looked at the garage. *"Oooo-kay!"* he said, apparently recovered from the aesthetic pain of the shabby mortar patch.

Archer completed his inspection of the brick exterior of the garage, a large two-car garage with heavy doors that slid back and forth on tracks. It contained a plumbing stack and a small fireplace and chimney, which intrigued Archer—he wondered aloud if the original builders hadn't lived in this solid structure during the building of the main house—and he alerted us to some insufficient brick repair, a cheaply repaired roof that had a visible crack in it and much debris on top that could be removed. With what seemed pleasant anticipation, he then said, "Let's march on down to the basement, shall we?"

"You like the basement," I said.

"It's where I spend most of my time," he said, taking long, duck-footed strides toward the back door. "Most of a house's mechanical systems—plumbing, electric, heat—originate and extend out through the house from there. It's where the foundation of the house is visible."

"The foundation is one of the main things you inspect."

He stopped and turned at me. "The entire *house* rests on . . . the *foundation.*"

"Right," I said.

Archer knocked at the back door. Its color implied warning, and the abuse it had suffered unnerved me, gashes of weathered wood scarring the red surface. A curtain with a yellowed floral pattern covered a rear window. Fingers drew it aside. The curtain closed, and I watched the handle turn.

We stepped through the doorway, Archer saying hello to the owner and asking permission to enter before descending into the basement, brick walls with arched doorways, cracked concrete floor.

"Ooo-*kaay!*" Archer said with serious intent. He'd turned on lights, poked his little electric meter into outlets as he passed to check activity—without comment, without even seeming to pause. I admired the eighty-bucks-an-hour efficiency of his movements. He poked his head into a few rooms to get his east-west, front-back bearings, craned his neck at the ceiling, then stepped into the center of the basement, which would be directly below the main staircase and hall.

The "record" button clicked on. "I'm seeing a lot of galvanized pipe," he said. "This is common in old houses." His words were soon to become like arrows through our excitement at actually purchasing this structure. He quickly strode first to what was the laundry room, regarded the "old concrete wash sink—*no, stone!*" he corrected himself, in what for him was a paroxysm of emotion. "That's really old!" He squatted at its far corner. "The legs here are rotted. If you're going to keep it, support that with concrete or bricks and mortar. If that were to fall—you have small children—it could squash one of them." The kids were being looked after at home; how he knew this, I had no idea. Perhaps he'd noted the car seat? But children, plural? The guy was good.

"Galvanized pipes are fine for a while." That word "galvanized" was not a good one when it came to pipes—I knew that. The only good word when you were talking water-supply pipes was "copper." I'd known galvanized metals from work in the boatyard, where it was fine—you'd want a steel tiller head galvanized, dipped in a solution that gives the metal an electrical charge to attract a bright silver plating of zinc. But galvanized pipes corroded after several decades, and here came the beginning of Archer's difficult descriptions.

"Plumbing drain pipes are cast iron and galvanized steel"—his active eyes running the length of the pipes as he spoke. "That's normal for a house this age. I suggest replacing galvanized steel supply pipes, *replacing* them. They tend to corrode from the inside, like a hardening of the arteries. Pretty soon you're going to run into problems. I see some mineral buildup at the joints of some of them, which means they've been leaking for some time. I can't see inside the walls. I can't tell you if you've got leaking pipes inside the walls, but I will look for water stains that might indicate leaking plumbing. If a plumber has to go inside a wall to repair the plumbing, that can be expensive." Many of the pipes were concealed by the moldering plaster-and-lath ceiling, which was in turn partially hidden by a crumbling tile ceiling. Archer followed these where he could, pointed a flashlight through cracks—"You might want to replace this plaster and lath."

"Is that expensive?" Donna asked.

"It doesn't require educated labor," he said. "It's a mess, and you need someone who will be careful to contain the mess and not damage the plumbing or wiring above it." He waited, staring hard at Donna. When she had no further questions, he returned to the ceiling. He was grunting and panting a little bit now, as he stepped on crates and boxes to look up into the ceiling. "There are areas that have lots of stuff piled up and stacked up, especially in the boiler room, areas I just cannot get into. I can't see the foundation or floors in this area." When he stepped down, he said, "I'm seeing a lot of *leaking, galvanized* water-supply pipes here."

He emphasized the words "leaking" and "galvanized" with such gravity it hurt.

"If a plumber were to try to repair these pipes, it's not unlikely that the pipe would break—and he'd have to go all the way back to the next joint, take it apart. It breaks, he has to go back to the next joint. Dominoes all the way up to the third-floor bath. I've seen this happen."

"We need to replace some of the pipes."

"If you only needed to replace some of the pipes," Archer said, "you would consider yourself lucky."

"Are you suggesting we replace *all* the pipes?"

"I'm not suggesting you do anything other than call a few plumbers and get estimates. This is not a small issue." He stared hard at Donna. Donna only sighed and turned to me.

"I've scanned the visible *gas* pipes here in the basement with a TIF 8800 combustible-gas detector and found several gas leaks, all small, but they're like dripping faucets—somebody's paying for gas. Get the gas company in here—they may well fix them for free.

"*Ooo-kay!*" And stepping back into the dank laundry room, he said, "This has been a dry July. Not a good time to determine how much a basement leaks. I can look for rot in the bottom of the stair stringers, rust on the bottom of the water heater and washing machine. There is some rot on the bottom of the door casing." He pointed. "I've seen stains on all four sides of the foundation. The basement leaks. I'm not getting the sense that the basement leaks to the extent that you need to wear tall *boots* when you're down here. But my protometer, sensitive to moisture, hits the top of the scale here at most of the foundation walls. And we're in a dry July."

He moved into electric, which we knew would be a problem and were prepared for it.

"Ooo-kay," Archer said, having removed the fuse-box panel. "Please understand I'm not here to do a code inspection. I'm not qualified and have no interest in a city's code. I can give you information regarding whether something was and is safe and correct according to the way the house was built.

"Right now you've got a combination of circuit breakers and fuses— nothing wrong with fuses if they're not bigger than the wire leading to them; they're more reliable, in fact, because they have no moving parts. But there's no main breaker in here that would turn off all the power. No breakers are labeled. I do *not* see a ground wire coming out of the panel, a bare copper wire that runs out and is connected typically to a cold-water pipe. This needs to be grounded. Above the fuse panel, you'll see some woven fabric tubes called 'loom.' Those are protection for wires in walls and ceilings, part of knob-and-tube-style wiring—wire wrapped around porcelain knobs about as big as a spool of sewing thread—which was used in houses as late as the 1970s. No longer used, but some electricians try to get extra work by claiming it needs replacing. Donna, it's OK to keep using it if it's in good condition.

"This panel needs to be revised if you intend to do any renovation. Talk to an electrician, describe your ultimate plan, know what kind of power requirements you'll need—for computer, kitchen appliances, you mentioned, Donna, wanting a washer and dryer on the second floor. You're going to need, for basic power, two-hundred-amp electric service, which would mean new meter base on the outside, new wire overhead, new wire up the wall, a new panel in here with one breaker that would shut off all the power in the house, and enough space below that breaker for all your individual circuits."

He carried on with basement systems—hot-water heater, heating system—but there were no surprises. We "marched" up the stairs to the attic, and he stopped at a second electrical panel here, covered by an elegant, unmarred mahogany door. "This is *really* old," he said, opening it. "Lead wire fuses!" He shook his head and carried on up to begin the structural inspection of the house from the top down.

The third floor had been painted long before, an eerie green and an eerie orange. These colors, combined with the dim lighting and stifling air ("I'd advise venting the roof," Archer said before he'd reached the top of the stairs) gave these three rooms, hallway, and peculiar crawl spaces—originally servants' quarters, surely—a subterranean feel rather than a lofty one shaded by branches of ash and silver maple. Archer performed his fundamental tasks, flushing the toilet, then rocking it to see that it was secure, checking water pressure, looking for structural flaws, heat, electricity.

As he entered the central room, what we hoped would be our daughter's room, he stopped to regard the doorknob and doorframe. This had been broken out in a particularly brutal-looking way; the wood was deeply splintered and crudely patched with an unmatching filler and a cheap, hardware-store knob. Archer closed the door, pushed on it to see if the latch held, then opened the door, ran his slender fingers over the broken spot, and frowned at it. He didn't comment on what was obvious: that somebody had broken this door down at one point. I'd begun to notice that there were a lot of doors in this house like that.

Nothing surprised him up here—in fact, it was probably the best floor of the house in terms of fewest city violations and work needed. "Nothing you can't see that I can—superficial damage, not serious," he said. We looked into each room, a small one to the left of the middle room, a large one to the right that had a padded floor, perhaps meant for dances, all connecting off a large main landing at the top of the stairs. "I'd love to be able to see the underside of the roof," Archer said, staring at the ceiling.

"I can only note that I wasn't able to inspect that. I can say that from out-side the roof looked to be in satisfactory condition, ten years old with about ten years to go. I know from the heat here that you'd be wise to vent not only the roof but vent the eaves as well to maintain good air cur-rent beneath the roof. Call a few roofers, get some estimates."

We descended the staircase, sweating, into the cooler, less com-pressed air of the second floor; again this staircase was a wide one, with a landing where we reversed direction. There were a lot of stairs in this house, and most people would be hyperventilating by the time they reached the third floor.

Archer did more toilet flushing in the bathrooms and water-pressure checking and poking around in the bedrooms. There were four—a small one in back, directly above the breakfast room; at the other end of the hall was a larger bedroom with a fireplace and broad windows look-ing out to the street and the drive; between these rooms was a bathroom with an enclosed tiled shower stall whose sill stood about two feet above the floor; I suppose you could stop the drain and fill it up for a shallow square bath. On the wall opposite the bathroom was a utility closet. The small central bedroom, with browning wallpaper intended for a young boy, connected through another bathroom to the master bedroom, which ran the width of the house, ending in a large walk-in closet with built-in cabinets and drawers. This room, too, contained a fireplace, con-necting with the living room chimney directly below. Archer tried to look up both fireplaces, recommended getting them thoroughly serviced—but he seemed to know most of what he needed from his scrutiny of the basement. He spent little time here or on the first floor. The dining room fed into the kitchen through a swinging door, which in turn led to the breakfast room. In the kitchen and in the foyer, Archer called our atten-tion to large water stains on the ceiling, wavy orange lines radiating out from beneath where second-floor shower and tubs were; the stains con-tinued to travel down parts of the wall. "Confirmation of what I sus-pected when we looked at the plumbing from the basement," he said. "You've got some significant leaks in the plumbing to both those bath-rooms. You'll have to do something about that." And that was all.

He paused to have one last look around, and this seemed to be a look of pleasure. We were in the main hall now; it was spacious and handsome with its raised-panel walls and the wide front staircase. The floor plan was a traditional layout, with a living room that ran the width of the house immediately off this hall; on the other side of the front door, a small study with its sliding pocket door—heavy paneled wood more than four feet wide—and bay window looking out into the front yard; next to this was a conventional dining room that also featured a pocket door and a large bay window; from this room back through the house were the kitchen and breakfast room. Archer was clearly finished—I would have applauded had it been appropriate—and he seemed to be taking in the house as a whole, considering it for his own pleasure. We passed through the long vestibule, descended two marble steps midway, then moved outside into the warm evening air, two hours on the dot, July's heat having lifted only a little. I was glad to be out in air again, smelling the warm, dry grass.

"I think I'm afraid to ask about replacing the galvanized plumbing," Donna said. "Do you see that as being the biggest expense?"

"It's *one* of the biggest expenses," Archer said. "I'm not in the contracting business. I'm not going to give you prices. I'm just not able to do that. But the biggest expenses will be plumbing and electrical. Tuckpointing—we talked a lot about that—materials are cheap, but it's a lot of labor. You want to get competing bids on that, because people charge what they want to charge." He paused. "Do you have any other questions, any big concerns that you might have had about the house that I didn't address?" Again he spoke to Donna. "If you do, if you think of something later, call me. I'll be happy to answer questions. There's no charge for follow-up phone calls. I'd be happy to discuss your concerns. You're bound to run into small surprises when you move in here and start your renovation. I wasn't here to predict those or to nitpick. You'll find little things I didn't talk about. But if you run into any big things I didn't talk about or expect, call me. If someone tries to *sell* you something big that I didn't say you needed, call me, feel free. I have zero to sell you beyond the information I've provided, I'm not in the repair business. But I'd be happy to comment on contractor proposals."

He paused one last time. He popped a tape out of one of the two recorders he carried and handed it to Donna.

"Thank you very much for using my company," he said. "I appreciate it. You'll receive a bulleted list of major issues in the mail in a few days." His expression was matter-of-fact. "Good luck with your project here. I'm assuming that you're intending to replace the current operating systems within what is otherwise a solid structure. If that's so, I like what you're doing."

"That's an opinion," I said.

"I'm off the clock," said Inspector Archer.

"In your opinion, then, is this a good house, from a structural standpoint?"

He held my gaze long enough for me to think he was reappraising me, then said, *"It's a tank."*

And off he marched, taking long, duck-footed strides and whistling, I believe, "Oklahoma." I looked to Donna, who watched him march along to his car. Marching Archer. She pursed her lips and raised her eyebrows. "I'd use his company again," she said.

5

The Concession

I joined Donna impulsively on two quick errands at the end of the day
not too long ago because I could see she'd had the kind of day during
which each of the simplest of errands had snarled on her, because my
writing had gone well and I figured I should quit while I was ahead, and
because, as I saw her buckling J. into the hot car seat yet again, I acknowledged that it was my fault she had to return to the grocery store (I, in
charge of the house's food supply, had neglected to put milk on the list,
thus wasting her time there). If I went along, one of us could hop out,
obviating the two-kids-loose-in-the-grocery-store tension she'd already
endured once today, which almost wasn't worth the milk. I ran out the
front door and nearly missed her the way she peeled out of the drive.
"What's the hurry?"

"I've got exactly enough time to get to the bank to make our
deposit," she said, annoyed at having to pause precious seconds while I
leaped in. "At least that will be *something* accomplished today."

Fifth Third Bank faced the grocery store, five minutes tops from our
house. The car clock said 5:25. She made one light, got stuck at the second, and turned the corner to the drive-through window at 5:29 to find
the shade being drawn closed.

My stomach fell—yet another of these little daily blows—and
maybe my fault for wanting to come along.

Donna rolled down the window and pressed the button anyway. J. began to scream in the backseat because A. took his toy hammer from him in order to achieve this reaction. The scream intensified Donna's resolve. She pressed again until the scratchy voice through the speaker said, "We're closed."

"It's five-twenty-nine," she said. "You're open."

"Donna," I said, "I can make the deposit tomorrow."

"I'm sorry, but we're closed," said the voice.

Donna turned to me and said, "Will you *please* deal with the kids?" Then, pressing the buzzer again, and holding it: "If you don't open this window, I'll call your manager and tell them you refused us." Donna had kept her athletic figure; she worked heavy creams into a complexion that had weathered ten Florida summers, but even so, she looked her age, thirty-nine. In our green Jeep Cherokee, she appeared not much different from all the pretty moms around here who drive SUVs and Volvos, child seats just visible in the passenger windows—but now there was a distinct Suburban Mom on the Edge tone.

The kids evidently were accustomed to this tone; they quieted without my saying a word. The shade lifted halfway, and a shadowy figure glanced out at Donna, then raised the shade completely. The teller didn't appear to be annoyed. She said, "One minute."

"*Thank* you," Donna said.

I was impressed but did not comment. She was on a roll.

"You have no idea what this means to me." Donna held up the check and deposit slip. "'Doing it tomorrow' means ten minutes to get both kids in the car, shoes on, buckled in, juice, finding J. has blown out a diaper, change the diaper, back in the car, and then to the bank," she said quietly to me. "She closed because she was lazy. I cannot *afford* for *other people* to be *lazy.* Look, there are customers still in the bank—she's not reopening for me. That thirty seconds it takes her to stamp a deposit slip saves me a half-hour headache tomorrow. And please don't tell me *you* can do it tomorrow. If you can do that, then I've got a lot of things for you to do. *I'm* doing it. Photography is not my job now, this is. This is my job, and I'm doing it so you can do your work."

I nodded, chastened and grateful again for her commitment to me. Donna took a breath while we waited for the teller to return. She put her hand on mine.

"Who was that chef in your book, said *all* people were *inclined* to be lazy? It's true. People's first response, whatever they do, is to do the least they can, not the most they can. Shouldn't you try to do the most you can? The best? The best and the most? Why do you have to *push everybody*? It takes so much of my energy. Ten minutes punching buttons on the phone just to reach a human who can respond to a question about the phone bill that that very company sent you. It makes me so *angry.*" The metal drawer popped out, opening its mouth. Donna dropped the checks in. "I shouldn't have to work like that to make a deposit. Everyone knows what they should do and shouldn't do. What's right. Why do you have to work so hard to get people to do what they already know they should do?"

Out popped the drawer; Donna retrieved the stamped slip and said a courteous, "Thank you very much." She pulled the gear handle into drive. "Now. Milk."

We'd been married eleven years, and I was still learning about my wife, watching her evolve. We all have a core that we're born with, that doesn't change much—the temperamental and chemical hardwiring of our personalities and bodies. And we all have a husk or a bark, an appearance, necessary but insubstantial. And between these two facets of our being, we have the changing, evolving part of us, the xylem and phloem tissue through which the food moves up and down the trunk. It's the shapable part of ourselves, the part that changes when you have kids or make a dramatic career switch.

Some people have a very thin layer of this changeable part of their personality. My father hit adulthood, I believe, on the day of my birth and hasn't changed since, has been on a more or less frictionless glide through the universe—suburban working man, homeowner, devoted dad.

But I think most people reveal a more vivid evolution, their whole lives variations on a theme of themselves that develops a meaningful pattern, one hopes, before the end. Work, I've found, is one of the main evolvers. My work has changed me. I used to be like most people, letting time go by, wasting moves, not being lazy but not being taut and efficient either. We forget things—car keys, wallets, the milk—because we're not thinking, and there goes more time. What was I going to do? Why did I open this cupboard? Unfocused and inefficient moves. Then, for a book, I learned the rules of the professional kitchen, and I started to hustle. I learned to cook. Now I always had a plan. I tried never to do one task without knowing, while I was doing it, what exactly I would be doing when I had completed the one at hand. No reason to finish one task and then sit around doing nothing while you figured out what to do.

Now I ran everywhere I went. I ran through parking lots. I had things to do. I had things I cared about. I get out of my car at the grocery store, I run to those doors. Can you believe all these people who just *walk*? *Look at them!* I wonder, Is this how you live your life, walking through parking lots, strolling, no hurry, taking your *time*? Don't you have anything to *do*? Don't you *care* about anything? You think you're going to live forever? You have one life, for godsake, use it. Some people make me want to scream. *Do something!*

Of course, this attitude, looked at from a walker's vantage point, appears a little off. I know a lot of very efficient and effective people who don't feel compelled to run everywhere they go. But chefs as a rule can seem odd when viewed through the window from the outside world. People say chefs are crazy. The ranting French chef has nearly become a cliché. In fact, chefs aren't crazy, but they are different. I used to think it was because chefs actually cooked their brains in all that heat (some truly have; notice the brownish, caramelized tint to the whites of their eyes—dead giveaway), but really their seeming whacked in the head is all a matter of perspective. In *their* world they're perfectly sane—it's only when they leave their world, expecting life outside to behave as it does in a kitchen, that they appear to be crazy. I'm not a cook. I'm a writer. But I was once a cook; it's hard and you've got to hustle all the time to stay in the game, and some of those gears in me still work even though I don't really need them. So I feel a little crazy myself when I run through parking lots in the middle of a weekday afternoon. I'm in both worlds, the kitchen and the "real" world. I'm like a snoop in the shrubbery, looking in through the windows of my own brain and thinking, How odd—glad I don't live in *there.*

But I do. I continue to run through parking lots because I can't shake the habit. And I do get more done this way. But sometimes I feel a little crazy and wish I were back in a kitchen.

I learned to cook, I worked a line, I changed who I was. Donna, a photographer by trade, changed when she gave birth. Those changes, I believe, ultimately caused her to pursue a permanent home with a singular intensity. First kids became her work, and thence began the changes. When work has wrought changes in a personality, the effects go deeper than, say, giving up cigarettes and alcohol, as Donna did when A. came along. Used to be, when Donna was awake, she had a super-low-tar chick cigarette going somewhere. More hours per day than not were spent wreathed in smoke. Donna was fun to drink with. She loved to dance. She shot pool better than most of my guy friends, and they respected this. She was intensely competitive—*hated* to lose, *loved* to win. When we were at home, we'd stay up talking and drinking and smoking until we heard the New York *Times* smack the door. I loved those days. We'd get into terrible fights—I didn't love those, but it seemed to come with the intensity of the relationship and the passions of youth. That passionate fighting part of our lives had come to an end with kids. We had arguments and disagreements, but we simply didn't fight anymore. We didn't shoot pool in sketchy biker bars. We didn't stay up late. We didn't even go to movies. We'd *evolved* past that.

As part of the attempt to become pregnant, which is as much a spiritual maneuver as a physical one, she quit smoking. She planned it. Donna makes up her own mind. She is solitary and deliberate, doesn't go on and on; it's between her and her. One weekend at an old friend's wedding on Cape Cod, she smoked with intense vigor and impressive volume. And when we got home, she quit. It wasn't pretty, but she didn't fuss, kept the misery to herself as much as she could.

So there were the abrupt physical changes begun by the pregnancies, in addition to the gradual ones of age and passing time, the wind erosion that begins during one's first thoughtless days of maturity when adult work is new and adult responsibilities are not yet crouching on one's shoulders. We'd moved to Cleveland more or less to make a change from Florida, bought a house to develop some equity rather than pay rent. When our daughter came along, right at the point when I needed to move to upstate New York for a year's project, Donna gave up her work as a photographer. To give up a trade you worked hard just to be lucky enough to do for money, work you loved, was a big deal. Work was always who she had been. She was her work. Then she let her work go.

Donna grew up in Queens and Long Island and at seventeen fled her home turf, put herself through a year at Rochester Institute of Technology in its well-respected school of photography and graphic arts, but found she couldn't justify spending that many thousands of her own dollars to hang around so many photo geeks. After a couple moves and a dead-end job that brought her to Florida, she crossed Royal Palm Bridge and the blue Intracoastal Waterway to arrive on the island of Palm Beach. Palm trees and bougainvillea and yellow Mediterranean stucco, expensive cars and mansions and, beyond, the great blue Atlantic Ocean. On this slender, lush island, the owner of Ramon's Camera Shop took her in like a daughter, helped her find a footing in the new place, and in due time the photo editor of the local paper, the *Palm Beach Daily News,* wandered in. Donna was happy and charming and beautiful—she radiated optimism and a can-do happiness whose naiveté is its fundamental power. It wasn't long before this photographer told her to come to the office and show him her book.

She quickly began to earn her daily bread with a camera. She'd gotten there with intelligence and gumption, on her own, and she'd just turned twenty-two. And to have done it all in such an unusual place, no less, shooting the likes of William F. Buckley, George H. W. Bush, Sophia Loren, Lady Bird Johnson, Donald and Ivana, Charles and Diana, in one of the most beautiful and wealthiest enclaves in America.

She loved her work. When she snapped her right arm clean in two diving for the Frisbee in a game of Ultimate, she demanded that the cast be bent at the wrist to facilitate her clicking finger.

These would be the happiest years of her life to date, in her early vigorous twenties, light brown hair streaked blond, brilliant blue eyes, and

tightly packed bright white teeth in a vivid smile. She had a broad forehead (her mom's), a prominent chin (her dad's), and a slender body
suited to Florida style. She had, if anything, too many good friends and
too many suitors. *And* she drove cool old sports cars. She parked her
white Alfa Romeo convertible beneath the palms outside the restaurant
to which she was forty-five minutes late for our first date ("Couldn't
find my keys").

The night Donna and I met began at an extraordinary house, the
most extraordinary I'd ever been in, and probably ever will be in: the
Henry Morrison Flagler Museum, a sixty-thousand-square-foot Beaux
Arts mansion built in 1901, featuring grand, gleaming white columns
and a barrel-tiled roof on Cocoanut Row. Each New Years' Eve the Flagler Museum hosted an extravagant party to benefit the Red Cross, and
to usher in 1988, it was called the Babes in Toyland Ball. Visiting my
mom, whose apartment looked across the Waterway down at the Flagler
mansion from West Palm, I went to the ball with a small group, led by a
woman who'd long ago baby-sat me, a friend of the family. Her name,
appropriately for the evening's initial task, was Crashy. We arrived without tickets, which ran many hundreds of dollars I couldn't afford.
Crashy was as sweet and innocent in appearance as the most sheltered
debutante but had nerves of steel and superior intelligence, a classic
overachiever who would soon have three kids and a thriving gem business in Manhattan. She flashed her blond-and-blue-eyed smile while
explaining to the gatekeeper that our group was from the Cleveland
chapter of the Red Cross and had flown here specifically for this
evening. I hung ineptly back. "Michael, come on," she called.

We were *escorted* into the ball. Here was I, a complete outsider suddenly in the center of the place where the coolest people were. And
Donna was there, also an outsider, and happy to be so, doing her job,
tonight shooting society photos for the *Daily News.*

She lived then above a garage set back among the palms in the north
end of the island and had planned to head there that night when her
work was done but had been talked into going to a party with her best
friend. She drove from Flagler's house to the house of the best-known of
the younger socialites on the island. Crashy, who always knew where

the coolest places were, brought me to the same house. Here I met Donna in the kitchen. I found her so attractive I immediately went over to her and said hello. She was it, and I knew it. But as I was in no shape at 3:00 A.M. to impress a woman whom I sensed I wanted to be in my future, I left her after several minutes of conversation. Later I stood beside Crashy as I watched Donna preparing to leave.

"Crashy," I said quietly, "see her? She's the one." Crashy regarded me with humor.

Donna wanted the new house in much the same way she had wanted to become pregnant, with the power of hunger, and she went about getting it with the resolve of the mom she was, a woman who didn't have years to waste searching for a house just as she didn't have a half hour to waste tomorrow for something that could be done in thirty seconds right *now*.

She enjoyed the new work, she loved being a mom. A woman can never predict how she will respond to motherhood; Donna surprised herself by how easily she took to it.

We kept on moving, first home to Cleveland from New York. We moved away again, this time to Massachusetts, and then home again, and we had another baby. This made it seven moves in just over ten years. Packing your entire life into a truck more than once every two years takes its toll, especially when the job of kids is involved. We got tired of putting things into boxes and taking them out somewhere else and then putting them all back into boxes again. Time now to stay put, somewhere, anywhere. The kids were growing up, their gathering physical mass an anchor, their downward vector intensifying with each new season, each inch and pound. They would soon need a stable, permanent home.

"Cleveland was supposed to be *temporary*," she said when evidence began to gather that I was liking the idea of staying in Cleveland

"We didn't know *what* it was supposed to be—I didn't anyway," I said. "It was supposed to be *not Florida*. And in that it succeeds."

"Michael," she would say, after the kids were asleep, after I'd read aloud the day's e-mail and our gazes turned to the broader landscape of our imagined future. "We can live anywhere. Your work doesn't keep you in any one place. Most people live where they do because of their work. Some people *have* to live in Cleveland. You don't. We can live anywhere."

Though timid in response to such direct questioning, I could honestly say, "I have yet to find a place better. If you know one, one that we can afford, show it to me, and let's consider it."

Donna had no real response to that, other than a sigh. This guy sitting across from her—not untraveled, he'd lived in England, traversed much of Europe, trekked in North and West Africa and throughout the United States—was telling her that in all the world he's never known a better place than *Cleveland*? How can you *respond* to that?

After a year of turning our options over in her mind, she accepted that for many reasons—cost-of-living issues and the general pleasantness of life with kids here—not to mention the deeper, more mysterious and unarticulated reasons she sensed *I* had for living where I grew up— she . . . what's the word? She *conceded.* OK, Cleveland. Once she conceded, then she began to hunt down our big brick tank. Cleveland would be home.

The heights of Cleveland sit on a glacial plateau more than two hundred feet above, and four miles from, the city's center. Because of its height, the land couldn't be developed residentially until the electric streetcar achieved efficient traction up the hill.

The downtown itself rests on a plateau above the Flats, the floodplains basin of the Cuyahoga River, which empties into Lake Erie.

Cleveland is a well-used, if not much lived-in, city. A common route takes me past it on my way to the West Side Market, a food bazaar opened in 1912, where the produce vendors shout at you to taste their goods as you shove through the crowd, the place I'd go if I needed a fresh pig's head right away. I pass the awe-inspiring ballpark, Jacobs Field, home of the once-again-loser Indians, and cruise straight over the

Lorain-Carnegie Bridge, a grand viaduct joining Cleveland's east and west sides, spanning the basin of the Flats and the crooked water, our famously flammable river. Visible from this viaduct is the whole of downtown, which is anchored by the Terminal Tower, built in the 1920s at Public Square, and across from it the British Petroleum Building, once Standard Oil of Ohio, a few blocks from the building where Rockefeller and Flagler formed their Standard Oil trust in 1870.

I loved traversing this bridge for this view of the city and its terrain, a city beside a river basin. And I loved Cleveland unabashedly, but like most here I have a bipolar relationship with it. I could adore it and denigrate in the same breath, often for the same reasons. But I didn't like when others did so.

A friend who planned to stay a night in the city on business e-mailed me from his Manhattan apartment to ask if we had running water and plumbing out here. A newspaper editor in New York who'd befriended me when I was young and unpublished asked me straight out, with obvious disappointment in a protégé, "Why are you living in *Cleveland*?" Some *Clevelanders* ask me why I am living in Cleveland.

Clevelanders go hot and cold on themselves but want to appear self-assured and confident to the world at large in their decision to live in the Mistake on the Lake (soon to be dubbed the poorest city in the nation by the U.S. Census Bureau). Which is why articles appear perennially defending the city and its honorable, work-ethical, ethnically diverse midwesterners. It is our community, and community is important, but we need to take our vitamins, remind ourselves of who we are and the qualities of our home.

"Our beaches ain't golden," Kevin Hoffman and Thomas Francis wrote in a recent essay called "Strange Love" that appeared in a local entertainment tabloid. "Our industry ain't high-tech. Our sports teams can't win. And every once in a while, we fuck something up and the whole Northeast goes black."

All true. This article goes on in solid, self-deprecating booster tones to discuss the lively cultural scene, the jaw-dropping prices of excellent houses, the ease of commuting, and the general approval of vices ("when it comes to the classics—booze, nicotine and fatty foods—

Cleveland knows no peer"), all of it under subheads such as "We've Got Your Culture Right Here, Pal," and making a so-uncool-we're-cool poster child of Harvey Pekar (creator of the American Splendor comics, "who proved that an ornery, socially retarded comic dork from Cleveland could be one of the coolest people in 2003 America").

This was an eccentric place, and it was my home, the hand I was dealt. Who was I to complain? While my East Coast chums might curl their upper lip at the mention of Cleveland, I knew that their clichéd response was a reflection of their own self-absorbed frame of reference and limited experience. I knew exactly how lucky I was. That luck was not simply a matter of having been born with every advantage in a caring, hardworking family, but also in a place that was worth staying in. It was once one of America's great cities. That it no longer is has as much to do with the changes in land use that swept all post–World War II America as it does with political and economic decisions made by the city's leaders and all the toxic crap we poured into a once fertile river and our mighty lake.

Cleveland is named for the man who lead the first surveying party into the territory known at the time, the 1790s, as the Western Reserve, which was owned by the state of Connecticut. A private group of Connecticut citizens, calling themselves the Connecticut Land Company, purchased a huge swath of the Reserve as a commercial venture, land speculation in the newly independent country. The group commissioned Moses Cleaveland, who'd been a general in the Revolutionary War—a tough, neckless man with heavy, dark eyebrows—to head into the wilderness, make friends with the natives, and begin the process of claiming and settling the land.

The general brought with him six surveyors, a commissary, a physician, and several other employees in charge of practical necessities, such as providing the group with food and trading with the Indians. These men and two of their wives were employed for as long as it took, up to two years. They brought along thirteen horses and some cattle.

The going was treacherous at the time. The lake itself had been named after the Erie Indians, called the Cat People because of the large, beautiful cats that lived all along the coast with this tribe, but the Eries had been killed off by Iroquois and Seneca. About fifty miles from the Cuyahoga River, the general's party ran into Mohawk and Seneca tribes, part of the confederation known as Six Nations. Cleaveland met with their representatives. "After shrewd persuasion," writes William Ganson Rose in *Cleveland: The Making of a City,* "the Indians relinquished their claim to the lands east of the Cuyahoga River in exchange for 500 pounds New York currency, two beef cattle, and 100 gallons of whisky."

On July 4 the Cleaveland party arrived at an opening of Lake Erie, named it Port Independence, drank heartily, and ate pork and beans to celebrate the anniversary of the twenty-year-old Declaration of Independence. They pressed on through territory they called New Connecticut, Cleaveland taking a small group by boat along the shore to the mouth of the Cuyahoga River. The heavily forested coast, lush now at the height of summer, had been mapped out by George Washington's studies of the Northwest, and Ben Franklin had already isolated the Cuyahoga as a promising site for a city in the Founding Fathers' newly united states.

Cleaveland strode up a bluff, looked out over the land, and decided to go no farther. Partly, it seems, because he'd had enough. They'd found the delta where the "crooked water" emptied into Lake Erie, the land around it marshy, the land above it thick with cedar and elm, maple, alder, and oak. Certainly the place was not without its advantages, Cleaveland thought, but really, who knew?

Cleaveland soon returned to the party's base at Port Independence and wrote a grumpy letter to the company, hemming and hawing a little because he didn't know if this was the best place to center their holdings, but then saying he didn't intend to travel farther and that, in effect, "if you want to get rich off our suffering, we've got your map right here, pal." He rejoined his men on the Cuyahoga, rested up, declared the site excellent, and prepared to head home while surveyors mapped out the city's first streets. Surveying land and starting cities back then was a job. He'd done it and would never return.

Two maps were made in 1796 outlining potential streets and naming them, Lake and Erie; the mapmaker crossed out "Broad" and wrote in

"Superior," which ran through a central square; Erie is now East Ninth Street, Lake is Lakeside, but these main avenues and a city center remain as imagined on paper that long-ago fall. Most believe that an early newspaper misspelling of the general's name accounts for the dropping of the *a* from the name, perhaps the original mistake on the lake.

In the late years of the century, the city saw its first businesses settled. Samuel Mather Jr., a member of the Connecticut Land Company's board of directors, traveled to Cleveland on horseback and returned home to invest more in this territory; his family would remain prominent in the city throughout the next century. Newcomers built their cabins along the banks of the river to form a trading-post settlement. Life was rugged. Meals consisted of coarse raw foods and game spit-roasted over open flames. Women made their families' clothes. If you wanted a bed that was more than a pallet on the floor, you built one using spruce poles and elm bark. Indians would sometimes walk into your log house without knocking, lie down by the fire, and take a nap.

"Neighbors were far and few between," writes historian Rose, "and there was a longing for the community life that had been enjoyed back home."

In the summer of 1798, nearly everyone living in the marshy, buggy Flats along the river got sick. When they recovered, they moved up and east, away from the pestilence, leaving the land for industry to take over.

Up the hill from these Flats, the large Public Square was created, dirt streets marking off four patches of stump-filled land where wild swine rooted.

Nat Doan bought some land several miles east of the city, built a cabin there that served as a tavern. He then built a store, a small plant to produce aerated sodium (baking soda, then called saleratus), and a blacksmith shop on what came to be called Doan's Corners, where tools were forged and horses kept shod. Nat served as clergyman, postmaster, and justice of the peace. He died in his tavern in 1815. The Euclid and East 105th Street intersection is no longer known by his name, but the creek that runs down the glen and out to Lake Erie is.

Terrain was once important. Settlers found the land here fertile for farming; apples and peaches and berries grew abundantly, maple trees gave sugar; salt, a precious commodity at twenty bucks a barrel, was not far away; and the lake teemed with fish. Cleveland came to be called "the Forest City" for its dense coverage of deciduous trees. "The ring of the ax echoed through the timberland, and self-reliance and resourcefulness were man's greatest assets," writes Rose of the early nineteenth century.

The city had begun the century with a population of fifty-seven. As more arrived, it followed a typical pattern of city growth. "Its people joined together for protection, sympathy, betterment and gain," Rose notes. Soon a doctor came and stayed, and so did a lawyer.

Lorenzo Carter built a big wooden boat with a schooner rig for shipping goods, beginning what would become a powerful industry centered here in the middle of the Great Lakes.

In the mid-1820s, the Ohio Canal was built, extending the Cuyahoga's commercial potential deeper into the state and connecting the state's resources, via Great Lakes shipping, with Buffalo, New York, where the Erie Canal, also newly opened, ran on to Albany. Canal commerce flourished, and the Flats of Cleveland soon thrived with industry. Coal replaced cheap, plentiful wood as industrial fuel. Log cabins became a thing of the past as properly sided houses sprang up. Settlers continued to pour in, largely New Englanders and German immigrants. Cleveland quickly became a boom town, as churches and taverns vied for superiority at a time marked by fervent evangelism, banks rose on Bank Street, and savvy businessmen sensed the first rumblings of industrial opportunity and prepared to take advantage of an era of unprecedented growth and profits.

A family of uncertain means headed by an itinerant snake-oil salesman, philanderer, and scoundrel named Bill Rockefeller, aka Devil Bill, a man indicted for raping a household servant and soon to become a bigamist, had driven his sons, John and William, into the bustling city in 1853 and set them up at a boardinghouse so that they might attend school. John D. Rockefeller was fourteen, his brother twelve.

Railroads had become a new force in the country that many people of the time considered to be almost magical, such was their power to transform the country. They provided a means of travel so fast as to be unimaginable when stagecoaches had predominated ten or fifteen years earlier. Trains could move masses of people throughout the country, as well as tons of freight, either raw products such as timber and iron ore and grain and salt or finished goods such as clothing or barrels. Increased passenger traffic by rail, into and out of a city, pumped up its economy and necessitated the building of hotels, the opening of stores to sell needed goods. In the world of commerce, trains added to already prosperous shipping on canal and lake. In Cleveland the sidewheel steamer was popular, but most cargo moved under the sails of one of the city's eighty schooners. The telegraph, a new technology that increased the distance information could travel and sent it there at an astonishing speed, joined the rail in America's economic explosion.

At the age of sixteen, in 1855, John Rockefeller quit high school, perhaps because of his father's itinerancy and the resulting need to help support his family. He pounded the pavement during a sweltering summer and into September before landing a clerk's position at a company trading commodities on commission, a job that paid him no money for three months. JDR biographer Ron Chernow, in his book *Titan,* imagines the teenager at his first job, which would eventually give him $25 a week: "Poised on a high stool, bent over musty ledger books at Hewitt and Tuttle, the new clerk could gaze from the window and watch the busy wharves or canal barges drifting by on the Cuyahoga River a block away." The young man began his day at dawn "in an office lit dimly by whale-oil lamps." John adored work, and he perched on that stool at a particularly auspicious time for a man entering business—many of America's tycoons were born in the 1830s, hitting mature adulthood and prime business shape as the Civil War ended—and in a city that proved especially auspicious for the talents John would soon find were his in abundance.

John worked at Hewitt and Tuttle for three and a half years. A gravely serious boy who accounted for his every penny, John had saved $1,000 before he was twenty and, with a matching grand from his unscrupulous dad, joined Maurice Clark at 32 River Street in opening a produce-commission business. Rockefeller & Clark earned money by transporting goods from one place to another, easily done here, via the Ohio Canal and the Great Lakes as well as by rail.

The very year that John, age twenty, became an independent businessman, Edwin Drake, a retired railroad conductor, drilled a well and struck oil at a depth of sixty-nine and a half feet near Titusville, in western Pennsylvania, an event that signaled the birth of the oil industry. At first the industry was wild and speculation reigned. Teamsters, who hauled barreled oil on wagons, demanded high transportation fees and thwarted opponents by destroying early pipelines. Prices rose and fell, and the market was impossible to predict. John Rockefeller saw a great market in kerosene, produced by refining the hydrogen and carbon that made petroleum, literally rock oil, what it was.

Until then whale oil or coal oil or candles were used for creating light, all of which were either expensive or sooty or both. John saw a future in inexpensive, clean, safe kerosene. With abundant oil in nearby Titusville, he began moving that product in addition to farm produce. But after the Civil War, the oil industry remained maddeningly unpredictable, and Rockefeller claimed that it was doomed unless refiners could get together. Only with consolidation could the oil industry become stable and predictable.

John quickly embraced the idea of oil and borrowed extraordinary sums to expand his business. He borrowed so ferociously, in fact, that he alienated his older partners, the Clark brothers, who thought he was crazy. They told him to cut it out. He said that if they wanted to dissolve the partnership, they should say so. They did, and to their surprise, John not only accepted but had already, with impressive sangfroid, put in place the levers to buy them out and begin fresh. In 1865 John sold his interest in the produce-commission business, dissolved his partnership with the Clarks, buying them out in a public auction for an amount that would today be $652,000, and setting up a firm with an ingenious Englishman, Samuel Andrews, whose techniques in refining crude oil were advancing the industry. The twenty-five-year-old now controlled the city's largest refinery.

In 1867 a flamboyant businessman named Henry Morrison Flagler came to town and married the niece of Stephen Harkness, by then one of the city's richest men. Not long thereafter Rockefeller negotiated an enormous loan from Harkness, who made his employing Flagler a condition of the deal. Rockefeller and Flagler became boon business companions in the new group that had been facilitated by Harkness's riches, a concern now called Rockefeller, Andrews & Flagler.

Rockefeller loved Cleveland because, Chernow writes, "it was the hub of so many transportation networks that he had tremendous room to maneuver in freight negotiations." He could confound the rail links feeding and coming from Chicago and Cincinnati, the New York Central, the Erie and the Pennsylvania, by shipping his oil on the Lakes and the Erie Canal.

Cleveland was ablaze with industry, American muscle, steel and oil, the city's air filling with their smoke. Rockefeller and Flagler continued to manipulate the transportation system and oil business throughout the city, and the city grew as a result.

Rockefeller had also begun the extraordinary business machinations that would make him notorious—buying the city's refineries, making them his own, further leveraging that industry and all those serving it. Within a year of the Harkness deal, Cleveland was the world's center of crude-oil refinery and Rockefeller was at its center, refining as much as his three biggest competitors combined. Given the size of his business, he was able to negotiate in secret a rebate deal with the Lake Shore Line, guaranteeing huge daily rail shipments in exchange for huge savings his competitors wouldn't enjoy, a deal many consider his "original sin," though the ethics of the deal can be argued either way. Some view it as justified because of the risks he took to guarantee the shipments in an infant industrial economy. Others see it as the first great economic conspiracy in America.

Rockefeller bought a house on Euclid Avenue, then considered one of most beautiful streets in America, "Millionaires' Row," representing the iron, timber, shipping, and real estate fortunes of the city and the era. His was a modest mansion, given its location on the south side of the broad, tree-lined street. He was "anchored in family life," according to Chernow. Here Junior was delivered by the city's first woman doctor, Myra Herrick, as were three Rockefeller girls. John and his wife, Cettie,

were active in their church and in the temperance movement. He epitomized the Victorian family man, a doting father, teetotaling church-
goer, devoted husband ("Oh, what I would give for wings to reach you,"
he wrote to his wife while away on business), his prudishness providing
the order and energy for him to be ruthless and revolutionary in his
work.

Flagler had bought a home nearby, and the two men walked the two
miles to and from work twice daily, from Fortieth and Euclid to Public
Square, planning their business strategies. Chief among them was finding some way of consolidating the world's oil companies, under their
roof.

Surely on these walks to Public Square they grappled with some way
to borrow the extraordinary sums of money required to buy up, or force
the sale of, all the other companies without giving up *control* of the big
new company, one of the most influential business deals in the history of
the country. The answer—which Flagler came up with, according to
Rockefeller—was to incorporate and raise money via stock, to form a
trust.

In January 1870, Flagler drew up the act on cheap legal paper, and the
Standard Oil Company was formed, John as president, his brother
William as VP, and Flagler as secretary. They could now acquire money
by offering shares in the company. The company began with $1 million
in capital, a huge figure, making this undertaking even at its outset,
according to Chernow, a historic moment in American business. Rockefeller owned more than a quarter of the original ten thousand shares,
with the rest divided between his brother William, Andrews, Harkness,
and Flagler (who would ultimately take his wealth to Florida, opening
the state's east coast, and build a mansion on the island of Palm Beach).

While investors didn't clamor at their door immediately, Rockefeller's Standard Oil bought up, or muscled into submission, virtually
the entire industry. Seven years after founding Standard Oil, writes
Chernow, "the thirty-eight-year-old Rockefeller, with piratical flair and
tactical brilliance, had come to control nearly 90 percent of the oil
refined in the United States." By the age of forty, in 1879, he was one of
the twenty richest men in the world. As Cleveland's wealthy were not

showy and its politicians were not violent, Chernow writes, Cleveland was "the ideal place for a reclusive magnate."

The devoted family man bought seventy acres a mile east of Doan's Corners and built an estate that ultimately comprised seven hundred acres, in addition to substantial landholdings along the entire eastern edge of the city and in the heights. From this Forest Hill estate, he would hop into his two-seater, lower his goggles, snap the reins on two fast-trotting horses, and zip five miles into the city along Euclid Avenue, where horse and sleigh races were popular pastimes, to his office in Public Square.

But his days in Cleveland were limited. "In an age of long-distance pipelines, huge volumes of crude oil were flowing to seaboard refineries, where they fed a flourishing export traffic, relegating Cleveland and other inland centers to an inferior status," Chernow writes. "Responding to the export boom, Standard Oil established sprawling refineries in Brooklyn, Bayonne, Philadelphia and Baltimore." In his quest for global dominance, Rockefeller needed access to more and more money; he needed to be at the center of America's industrial economy. It grew clear that Standard Oil couldn't maintain two head offices. And in 1884 a forty-five-year-old Rockefeller moved his offices to 26 Broadway in New York City, and his family to 4 East Fifty-fourth Street.

John Rockefeller changed forever the way America did business, and not surprisingly his impact on Cleveland is proportionately great and can scarcely be overstated. Standard Oil of Ohio helped to power the main industries of the city, iron and steel, shipping and construction. His efficient business strategy extended to owning the forests and the mills and the cooperages that would make the barrels to carry his oil. Banks thrived from the sheer volume of his borrowing and deposits. Thriving banks allowed all manner of unrelated enterprises to thrive as well. He revolutionized the form of giving itself, in that his grant-making foundation became a model for future philanthropic foundations. His charitable gifts to the city toward parkland, buildings, and education, though unnamed, remain powerful here. His company made many men fabulously wealthy, and these men put their money back into their city: Stephen Harkness; Colonel Oliver Payne, one of the original sources of the Bolton and Blossom fortunes; John Huntington, who built the city's Museum of Art; Louis Severance and his son, who built Severance Hall, where our orchestra plays. Standard Oil money continues to pour over the edges of this city as if from a fountain, a city Rockefeller remained devoted to till his death in 1937 at the age of ninety-seven.

He was buried beside his wife and mother under a gigantic stone obelisk in Lake View Cemetery, a rolling verdant hill at 12316 Euclid Avenue, just up from his Cleveland estate.

By the end of the nineteenth century, Rockefeller's direct influence dwindled, though he spent much of his time in Cleveland and owned and influenced real estate in what would be the eastern suburbs, now farmland and rock quarries. The growing city continued to push east. A small electric railway, the country's first, opened the year Rockefeller left for New York and closed fairly quickly because the underground cable didn't work in wet weather, which we have a considerable amount of here. Frank Sprague is the man who created the first viable electric railway, in Richmond, Virginia, in 1887, using an overhead trolley. Traction companies here and in cities throughout the country sprang up to take advantage of this new technology, obliterating the horse-drawn streetcar.

It was now possible to get masses of people easily up and down embankments. This ability, coupled with the growing desire of families to live in a cleaner, prettier environment—away from oil refineries and steel mills—convinced a stranger visiting the city for a day on business, a railroad lawyer named Pat Calhoun, to buy a swath of land in 1890 on speculation. He wanted to develop an aristocratic residential village, not unlike Llewellyn Park, and toward that end he also convinced a streetcar company to run a rail up to his village. Calhoun's company, the Euclid Realty Company, would soon construct the first of many houses on those three hundred acres, ours included. The streetcar suburb was about to happen here.

And it was to this streetcar suburb that I brought Donna, and to which, all things considered, she was willing to *concede*. To this suburb and to this city on a lake in the Midwest.

And upon this concession began the house hunting, or rather house stalking—Donna stalked it as if it were prey.

"If we're going to live in Cleveland," she said, again at night at the table in our cramped kitchen, "then we have to find a house we love. We know we don't want to live in this house forever. When I do work on our house, in it or around it, I want to know that it's going to last. *I* want to be able to enjoy it. For a long time. I want to do things right."

And so we purchased the structure and a property that we could not quite afford, built a hundred years earlier at the end of a streetcar line in the industrial midriff of America, one that needed all new plumbing, all new electrical wiring, with virtually every interior surface and exterior surface in need of scraping, sanding, or cleaning, then priming and painting. But a fine and durable one worth renewing and caring for. A tank, after all.

6
Ghosts

Following the Archer inspection, we were able to reduce our offer by five grand to compensate for wood deterioration and the extent of the plumbing work the house needed. This did little to ameliorate Donna's resentment of Steve over the furniture issue, but the owner wasn't budging further, and I didn't want to push the issue, ever fretful of a sudden collapse of the deal. The whole process had been wrenching and emotional, we'd become bitter and suspicious about our former friend and neighbor, but it was at last done. All were agreed, a contract was signed.

Impossible to know why this had been so difficult. My mother, who brokers deals for multimillion-dollar residences, described astonishing stories of the wealthy, one of whom, for example, after selling a $9.9 million home, took all the showerheads before vacating the premises. Why wealthy homeowners would risk botching a real estate deal they'd initiated by stealing the fancy but by no means invaluable showerheads displays in some sense the irrational, even disturbed, emotions and acts attending the sale of a house. But it didn't have to be that way. The ease with which we sold our house was surreal by comparison to what we'd been through as buyers.

We'd simply followed the known rules for success, supplied by the impeccably professional Mary Ann, a colleague of Steve's, in fact, whom we'd engaged to help us sell our house as quickly and efficiently as possible, our relationship with Steve having become untenable by then, which no doubt annoyed him, as he'd been counting on a commission from the sale of our house as well.

We took care of all point-of-sale violations; we cleaned the house, moving everything extraneous to the garage, hiding away anything that made a house personal (framed photographs, kids' fridge art); and we determined a reasonable asking price (more than double what we'd paid for it ten years earlier). We then departed for a long weekend vacation, while Mary Ann hosted an open house. The Sunday we returned, Mary Ann was waiting with two couples and their agents, making offers. One couple, who seemed virtually identical to the couple Donna and I had been when we'd bought the house, offered exactly what we'd asked for and could be flexible about possession date. We accepted. What's so difficult about that?

As the title-transfer date neared, I finished up my work in the pediatric intensive care unit, the last of the information gathering before I sat down to write. An ICU nurse named Ruth, an old-timer, checked lines and meds in the sedated, paralyzed, intubated infant as she described how different the ICU was today from the horrifying and brutal early days when open-heart surgery on neonates had been brand-new.

The pager on my belt buzzed, and, still unused to the thing, I jumped as if I'd been goosed. Donna. I finished up my conversation with Ruth, stepped into the ICU corridor, and saw Emad, an anesthesiologist, standing in an unoccupied ICU room staring at the ceiling-mounted TV screen. A nurse was there, too, and I think one of the ICU attendings, but it was Emad, a native of Egypt and a highly regarded doc, whom I will always remember, the look on his face. What could be so compelling?

One of the World Trade Center towers was hit and smoking—this alone, an incredible sight of course. But I'd arrived in time for a replay of another plane bombing into the second tower. I covered my mouth with my hands, and my stomach turned. The pager had to go off again before I could look away from the images.

I found a phone behind the ICU desk, and Donna answered quickly. "Yes," I responded, "I know."

"I need you here," she said.

"I'll leave shortly."

"I'm going to pick up A. from school."

"Good."

When I arrived home, the Jeep was gone. I knew that the house would be vacant, but when I entered, I was unprepared for the disconcerting emptiness. I felt as if the world were collapsing with those towers. I managed to find the remote to turn on the TV in the kitchen. The sound of tires crunching on gravel calmed my breathing almost instantly. They were home. J. crawled out of the car himself with a hulking sense of accomplishment, a grin between his plump, muscular cheeks. A. thoughtlessly swung her purple lunch bag as she strolled away from the car, uncomprehending, enjoying the novelty of being taken from school in the middle of the morning and ignoring the urgency of the hug I gave her and her mom, in tears at our touch on this cloudless September day.

Within an hour my father was with us. We as a family were far removed from the tragedy, and we knew not a single person who perished; nor did we know directly any family rent by the attack, knew no children who'd lost their mom or dad or both. We shared only the same historic sense of loss and irrevocable damage the rest of the country did, and we acknowledged anew our vulnerability, a vulnerability from which I believed a house could in many ways, if only spiritual ones, protect us.

Donna and I were about to make a big change in our lives at substantial financial cost. To be making such a change amid the immediate aftershocks of 9/11 created an ominous backdrop to the taking possession of this house. On Wednesday, September 12, we'd made the bad decision to try to help the owner move boxes out of her house and left in an uneasy and irritated state. The day after that, I found myself spying on the owner, still incredulous that the house would actually be vacated as promised. When I returned at noon, the house was empty, the street still. I rolled up the driveway that was now my driveway. I stood on the stone step at the battered red door. I jiggled the handle—locked but loose enough almost to force open without excessive effort. I pushed the key in.

I repeated these actions three hours later, keeping an appointment with an architect. I paused before opening the door but heard no footsteps. Only then did I question what I'd heard the first time. Had I heard actual noises? Yet there was this behavioral evidence: My response had been instinctive, not cerebral. I didn't think, I paused in surprise, then bolted for the front. At the time I had no doubt whatever that the sounds had been real.

I reentered our new house through the back door, took the five steps to the left up into the breakfast room. I moved through the narrow kitchen and into the dining room, taking down in my mind all the walls from here to the back to create one dining room/kitchen/breakfast room expanse. I saw the architect advancing up the walk and went to open the door for him.

The man was either in his sixties or still in his fifties but unhappy. He walked with a limp and took every opportunity to lean against counters and doorframes when we weren't actually moving through the house, sighing conspicuously each time he came to rest. The first concern was with the kitchen—namely, could my plan to have a completely open space here be realized, or was there a load-bearing wall that posed a problem? The architect stopped in the kitchen and leaned heavily against the steel counter. He looked up at the stained, buckling kitchen ceiling, inhaled and exhaled deeply before saying, "I hope you didn't pay a lot for this house."

How to respond? *Say no more, you're hired!*

I said, "You think we've made a mistake?"

"I just hope you intend to stay here for a while. If you planned to turn this house around, you're not going to make your money back."

His pessimistic, even defeated, tone annoyed me, given that he had no idea who we were or how we hoped to use the house. I might have told him that I already had my own parents, thanks, or I might have just said good-bye right there. How did a man like that get anything done in life? I hurried us through our meeting, each of us thinking the other a fool, no doubt. I hoped this wasn't going to be a problem, finding someone appropriate to do the work. The clock was now running—we had ten weeks before our move.

We arranged a time for him to return to take measurements for a set of drawings; we needed floor plans, which he would draw, in order to make exact plans for the renovation. I said good-bye to the sad man and really, then, for the first time had an undistracted stretch to think about the house. It was perfectly empty; all had been removed except for the dining room set, as agreed, and a hanging mirror in a second-floor bedroom, either unwanted or forgotten.

Though the rooms were vacant, the carpeting, wallpaper, and the unfamiliar scents underscored the sense that this still felt like someone else's house, not mine. And not a blank slate but a palimpsest of other lives. Those lives that had lived here outweighed my presence, many lives, many families, beginning with the Harding family, the head of which, we'd been told, was the brother of Warren G., twenty-ninth president of the United States, born in 1865 southwest of Cleveland. So we had reason to believe and liked the fact that the house had a pedigree. Certainly the interior felt very spacious and so would have accommodated abundant lives over the decades. The upstairs hallway was wide, the ceiling high. I stopped at the banister to look down at the landing, through the Gothic leaded-glass windows to the backyard—double-hung sashes, amazing. These ornate windows were designed to slide up and down. I descended the stairs slowly, held the banister as I hit the landing. I could imagine the tread of girls my daughter's age on these stairs. I continued to the main hallway.

I would stroll this way through the quiet house over the next several days, trying to imagine what had happened here—it was such an old house—and also what might happen. Because of the intricate spaciousness of the house and its rich details, it seemed to me to teem with life, with past spirits, with, metaphorically speaking, the ghosts of those lives played out in these rooms. I stepped off the dimensions of our kitchen table where I wanted it to go, hoping we would no longer be as cramped as we had been but also wondering what kinds of families had been in this room before me.

I continuously tried to imagine the new kitchen space, but it had an I-shaped construction of walls smack in the center, so it was difficult to know certainly how the open-kitchen idea would affect the house.

I stepped through the swinging door into the dining room. Immediately beside this door was an elegant built-in cabinet with leaded-glass doors. This wall would likely be taken down, but we'd be able to save the cabinet and its doors, perhaps build it into the new kitchen.

The dining room set was still in its place, the buffet against the vivid red wall. Above the white chair rail here was white wallpaper with red flocking. It was a deeply crimson room. The furniture and the dramatic color made this room seem, more than the others, still to be somebody else's and me just a visitor. I admired the furniture. It was mahogany, I guessed, very dark and richly textured. The legs of both table and buffet shared the same feathery carved pattern. It was a little more elegant and formal than was our style, but it fit the rugged Victorian impression of the house. The pieces were very good furniture and had gone a long way in compensating for the decrepit plumbing situation we'd discovered. Looking for the name of a carpenter or other distinguishing mark and also simply scrutinizing its construction, I removed the top central drawer from the buffet and set it on the dining room table. The pull for each drawer was a brass lion's head, the ring hanging below the snout. I removed the bottom drawer as well and noticed the newspaper clipping resting on the panel under the bottom drawer. I set this drawer, too, on the table behind me and looked at the clipping. It was a small square of yellowed newsprint. The headline read STABBED MAN'S BODY FOUND IN CREEK above three inches of type:

> The body of an unidentified white man with multiple stab wounds was found yesterday afternoon in Doan Creek, near Parkgate Ave. and Martin Luther King Jr. Blvd.
> Homicide Detective Melvyn Goldstein said the man ap-

peared to be 18 to 21 years old, 5 feet 5 inches tall and 138 pounds. He was found by a jogger. He had probably been in the creek two days, Goldstein said.

Goldstein said police believe the man was killed elsewhere and dumped in the creek.

He was wearing blue jeans, sweat socks and a Reebok T-shirt.

He suffered stab wounds to the neck, chest, elbow and wrist.

That was the story as printed, but somebody had written on it in black pen two phone numbers labeled "mother's" and "daughter's," both with Chicago area codes. Why save this thing? I wondered. Whose mother, whose daughter? It had once sat atop a full-to-the-brim drawer, apparently, and when the drawer was pulled open, the clipping had been pushed back off the edge and lay hidden beneath the drawer to become forever a part of the house.

Carl and Rob, the heads of the construction company we hired, Bleick & Kessler Construction, were indeed capable folks. We were all about the same age, we all lived in Cleveland Heights, our kids went to the same schools.

We liked Rob for his quick-talking enthusiasm and love of old houses. He was of medium height, brown hair receding across his dome-like pate; he had a teddy-bear belly not inconsistent with his age or the fast-food lunches he'd eat standing in someone's gutted living room or kitchen. Rob was a contractor, not an architect, but he made architectural decisions regarding what ceiling could be cantilevered here if the demo crew were to remove that load-bearing wall or if this room or that could be converted to, say, a laundry room.

Because he loved old houses, I trusted his ability to restore a great old suburban home to efficient working order for a contemporary family's needs (larger bathrooms, expanded kitchens) without diminishing either the integrity of the actual structure or the integrity of design and spirit of the house. "We can do that" was his motto.

During our courtship phase, he'd brought us to his brother's house, an ornate Victorian circa 1895, behind us on our new block, one of the oldest homes in the neighborhood. It featured an imposing entryway and front rooms all composed of extraordinary woodwork that had been lovingly restored and varnished. The kitchen had been redone, as had the third floor, which was now office and recreation space with wet bar, TV and stereo, computer and work area. The house was still very much of the previous century on its first two floors, and yet it was a practical and efficient living space for its owners. B&K had done the renovation, and Rob showed it to us because it embodied the kind of work they did.

We wanted to inflict much the same kind of renovation on our new purchase, but we couldn't do anything or hire people until we actually took possession and they could get into the house to give us actual information and estimates. And because we had to be out of our house end of November, we had to act fast once we took possession. So we got Rob quickly to the new house.

In contrast to the sad architect, Rob, who was the salesman and did all the numbers and estimating, grinned as he strode through the new house the following day, admiring the stone lintels, the unusual arch above the main staircase, and the leaded glass at its landing, responding to my every structural hope, "We can do that" and "We can do that." His whole being seemed to be trying to absorb all the details of a pre–World War I construction. He appeared as excited as we were, excited for us. Timing would not be a problem, he assured me.

Pages from early notepads during those days are headed "Questions for Rob and Carl," with cell-phone numbers scribbled in the margins and starred notes reading "When can we see actual numbers?" and "When will you begin work?" But in fact, almost from our first meeting, there was little doubt whom we'd hire. Indeed, I'd taken a walk through another house they were renovating—"This is what your house will look like in a month," he'd said of the gutted hive a mile from our house—then stood with Rob in the driveway's apron and tossed him the keys to our house. I hadn't seen an estimate or a contract. But I could tell we wanted these guys, knew their price wouldn't be unreasonable, and, critically, if we intended to be able to move in two months, we couldn't dither. It drove me crazy anyway, to dick around with estimates and interviews, wasting all that time, yours and theirs—you can suss out the situation by reputation, by taking a look at their work. We knew them peripherally through school, and we'd heard only good things.

Certainly behind much of the urgency to hire a contractor and get the work under way was the idea that if we didn't, I'd have to move us in with my father till the work was finished, a situation devoutly to be avoided. Also, I didn't want to have to move twice when one move could do it.

"We need to be in by the end of November," I repeated to Rob.

"We can do that," Rob said—no grin, only plain confidence, certainty.

It was of course with mounting anxiety that we watched the next days go by, our big brick house dark and silent. All day long. And then after a week, still nothing. "Don't worry, we'll get the demo crew in a couple days," Rob kept saying from his cell phone.

A week and a half after we'd taken possession of the house, a Saturday, Donna called from the car. "There's a big red truck in the driveway," she said, all but ecstatic. The demo crew.

Fairly quickly I finished up work at my desk—Donna had both the kids and so didn't poke her head in—and hurried to our house.

A crowd of men, African-Americans all, had arrived in the bed of an enormous red pickup truck. Their instruments were crowbars and sledgehammers. They wore hats and bandannas on their heads and masks or bandannas over their noses and mouths. When I arrived, they filled the dusty basement, a whole team of them, a dozen or so, yanking and clawing the moldering plaster-and-lath ceiling down around them. Debris covered the floor. They worked silently—no sounds but for that of hammers, the resonant creak of rusted nails rent out of wood, splintering boards. Electricity had been shut off. Their bright eyes turned on me from within sweat-gleaming faces, light shafting through propped-open ground-level windows. I felt as if I'd descended into a mine. The light illuminated rectangular columns of dust. Men filed past me carrying long, splintered pieces of wood on their shoulders, took the steps two at a time, and headed straight out the back door to toss the debris into their truck. Another man broke planks that were too long by pushing them against the base of the garage until they cracked and snapped in half.

Men upstairs tore out bathrooms. Much of the carpeting was already out. We wanted everything gone. The gold carpeting was next. Anything that wasn't bolted to the structure—and much that was—gone, all surfaces taken down to their bare origins, wood, brick, or plaster.

The site of the powerful crew who did this work enthralled me. The house needed this kind of force. The ripping out was good for it, like lancing infected boils and carving rot out of healthy muscle. The violence of their work felt cathartic rather than destructive.

As always, there was nothing for me to do here. So I continued to wander the rooms of the house, envisioning the changes. After a week and a half of anxious silence, the demo crew had brought the big brick house to life.

I descended from the second floor by way of the main staircase and heard a crack, followed by screams, one man's screams. When I hit the landing halfway down, I could see him through the Gothic leaded windows. He rolled and writhed in the backyard grass, both hands covering his face, blood leaking through his fingers. He was an older member of the crew, I saw when I'd reached him. He continued to roll in the grass in the hot September sun, moaning and stomping his foot. One crew member knelt at his side. The leader of the crew saw me and said softly, "Cut his forehead, needs help. Do you have a phone here?"

"Yes," I said. "I'll call." I went to the kitchen, dialed 911, and returned to the yard, where the man continued to rock, now silently, in the grass, clutching his face and his gashed forehead, kicking his heel into the ground. The crew had returned to work. They filed past me one by one, down into the basement. Occasionally one of the men, having hefted a load of debris to the truck, knelt again beside the man, laid a hand on him; they seemed to be speaking another language, but I couldn't be sure. "What happened?" I asked the foreman.

"Board snapped, hit him in the head." The foreman watched the old man in the grass with a grave expression. He turned to me, cocked his head back to regard the house, then he looked at me once more, and his nostrils flared. It wasn't blame exactly, but it felt like something close to that. As if he knew something about the house. He reentered it, and I waited for the medical emergency squad, which turned out to be two plump men carrying large padded shoulder bags. One knelt at the man's side to examine him. He clutched the old man's wrists to stop his rolling back and forth and pulled the hands away to reveal the gash—it ran from the top of his forehead to the right inner side of the bridge of the man's nose. It wasn't the blood that turned my stomach or the hamburger-like texture of the wound's edges but rather the crest of pure white bone that ran down its center. The EMS tech released the man's hands and took the antiseptic and sterile gauze his partner had opened for him. The old man would be taken to Emergency for stitches. As he was lifted onto a stretcher, I turned and left for my car—there was nothing to do here today, and the sight of the gash in the bright morning sun had unsettled me.

7

Gut to Studs

The previous summer we filled legal pads with columns of figures and costs, mandatory renovations and wished-for additions, in order to arrive at a purchase offer, ignorant of the exact nature of the house and its condition. Before the Archer inspection, we still thought in terms of electrical and plumbing "repairs." An item on a long list might read "Repair damaged areas of the basement ceiling," rather than acknowledge what actually needed to happen: "Tear down and remove the basement ceiling." "Bring electric up to code—$5,000?" should have read "Completely rewire house—$20,000." In a spot where we might accurately have written, "Remove all old pipes and replace them with new ones, half of them made of expensive copper—$25,000 min," there was nothing, *zero*. Plumbing in those early lists did not even exist ("No, Donna," I remember saying, solemnly scribbling numbers, "let's be very realistic here"). Yes, items such as "Pave driveway—$9,000" were on there, quite a bit more than it would actually cost once we got around to it and not really a necessity (we could regravel to fix the violation), but what those lists described was not what needed to be done and how much it would cost; instead they caricatured a wildly deluded couple.

List making served mainly to throw dry wood on the fire of our houselust. Almost every single item had a corresponding cost next to it, which I'd based on no real knowledge of anything at all. The figures were no better than goofy quiz-show guesses. "Carpet 2nd and 3rd floor—$7,000"—where the hell did I get that? What was going on in my head? Houselust had become a kind of pathology. I functioned in the real world, but it was also a world in which an imaginary work crew would remove all carpeting and all wallpaper for an astonishing price ("Carpet/ wallpaper removal—$1,500").

This exercise made it possible for me then to attach a total rehab price on the house of $135,000—amazingly, just what we could afford! Look, honey, we can do it!

Thus we'd made our offer, paid five grand more than we'd initially agreed upon between us, and engaged the contracting company Bleick & Kessler Construction, more or less with a toss of the keys to Rob, and now the exciting business of renovating a home was immediately at hand. We wanted to restore this old house, to give her renewed life after decades of unacknowledged or hastily patched deterioration.

The house was huge for us—roughly thirty-six hundred square feet spread over three floors (not even counting the basement) this way: Third floor: two bedrooms, a bathroom, and a playroom with lots of deep, oddly shaped closets and sloping ceilings (due to four gables, one on each side of the house). Second floor: four bedrooms, two baths. First floor: living room, a wide entrance hall, study, a half bath, and the dining room/kitchen/breakfast room we hoped to make one long space. Hardwood floors had been beautifully preserved beneath the tarpaulin of carpeting. Raised-panel woodwork in the entrance hallway immediately gave one the sense of intricacy of design. We didn't intend to have more children. Donna wanted to get back to adult work. There was never any question about having enough room for the four of us. This meant that we needed only to decide where each of us would go, who called which room.

Early on, it was clear that the kids would be high atop the house on the third floor, which spread out over three rooms. On the second floor, three of these six rooms would be given new purposes, would have new careers in the life of the house. The back bedroom would be a laundry room. The central and smallest bedroom would become a master bath, and its bathroom, shared with the master bedroom, would become a walk-in closet. All this space provided luxury. A twenty-five-square-foot shower with an attached bath, for instance, to be enclosed by heavy, ceiling-high glass doors.

Indeed, turning a bedroom into a bathroom presents a problem of having too much space. How do you fill it? For instance, the far wall, the only place for dual sinks, was about nine feet long. What kind of vanities to put here? Even the cheapest of them cost hundreds of dollars, and we didn't want a Home Depot bargain in what had the potential to become a grand master bath. The answer was simple. The house purchase had left us with two dining room tables. The house's and ours, a farm table, a Country French number made to look as though it had been through years of loving abuse and jovial meals of wine and cassoulet. This would make an elegant and spacious double vanity. Cut lengthwise and affixed to the wall, our erstwhile dining table would have a second life holding two sinks, lotions, hairbrushes, and toothpaste for the cost of a few hours of labor and cutting expertise. All four legs would be retained and elevated three inches, and we'd use the sawed-off edge of the table as a backsplash. Sanded and varnished, it would look spectacular.

The major structural change, the most exciting part of the renovation, would be the new kitchen. Here, as little expense as possible would be spared. Food and cooking comprised at least half of my writing life. I'd worked in professional kitchens and so had been spoiled by professional equipment. I was currently in the last stages of a second cookbook with a four-star Manhattan chef, and I hoped to write more books on food and cooking. I didn't just deserve a good kitchen, I needed one for the work. Or so I reasoned.

Personal justifications aside, the kitchen was invariably where the family would benefit from a thoughtful design—it was where we spent most of our time together. During one of our early visits through the house, Steve had held the tape measure to the far wall of the kitchen while I stretched the tab end to the opposite wall, in the breakfast room. "Is twenty-three feet good enough for you?" he asked. I smiled greedily, incredulous—one day to have a kitchen twenty-three feet long and, with another quick calculation, thirteen or fourteen feet wide within one of these old Cleveland Heights houses, where rotten kitchen space was considered a fact of life, this was amazing. A kitchen almost as big as our living room, and that, too, was huge. "Yeah," I said. "That's good enough."

The current floor plan of the house described a classical Colonial pattern suited to most of the last century. The dining room was off the main hall. One entered the kitchen from the dining room through a swinging door. On the right side of the narrow kitchen, a stainless-steel counter ran the length of the twelve-foot space, the sink positioned below one of two windows looking out to the driveway. On the left were stove, counter, and refrigerator. One walked through this alley into a breakfast room with laminated cabinetry running the fourteen feet of the farthest wall of the house. One window on the adjacent wall faced two windows on the driveway side, making the room bright. If you made a U-turn here, you would enter a dark hallway, passing a half bath, that led back the same length of the kitchen to a second stairway. This part of the house's layout reflected its era, one in which even the middle classes had live-in servants who required a convenient private path to their rooms on the third floor.

The design unknown was a structural one: Could we blow out the three walls, connected in the shape of an I separating dining room and breakfast room at the top and bottom, kitchen and back hall on the sides, in effect connect the dining room and breakfast room via an open kitchen with a central island? Completely open this place up into one long expanse?

"We can do that," Rob said.

On September 28, Rob delivered an initial estimate on behalf of Bleick & Kessler Construction. Demolition included carpet removal, basement-ceiling removal, gut to studs kitchen and half bath, gut to studs both upstairs baths and middle bedroom, among other less violent work. "General Work" included a new heating-cooling system for the second and third floors and installation of new PVC stacks, drain lines, vents, and copper water lines for all upstairs bathrooms. Allotments for the big shower area and new electrical panels and wiring for second and third floors, guesses at major expenses Rob would hire out and bill us for, were $8,000 (upstairs baths) and $15,000 (electric) respectively, expenses that might change but that we ought to ballpark now. Total estimated cost: $82,500.

See, more than reasonable, as I'd expected B&K to be. I hadn't been wrong to blithely toss the keys to Rob the week before.

The estimate even included under an all-caps heading of "NOT INCLUDED" such items as tile, plumbing and electrical fixtures, shower doors, and the like. Had "tile" ever been included on my private legal-pad list? Are you kidding? Tile comes with the house, doesn't it? So do plumbing fixtures, right? Shower doors could be pricey, no doubt, hadn't really thought of that—couldn't very well put a curtain or cheapo slider in here. The initial estimate also didn't include most of the first floor beyond gutting the whole kitchen area. It didn't include numerous minor details, such as, oh, kitchen cabinetry. It didn't include the landscaping Donna really wanted, nor the storm windows that were needed to keep our heating bills out of the stratosphere, or the new gutters, or the wallpaper stripping and priming. All I saw was the $82,500, and that fit comfortably within the $100,000 total we'd originally counted on. Not bad, actually, right? Rob had said we could be in by November. Life was good.

The demo crew did the destruction work quickly, removal of the big debris—the gut-to-studs work. Gut to studs—I loved that phrase, with its Anglo-Saxon intonations of a violent evisceration. John, who ran the B&K crew, was a young man built big and fit, a father of three, who typically passed me carrying a huge, heavy door out back to take some height off it or, in the demoed kitchen, running a Skil saw through some white birch plywood that would become shelves. He once fell off the roof of a three-story house, landed on his back, stood, regained his breath, then climbed up again to finish working. In high school he'd lost control of his car when driving too fast, smashed it through the front of a house, and not only was he able to simply walk away, he wasn't even late to class that morning. The guy was indestructible. He ran the crews.

I'd traveled to Vermont—when airports were so quiet they were spooky (little or no conversation, an absence of children, flights taking off early)— on cookbook work with Eric Ripert, chef and co-owner of Le Bernardin, a great Manhattan restaurant. Eric wanted to make meals in four different locales, and this was our final one, a farmhouse at the peak of fall, azure days, cold nights, the foliage gone to blazing oranges and reds and browns.

A wide fireplace anchored the far end of the open kitchen/living room area in the house Eric had rented, its hearth raised a foot off the ground. The old electric kitchen stove did not inspire him, but the fireplace did. "We're going to be using that a lot," he said. It recalled a farm in France where he'd lived for six months, where cooking for all the workers had been done in the fireplace, over flames and wood coals. It was fascinating to watch him master that fire, to explore it. He was *in* it, blowing flames, shaking coals off burning logs, shoveling them under grates to heat a big pot of beans packed with chunks of Italian ham and sausages, or grill magret duck breasts, hauling in wood from the barn as we needed it. Cooking in this elemental way inspired me: We, too, would have a fireplace.

"You must have a fireplace, Michael," Eric had said when I mentioned the idea.

We'd never have thought of the idea had we not been told that this breakfast room once had a fireplace, obviously the reason for the chimney rising up the back of the house. Donna and I began to talk about it, first hopefully and then as if it were a given, how great it was that we were going to have a fireplace in this new kitchen of ours. When I called Donna from Vermont, she delivered the bad news.

"There *was* no fireplace here," she said. "We were misinformed."

"But there's a chimney there. What was the chimney for?"

"I don't know. Maybe for a furnace, maybe for a second-floor fireplace. There are some supports beneath the laundry room floor we can see, now that the kitchen ceiling is down; they may have been put there to support a hearth. All the cabinets are gone, and the wall is all original plaster. We won't know if it's a workable chimney till we break through the brick. And even if it is, Rob says building a whole new fireplace is going to cost five thousand dollars. We can't afford it."

"We've got to have a fireplace," I said.

"Even Rob says we shouldn't do it."

When your contractor recommends you don't spend money, you've got to take that seriously. Five grand was a lot for us, and we were already a little panicky about how fast extra charges were ringing up. Did we need to add another expensive luxury?

"Let's just think about," I said. "Rob really said we shouldn't do it?"

"He said if we're worried about cash, that isn't the best place to spend it."

I told Eric about our dilemma. Eric said only, "You *must* have a fireplace."

I nodded and said, "You're right, we will."

Eric maneuvered a pan of oxtail over some coals on the left side of the firebox to sear them and get them braising, then stood and swayed red-faced away from the blazing logs on the right, nearly tumbling over and saying, "Ho, shit, that's an adventure."

"Donna," I said. "We have one opportunity to do this. We're not going to go back. Now is the time. We have to do this."

"I told Rob cooking was part of what you did, how important it was to you and your work. He didn't know. Their mason's going to come in tomorrow and evaluate."

"Thanks, Donna." How many women understand how important fire is to guys?

"What else is happening in the kitchen?" I asked. "Can you see the space yet?"

"All the walls and plumbing and wiring are out, but the studs are still up. Michael?"

"I'm here."

"The walls were *filled* with nests, rodent nests."

"I remember seeing some mouse droppings in the cabinets," I said. Houses have mouses—it's one of their characteristics.

"No, Michael, not mice. *Big*-rodent nests. The walls were filled with them. John couldn't believe it. He'd never seen so many nests."

"What, squirrel? Rat?"

"I didn't want to ask. Too creepy."

"Well, they're gone now," I said.

"And did I tell you I talked to Hope?" Hope lived across the street, the mom of one of my high-school classmates, loved to garden and cook.

"What about?"

"She heard screams coming from the house."

"When, at night?"

"No, middle of the day. She was in the garden."

"What kind of screams?"

"I don't know, screams, really loud screams, like someone in pain."

"An ambulance or anything?"

"No, that was it."

"Must have been the demo crew."

Donna said, "Must have been."

I told Eric about the house. Gut to studs could take care of squirrels and rats, but it didn't take care of ghosts. Eric believed in ghosts unapologetically. In fact, he'd told me that the ghost of his paternal grandmother had been with us at the summer location.

Eric said, "Michael, you *must* have the house exorcised."

"How do you do that?"

"There are ways to do it yourself, but I would recommend hiring someone." He described a method whereby one leaves pans of salt in various corners throughout the house, and the salt draws the impurities out of a place as it does blood from meat. Then there was a special means of disposing of the salt and some sort of ceremony that had to be done in a room in sunlight, which was a rarity in Cleveland from November through April, a sticking point on the do-it-yourself exorcism. I asked Eric how one found such a person to hire, an exorcist.

He shrugged, said, "Yellow Pages," and munched on some celery root.

I returned home and there, hitching up baggy jeans and chewing a half-smoked, unlit Backwoods Smoke cigar, was John Basar, the mason. There was a hole about a foot in diameter in the wall leading into the chimney. "Yeah, I can put one in," he said. "I don't know how big the box can be. I think you've got an eight-inch flue. I gotta check my chart." The size of the flue limited the size of the firebox. I wasn't going to get a pizza oven in there, but we were going to have a brick fireplace in the breakfast room; it would become a permanent part of this house.

Fall rolled on with an escalating sense of urgency, an odd emotional mix of financial panic and the thrill of the quick pace of the project. I'd return from the hospital midmorning and have to search for a parking space, the street was so crowded with the cars of the paint crew and the trucks of the various teams working on the house (plumbing, carpentry, electric, heating and cooling). The house was a hive.

On one fall morning, a cherry picker rolled up our front lawn, its fat tires gouging grass into troughs of mud, to unload a ton of drywall, four-by-eight-foot panels of gypsum and cardboard that would become the walls of the new bathrooms and closets and bedrooms and kitchen. The sight of this monster truck pushing the panels through a second-story window in that golden autumn light was so dramatic that Heather from across the street came out with her camera and took pictures.

Drywall: solid smooth walls that can go up in a matter of hours. To imagine how the walls of this house had originally been created boggled the mind, given how easy it now was. Thin strips of wood, lath, were once nailed in place, with narrow gaps between them, then plastered over, plaster and horsehair squeezing through the cracks and making the lath secure, followed by more coats of plaster, the final one creating a perfectly smooth surface. The process required not only several days' work, but real skill on the part of the tradesman. It wasn't easy. No skill is required to make a smooth wall today. You buy it and screw it in.

But we pay for that convenience. Plaster-and-lath walls were very strong, fire resistant, excellent sound barriers, and they didn't loose their strength if they got wet. Sound passes through drywall as if through a drum skin. Drywall burns well. In a damp room, such as a bathroom, it grows mold. If it gets too wet, it falls apart. But plaster-and-lath is prohibitively expensive now that drywall's available. Drywall is so ubiquitous that few people even know how to plaster anymore. Were I to have unlimited funds to build a house, I would hire someone do plaster-and-lath walls, if only to keep the knowledge of how to do it alive a little longer. But I was just like everyone else—I couldn't afford that.

Our funds dwindled by the hour. Our first bill came due a few days after I returned from Vermont. Fifteen grand. No problem, we expected it and had it; it felt good to pay for what already appeared to be great progress. But writing the check and doing the subtracting in the ledger encouraged some easy computations. We had demanded to be into the house in a month and a half, by which time B&K had agreed to complete what was now $90,000 worth of work and would expect to be compensated as agreed upon in a timely fashion.

I remember it vividly, the exuberant easiness of having taken the kids to see *Shrek* a second time (thirty bucks for a movie, candy, and popcorn—"Thirty *bucks*?" I tabulated, digging a second twenty out of a near-depleted wallet). An easy Sunday afternoon returning home from a movie, and suddenly my hands are sweaty gripping the steering wheel, all ease melted away, and my throat's knotted up as the truth of the situation appears like a bank of black clouds behind me, rolling inexorably over blue sky.

My God, what were we thinking? We can't do this. We're gonna have to sell the house before the year's out and rent an apartment. That old architect was right. Jesus. Fireplace? What was I thinking? What are we doing?

I returned from the hospital the following morning to the familiar line of cars and trucks outside our house, vans containing entire hardware stores, whole carpentry workshops inside them, sawhorses set up outside for woodwork, someone else fabricating gutters, vans with big lengths of pipe strapped on top.

What are all these people *doing* here? I thought. Go away! I felt as if I were suddenly, in the course of twenty-four hours, meant to pay the bills for the screaming families of a dozen tradesmen.

I didn't reveal the depth of my panic to Donna. That's what it was— panic, never a good thing. A serious case of inner flop sweat. A panic whose locus was always my children. I would look at J., glowing, smiling, beautiful, innocent, and think, How could I put him in jeopardy? Or at A. and say silently, My sweet daughter, I want to give you everything and I've blown it. This houselust will deprive you of what will make you happy and good. I've thrown it away. I confessed to Donna only that I was "suddenly very nervous."

She stroked the side of my head and said, "I know. It's a risk we're taking, but we'll be all right."

She looked at me again. "Don't *worry,*" she said, kissed me, and returned to some catalogs in search of plumbing fixtures—what kind of showerhead and knob for the guest bath shower? Hmm. And as I watched her, the panic melted away.

We saw less of Rob—he'd appear now and then eating something between a bun, resting a fast-food soda cup on a windowsill next to John's Kools, and have his lunch while he and John discussed the progress and Rob finalized his list of first-floor specs—and more of Carl, who had started the business. Rob wore Topsiders; Carl wore work boots, Carhartt pants, and T-shirts, a tape measure on his belt beside the cell phone. He was the real contractor, the guy who could do the work, the general practitioner for houses—he could put in moldings, hang a door, drywall a room, do basic plumbing and electrical—and he had put this knowledge together to make a business in which he'd oversee the specialists in each area.

Carl looked, sounded, and acted like a tradesman. Even his name had stolid Germanic midwestern earnestness to it, a hammer hitting a nail. He wore his dark hair short and trim. He was solidly built with a lack of middle-aged fat that seemed an admirable indication of both his trade and his moderate appetites. He had a tradesman's awkwardness in articulating complex ideas—not for any lack of intelligence, I imagine, but rather from a lack of having had to do so. People who did physical work, work that didn't require advanced language skills, didn't develop the muscles to do that work, nor did they care to—nor should they, as far as I'm concerned. That was one reason they liked the work. They were more comfortable working with their hands, manipulating physical objects, than talking about it, and moreover, in this instance, doing so in the service of beautiful houses. Rob was the talker; let him do that work.

In the crisp fall weather, in his clean, well-worn work clothes, Carl radiated good, solid, dependable guyness.

And when such a guy delivers an envelope containing a bill, it's somehow easier to pay. On October 10, Carl handed me our first invoice. "For progress to date," it read:

    a. Permits
    b. Interior demolition
    c. Rough electrical work
    d. Rough plumbing to date

"TOTAL PAYMENT REQUEST," it concluded, all caps, so we wouldn't miss it, I suppose, "$15,000.00." And Donna wrote a check four days later. You don't realize it at the time, but paying a contractor goes from easy to hard. It's easy to write that first check. The bank account full, you're glad and amazed that work has begun and is proceeding so quickly; you're eager for it to carry on, excited by it. But the invoices keep coming and keep coming, and after a while you find yourself increasingly less glad to pay them, until finally you're actively not glad—in fact, so unglad are you that you don't pay them; instead you write a withholding-payment letter, to make your ungladness official.

At the time, though, one month after buying the house, excitement only built. Look at all that had been done. The internal demo was complete, the width of the house now cleared. I could stand with my back to dining room window, the very front of the house, and see all the way to the rear wall where John the mason was laying the bricks of the fireplace. Both upstairs baths had been gutted, the walls removed, the debris from the crumbling built-in shower gone, the tubs and toilets gone, nothing but darkened, thick studs—the heavy, dense studs of pre–World War I construction, first-growth wood, and they were actually two inches by four inches, so clearly superior to the "two-by-fours" of today, which are balsa wood by comparison and a half inch shy of both two and four.

Electric was being put in from top to bottom by Vern and his crew, an affable threesome who filled the walls and ceilings with the vessels through which the current would flow. A company called Classic Floors, a team of sylvan youngsters, laid tongue and groove in the new kitchen and prepared to sand and varnish all upstairs and downstairs floors.

Jim the plumber, our age, with dark, curly hair, worked alone to take out the old iron stacks, replacing them with PVC stacks, soldering what seemed like miles of copper pipe from the main supply entering the front of the house and zigzagging below the floors and up the walls to the four bathrooms, laundry room, and kitchen. Jim installed new pipes in what had been bedroom walls while John framed the new shower area, nailing two-by-fours into ceiling joists and into walls still covered with decades-old wallpaper, Vern's wires dangling loose out of both ceilings and walls.

The first-floor specs were completed, and as Rob looked them over in the demoed kitchen, where we tended to do our talking, I saw the final figure, another forty-two grand, a punch in the stomach. I swore. Rob looked at me innocently and said, "More than you expected?"

"We've got to get that down somehow."

We didn't. What were we going to do, fire them? Get estimates from other companies? Not at that stage. Rob had us by the short and curlies, and he knew it. That was the last we saw of Rob. He'd done his work. Sold!

The calendar days went by, and we kept our sights on moving day and our main necessity: a finished third floor. Which meant working plumbing by Jim, who couldn't finish *his* work till Dennis the tile guy

finished *his* work. The logistics of what-happened-when were tricky—
Carl had to make sure Jim did the initial big plumbing, and then have
Vern put in the electric for this third-floor bath (when Jim wasn't there),
then have Jim stop at the right point so that a tile floor and tile shower
walls could go in, after which Jim could finish his work of installing fixtures (after Donna had primed and painted the new walls, which was
much easier to do without toilet and sink in place).

The street in front of the house remained crowded with cars and
workers. Neighbors strolling down the street stopped to look at the
house, stare at it, perhaps trying to fathom all that must be going on
inside. The main visual clue, besides the crowds of workmen and the tire
gashes in the lawn, was the gigantic blue Dumpster filling up with iron
pipes, a smashed iron bathtub, piles of lath, old appliances, large pieces of
anonymous debris that might have come from a shipwreck. The weather
grew gray and cold, Halloween passed, and the small house we were
leaving began to fill up with boxes.

8

The Morning Paper

M oving day, a day so dreary and gray I thought light might never arrive, began with the suspicion that forces beyond our will were working to thwart us. The source of these ominous powers, I believed, was a carpet-installation dispatch man.

To buy and install carpeting even in the best of circumstances— when you're not moving, have no children, and are in no hurry—can be a trial. I don't know why this should be so. Last time we tried it, huge quantities of the wrong carpet were to be installed by a man missing his two front teeth, who'd brought along his pregnant wife and a helper. The toothless man explained that his assistant, a man with a smooth, domelike forehead and deeply sunken eyes, was beginning his first job out of prison—"but he's all right."

This helper, in his early thirties, I'd guess, had addressed my then six-year-old daughter as "sexy thing." We all stood out on the front lawn, Donna and the toothless man hashing out the carpeting issue (wrong carpet!). The ex-convict looked up at the street address on our house and announced it to the air, as if committing it to memory.

Donna resolved the carpet issue, and the toothless man left in the van to retrieve the correct batch, having instructed the ex-con to start on the preliminaries. Inside our house the ex-convict spotted a box of cornflakes on the kitchen counter and said with the friendliness of a child, "Can I have some? I haven't had breakfast." More surprised than anything, I said, "Sure," and poured him a bowl, poured the milk. He tucked himself in at our kitchen table, and I set down a spoon and a bowl of sugar. He lifted the spoon, but before dipping it into the sugar, he looked at me abruptly, suspiciously, and said, "You don't have *roaches* here, do you?" I shook my head, and he shook his, smiling and saying, "Naw, we don't have them either," and spooned it onto his cereal.

It was nine-thirty on a lovely summer morning. A stranger ate cornflakes at my kitchen table.

He glanced up to ask me, "You know Franklin Delano Roosevelt?" I nodded. The man said, "He was my *uncle!*"

This time we'd further tempted the malevolent carpet*geists* by arranging to have it installed three days before we were to move in. The scheduling constraints were unavoidable—but we'd thought it all through ahead, given ourselves room for the unexpected, so it would work out perfectly. It's a matter of planning.

As the third floor would be our residence while the lower floors were being worked on through the winter, we needed that floor completely finished before we moved in. New bathroom fixtures (a tiled shower stall replaced the old iron tub), tile floor in, walls painted; all other rooms primed and painted, but only after the heating and cooling guys ran the conduits from two furnaces into the crawl space overhead and Vern had the place rewired with all new switches, outlets and hardwired smoke alarms. After the painting was done, the carpeting would go down on the wide pine boards, two days before the movers arrived with furniture and boxes. We'd choreographed it to the last detail.

A few minutes before 8:00 A.M. Monday, the inevitable call arrived. "I can't install the carpet!" the installer screamed.

"Why not?"

"It's got to be warm. All the radiators are out in the driveway! The house has to have heat!"

"There's heat upstairs," I said. "Have you been up there?"

John arrived a few minutes later, let the guy in, and he set to work. Donna hustled over to make sure he'd arrived with the right padding and the right carpeting. He had, she said from her cell phone, but he was complaining about not having an assistant, who'd called in sick. When I arrived later in the morning, the installer, a tall, lanky man with a bushy red mustache, had carpeted what was to be J.'s room. Rolls of padding filled the other two rooms, but, he said, he didn't have enough of the right carpeting. I asked for a fuller explanation. He said they hadn't given him enough. And he was gone. So was the day.

Tuesday nothing happened because, we were told, they'd needed to reorder. I remained optimistic. It takes only a day to carpet—not even a day. Wednesday would be that day. And this would give John the time to fix the floorboards before carpeting went over them. Either he or Jim the plumber had sawn through two wide pine boards, discovering after each cut that this was not where they'd needed to enter into subfloor space— but hadn't repaired them. Now the planks bent down an inch or two when you stepped on them. I asked John to fix it, and he said sure.

Wednesday, after considerable irate conversation with Vince at Home Depot, from whom we'd bought the carpet (on sale! what a deal!), more padding and carpeting arrived and was cut and spread out across the paint-spattered boards—by two new guys—but it just lay there in folds and covered with scraps when they departed. I never got an explanation, but I'd spoken with Vince at Home Depot, who was organizing this installation, and he assured me, no problem, done deal, sorry for the delay, it would happen first thing in the morning. He gave me the number of the company who'd sent the installers on the off chance something went wrong, which it *wouldn't.*

I woke early on moving day with a plan to start calling that company just after six. There was still a lot to do before the movers arrived.

Rain pelted the black windows as I poured coffee in the too-bright kitchen and dialed the dispatcher.

"What's the name again?" the man who answered said. He had a vaguely southern lilt, and I pictured a guy in his late fifties with thinning gray hair who ate a lot of medium-well beef with buttery potatoes, a union guy, you could hear pro-labor in his voice. I heard papers shuffling, and so I spelled our last name. I heard more papers. I spelled our name again.

"I don't see your name down for today," he said calmly.

"What do you mean?" I asked. I knew it!

"No one's assigned. You're not on the list."

"Not on the list? You mean not at all? Nothing is going to happen today?"

And here the voice matched my incredulity with an equal amount of satisfied arrogance: "That's right."

"We were assured it would be completed this morning."

"Who told you that?"

"Vince at Home Depot."

"Who?" More sounds of shuffling paper.

"Vince."

"Who's Vince?"

"I don't know—Vince, some guy named Vince, for chrissake." No one was accountable. Why hadn't I gotten Vince's last name?

"I don't know any Vince."

I was pacing the kitchen now. In addition to coffee, I'd also grabbed a Granny Smith apple. I'd needed something in my stomach. During the pause, and in my nervousness—either we got carpet today or we didn't, and these next moments would determine which; I couldn't blow it— I'd taken a big bite of juicy apple. I was still chewing when I said, "Regardless"—chomp, chomp, swallow, chomp—"we need to have this carpeting completed this morning."

"Are you eating something?" the man asked. "Sounds like you're *eating* something!"

The guy sounded pissed. I swallowed, set the apple down, and lied.

"You are," said the man as if he couldn't believe it. "You're *eating* something."

"No, I'm not," I lied again.

"Then something's wrong with this phone. I'm hearing something!" He whacked the phone hard against a meaty palm. "Maybe that did it," he said.

Minor catastrophe averted, I pressed on. "What can we do?"

"We can schedule you for tomorrow—no, I'm sorry, Monday."

"What? *No!* This was supposed to be finished *last* Monday, three days ago." As I grew audibly upset, the man grew calm.

"We don't have any installers for you today. They've all been assigned, they're on the road."

"So what you're telling me is we're *fucked.*"

Pause on the other end. A long, menacing pause. Then very calmly, fat sheriff in the small southern town, he said, "Excuse me?"

"So we're screwed," I rephrased. Then I began to plead in my most humble, no-profanities, God-fearing voice: "Sir, please understand. We've been planning this carpet installation for two months. Your company had promised to have it installed last Monday. It's still not done. We're moving this morning into the rooms that were supposed to be carpeted by now. The movers will be here in an hour." J. began to cry. Still holding the phone to my ear, I hustled upstairs to find him standing in his crib in the dark. "Please, can you help me?"

"*Last* Monday?"

"Yes," I said. I had J. on my shoulder. He'd cried only to be saved from the dark, and now he cooed and ahhed.

"Sounds like you've got a little one there," the man said. His voice had changed. I could hear it. Something had happened. It was like storm clouds moving off.

"Yes," I said.

"Last Monday, you said?"

"Yes."

"Ruhlman."

"Yes!"

"OK, here you are. I see what happened. You're right."

And just like that it was fixed. I don't know really how or why; I only know that when you decide you need carpeting in your home, you're stepping into a parallel world that looks very much like your own.

I filled a sippy cup with orange and cranberry juices for J. and fell back into the chair. Rain continued to beat against the window. Moving day had begun under circumstances consistent with my understanding of the universe—the carpet-dispatch man didn't act much differently from God, I figured: He didn't know me personally, but if I were in a pinch, I could complain earnestly and not with my mouth full. He'd find my paperwork and, with only a little luck and uncertainty thrown in, make sure things came out more or less . . . well, not perfectly but generally as expected in my life, which He could see was pretty comfortable. Then He'd disappear for a long time, maybe forever; He was busy, a bit arrogant, but He was God after all, and *busy*.

I was already wiped out. J. banged a whisk against some pans that would not fit into available boxes, scattered and stacked on the wood floor among the dust balls and kitchen refuse not likely to make the cut—a crumpled box half full of plastic spoons, a glass pitcher that never did pour very well, a sticky bag of once fragrant black cumin. I couldn't rise from the chair and so thought of nothing and moved not a muscle for several minutes.

The Berea Moving & Storage truck slowed in front of our house at exactly eight, hydraulic brakes shrieking and hissing. A few minutes later, four kids and a supervisor showed up at our back door, in rain that had turned to mist. Granted it was a local company, not one of the big movers, but I expected more bulk, a few guys named Bluto. These guys seemed to me kind of runty. One looked like he had some genuine heft, but the remaining three were a mixed bag, a scrappy black kid in a zip-up sweatshirt, the smallest and quietest of the group; a tall, skinny man-child with pink-rimmed eyes and the sniffles (in fact, a divorced father whose insane wife still had custody of the kids—"She's crazy, but I love her," he told me morosely); and a bespectacled student from Denmark, one ear dripping with rings and wearing fashionable wire-rimmed glasses, designer denim cargo pants, and yachting sneakers.

The leader, a ringer for a young Frank Sinatra who would do no lifting but instead arrange the goods in the unnecessarily long truck, was smart and efficient, an adult in control of the situation.

As unlikely as it was that these guys could move all our furniture from one house to another in a day, I found them oddly comforting. They weren't impersonal brutes but naive, apparently goodhearted, well-meaning kids earning a working wage. They huddled around me and shook my hand definitively, each one of them locking his gaze on mine and speaking his name. This act said, *We're not strangers—you know us now, and you can trust us with your personal stuff.* Clearly these guys weren't going to get mixed up in the carpet-installation business.

Donna dressed and drove A. to school. My daughter could only have partly understood that the contents of her home were about to be removed, stuffed smartly into a very large truck, and carted less than a mile to the creepy old brick house with the Dumpster out front and a hole in the kitchen floor.

Donna had promised her, "You'll be surprised at the change you'll see. It's going to be different." A. sensed that Donna was a little more enthusiastic than was necessary and so remained skeptical.

I was as hopeful as Donna. A. couldn't know the transforming magic that happened when thick padding and fresh carpeting are stretched across all that dark, messy flooring. And she'd really known this third floor only at its worst—attic heat in July when we began looking to buy the house, stuffy still air, the smell of age, the dim orange and underwater green of the plaster walls, dark in the daytime. We'd mainly kept her and J. out of the house, for no other reason, really, than that once the demo crew had entered and work began, it was a minefield. Less than two weeks earlier, I'd stood in the attic bathroom and stared somewhat disoriented twenty-five feet down to a pile of rubble on the gutted kitchen floor. To behold her new rooms, this new space, would surely be a positive surprise.

The crew worked efficiently, I among them, hedging my claim to adulthood by carrying load after load to the truck and passing the people I was paying on the truck's ramp. I wasn't in stodgy middle age, unable to do some heavy lifting to save cash.

In a little more than four hours, the truck was packed.

I looked upon hiring a moving company as a milestone. I'd been moving since age eighteen—so had Donna—and we'd kept moving, pretty much continually. Hiring a moving company for the first time was a definitive indication of adulthood. I'd always thought of U-Haul as an unfortunate but necessary fact of life. With every move after college, I would put a rattling old truck into gear at some early hour (almost invariably a Saturday morning) and grind from the U-Haul center toward home, preparing for a long day of packing, followed by a second long day of driving, followed by a third long day of unpacking. With any luck I wouldn't take out too many branches or stop signs, and the manual-transmission truck wouldn't overheat just after emerging from, say, the Holland Tunnel into New Jersey, seven hours from my destination.

U-Haul itself all but bragged that one in five Americans move in a given year, that the average American moves eleven times throughout his or her lifetime (that's once every seven years of your life if you live to be seventy-five or eighty), and that three out of four people who move do it themselves. These U-Haul fun facts are published in an effort to encourage people to buy a franchise and so may not be unbiased, but they jibe with my history and that of most of the people I know. I first U-Hauled into New York City with my face comically swollen from a bone-splintering removal of wisdom teeth, and then, about twenty-two months later, I U-Hauled out of New York City. I U-Hauled down to Florida about a year later, and then Donna and I U-Hauled to our first shared apartment. Two years after that, we filled the truck again and, Donna, my new partner in U-Hauling, tailed me in the new Nissan Sentra (she'd decided to give up the sporty but impractical Alfa) all the way up through the southern states, across the mountains of West Virginia, to the southernmost point of the country's northern border, Cleveland, Ohio, on Lake Erie, where we stuffed all our crap into my dad's garage while we hunted for apartments, the finding of which required, two months later, yet another U-Haul.

All of this necessitated thousands of trips to and from the truck under the weight of books and clothes and furniture; in Florida, Donna had become fond of using small cement pillars as table bases and plant stands. She became, in fact, a collector and connoisseur of these hundred-pound fuckers. I've never thought much of them, but Donna did, so we—I, rather—carted every one all over the country from then on, to at least three other states.

The U-Haul from apartment to our first house—this house, where I sat listening to the rain and to my toddler son banging a pot in the emptied kitchen—was not the last U-Haul by far—four more big ones awaited, ten in all over a fifteen-year period—but it was the biggest, because we had by then begun to amass a lot of stuff while maintaining almost no income.

Some have noted that the age when you become an adult continues to go up with each generation. My father was an adult, I believe, at twenty-five, the result of a baby and the work that continues to occupy him now. I know a woman in her mid-forties who considers age fifty to be the *real* cutoff point, the age at which you have to admit, no excuses, no whining, that you are now irrevocably an adult.

I am confident in marking my adulthood, not at or before my marriage, not at the birth of either of my children, not at the publication of my first book, but rather at the desire and ability to hire a moving company.

The boys wandered down our street to look for some lunch, and I went to check on the carpet. Still not finished, but close. There were the usual problems—the wrong padding had been installed in the closets, and there was a roll stain for which we'd be compensated five hundred bucks—but these seemed small issues at the time. All I cared about was that we'd make it in.

The scrawny movers, as they reversed their morning efforts, felt almost like friends of the family by then. They commented on the house. "This is a great old house," said the guy with sniffles and the crazy wife. "You guys are doing a lot here, that's great. I love these old houses."

The student in designer wear stared intently at me, having brought some darkroom equipment to the basement. "This is a good house," he said. The basement followed almost exactly the floor plan of the ground and second floors, brick walls now painted white. "Look at the arches above these doorways," he said. We paused to admire them. They did have nice arches, two rows of brick ends in a gentle curve.

And the scrappy black kid told me he'd left his sweatshirt at the old house—would I mind going back to get it? And while I was at it, could I pick up a two-liter bottle of Mountain Dew at the Medic drugstore on the way back? He extended a buck and some change as he asked.

After three hours of this hefting and moving, hustling as darkness gathered around us, the boys grew a little whiney, moaning when Frank handed them a box marked "3rd Floor" because the third floor was a serious hike—first stone steps up to the front porch, then two full stairways with a change of direction on each and two hallways in between them, forty-one stairs up and forty-one back down. The installers had finished up and actually passed the box-laden crew on the way out—the last of the carpeting fastened to the house in the nick of time. By five-thirty the very last boxes were leaving the truck. A good thing, because there were neither light fixtures nor electricity on the first floor, and it was almost too dark to see.

They sat on boxes and a table in the living room as Frank tabulated hours and wrote out a bill, leaning closely over the paper in order to see it. He was also on the cell phone with the home office, presumably in Berea, receiving job assignments for the following day. Everyone was working the following day except the guy with sniffles. "I can't believe it—why?" he was saying as I wrote out a check for an even $1,500. I tipped them fifty bucks, said thanks, and left them in the chilly darkness of my living room. I'd never see them again.

The house we'd left wasn't completely empty, and the new owners took possession of the place at eight the following morning. There remained some framed pictures, a couple of lamps, a few stray open boxes, two plants, a bucket of cleaning materials, a vacuum, and stray trash still needing to be picked up. I could get it all in the Jeep in one go, then close the house for good.

I'd asked A. if she wanted to join me, see her old house for the last time and say good-bye. We entered the house that had been hers when she'd left for school that morning and was now empty of all she'd ever known. I turned on the dining room and kitchen lights, which illuminated the harsh, dusty barrenness of the place.

I could sense the depths of her melancholy as she gravitated to the center of the room and stood there in her yellow rain jacket, sweeping her gaze across the scene, bewildered. Her feelings seemed almost palpable to me. She was thinking, in her six-year-old way, How can it be? Where did everything go? She was possibly seeing the ghosts of our family in many of its better variations, the fun we'd had here—remember the pool table in this room, covered by an enormous dining tabletop? the birthdays, how we'd chased her around the table? Where was the table under which she'd spent her pensive spells? Where was the rug? Where were the Christmas dinners? Where now, in this empty, dust-ball-y kitchen, were the everyday comforts, the lunches with her friends Emily and Hannah, the cracking of eggs on Sunday mornings, all our weekday dinners. Where were they?

Gone.

Honestly, she looked baffled.

I began to load the Jeep, really starting to feel the effects of the day, moving very slowly and swaying a bit from fatigue. I walked through the upstairs rooms picking up the last discardable bits from our life here— crumpled paper, used scraps of packing tape stuck to the floor, a couple of hangers. I paused in the second-floor family room, stared at the spot where the couch had been, obvious from the neat rectangle of unfaded carpeting. On this rectangle a spread of litter—like tapenade on a giant piece of melba toast—popcorn, popped and unpopped, and bits of paper and chips of plastic toys, surely plenty of stray hairs, more dust balls. I left it for the new owners to clean up. Sorry, guys, I'm spent.

A. moved through every room, stopped to consider the change in each, visiting her specific favorite spots. Intense and moody even in everyday situations, she took her time to allow the experience to resonate fully. I made a last pass through the house turning out lights, then stumbled downstairs. A. had made it to the living room by then, and I waited for her by the back door as she came full circle.

She said, "OK, Dad."

I opened the back door, and she passed through it, a stoic.

———

While I'd been moving boxes in with the boys, Donna had remained in the aerie, directing traffic, keeping muddy shoes off the couldn't-be-newer carpeting, ensuring that the right pieces of furniture were set down in the right spots—beds, dressers, the couch (a doglike eighteen years old and in its final days), bookcases, the kitchen table. And then she had set about organizing everyone's space and clothes, starting by locating clean sheets and pillowcases to make up beds, a first for J., who through this morning had slept in a crib that now joined a heap of trash on our ex–tree lawn. Clean sheets, made beds, were symbolic for Donna of a successful move into a safe new place.

"How's it going?" I asked her.

"Great—I'm getting us really organized," she said. She passed me, not wanting to break her efficient stride, but stopped, took one step backward, clutched my waist, kissed me hard on the mouth, and then carried on.

I almost didn't want to halt her momentum, but I reminded her of the plan to head to my father's for a carryout dinner, away from the sight of boxes, everywhere boxes, boxes that needed unpacking, stuff that needed placing even in our temporary tree house. We left, ate, rested, and returned, windshield wipers clicking, to a very dark house, our new house, our new old spooky demoed house. We couldn't go back to the old one if we'd wanted to. This was our house now.

Reentering it was hazardous. I'd left a utility light hanging by a nail in a stud in the gutted kitchen so we could see, once I got the door open. John, in maneuvering an old fridge down the basement stairs weeks ago, had busted the back-door glass, and it had since been covered by ply-wood. The boarded-up door opened onto a small landing and a hole that had once contained five steps, a space that now dropped to rubble in the basement, over which a ladder had been rested. This is what squat-ting would be like. We were squatting in our own house. I went first across the ladder, carefully, a sleeping two-year-old slung over my shoulder, followed by an even more careful A.—not her idea of fun! why had we moved here?!—followed by Donna.

I'd set a flashlight on the windowsill and used this to guide us up two flights of stairs.

I laid J. on his new bed—a mattress set on box springs set on the floor—untied his shoes and removed his pants. Donna dutifully stuck her nose in his diaper to make sure he'd have a comfy snooze, covered him, and went to find A.'s pajamas. She had already set out tooth-brushes for us, hairbrushes, some water glasses—we were camping, and she was prepared. She'd stocked a large cooler with milk for coffee and cereal, juice and fruit for the kids, a bag of ice. A. fell asleep while I was reading, something she rarely did, but it was now past eleven.

And at last I could relax completely. Donna was already in her own pajamas and a bathrobe, and pouring herself a glass of wine. I got myself a whiskey and joined her, exhausted and exhilarated.

We were in. We'd done it. I gazed, a little deliriously from the fatigue, at my wife's flushed face and bright blue eyes and freshly brushed hair. She was happy. From that Monday dinner in early July when Donna first told me of the house, events had cascaded in our favor, inevitably toward this moment. We were inside.

I slept way down deep in dreamless sleep, physically spent, on the top floor of the house I hoped would be our center. We were strangers to the nighttime house—it held none of our own ghosts, none of our routines—and, after both kids had migrated into our sheets, none of us stirred or even altered our positions much, slotted tightly as we were, four of us in a queen-size bed. It was still dark when J. began to rotate nearly 360 degrees over the span of thirty minutes. At 180 degrees, his heel whipped sharply into my jaw to bring me to the surface, but I sank back under for a few minutes, already sensing the aches yesterday's move had left behind. I'd actually learned to sleep soundly through blows to the head, an important skill if you sleep with a toddler, so it was A. who forced consciousness on us.

"Daddy?" she asked. "Do I have school today?"

"You sure do," I said, stretching. She grinned, not only because she loved school (she cried bitter tears when sickness prevented her from going), but also I think she was comforted that this routine remained despite the total upheaval of moving into what to her was still a "hideous" house. I rolled over and reached down for the travel alarm on the floor: 6:55. I'd left the lights on dim in case any of us woke disoriented among the strange walls of boxes, and I could see twilight through the windows on the western side of the house, windows flanking the protrusion that would be the chimney originating way down below in the living room.

I hauled myself out of bed and donned house pants and bathrobe, which Donna had draped over the back of the kitchen chair at our kitchen table now at the foot of our bed. I maneuvered around some boxes and switched on the coffee machine I'd set up last night, retrieved a carton of OJ from the cooler, and poured myself a glass and a cup for J., who'd be calling for it soon.

It was now just light enough out for me to walk down two flights of stairs without a flashlight. I did so anxiously—not wanting to be disappointed. Of the thousands of items scratched off our to-do list was the paper-delivery change—we got the *Plain Dealer,* now the city's only major newspaper, and the *New York Times.* I descended the stairway, barefoot and scanning for debris—loose box-cutter blades, torn-out toe molding lying rusty-nail-points-up—already anticipating the letdown. Seeing the *Times* in its familiar blue bag would be just too much to ask. I stepped over a stack of plastic painters' tarps and around several five-gallon drums of paint, toward the front door.

Since our move into the suburbs, when I first began bending over in my bathrobe for the morning paper, the image of Ray Liotta as Henry Hill in the final moments of *Goodfellas* appears in my mind. He has been removed by the witness-protection program from the gritty New York gangster world to anonymous, new-development Middle America. He, too, bends over in his bathrobe in Technicolor vividness to retrieve the paper in anywhere-suburban sprawl, pauses to stare at the camera, smiling ironically, as his voice-over says, "There's no action. I have to wait around like everyone else. . . . I'm an average nobody. I get to live the rest of my life like a schnook."

Look at him, the director commands, see what he's reduced to. Just like any other middle-class stiff. The act of bending over in your bathrobe to pick up that relentlessly arriving morning paper was freighted with symbolism: It was the act of a nobody, a schnook.

Lo! There they were—my heart rose—shadowy objects in the chilly gray twilight in the center of the front walk. The *New York Times* and the *Plain Dealer* had acknowledged our move, and I could continue my morning routine without breaking stride. This was amazing. A *good* thing. I struggled with the door, scooted onto the front porch and down the stone steps, snatched up the papers, and hustled back in on this chilly, wet morning. With a light heart and a sense that the transition into a new house, a new phase of life, would be a smooth one, I shoved the heavy front door of our house closed with my shoulder.

9

The Perfect House

Morning papers tucked beneath my arm like a football, I hiked back up the stairs two at a time, slowed to one, panting and swaying when I reached the carpeted landing of the third floor. On my way to the main room, I hit the spot. I stopped. I turned and looked down at where my foot had been. I pressed down on it again, and the board beneath the carpeting creaked and bent—John had not fixed it. "Damn it," I said. Donna was still in bed, awake but with eyes closed. I said, "John didn't fix the floorboard."

She propped herself against pillows. Eventually comprehending, she said, "He was up working on it—I thought that's what he was doing."

I poured some coffee and said, "You know what's going to happen, don't you?"

"About what?" she asked.

"About that broken board under the carpet. Every time you step on it—it's in the most walked-over spot of this floor—it's going to bend down. Over time the carpet will stretch, it will grow a little discolored because the vacuum won't clean it just right and it will pick up more dirt anyway, and we're going have an off-color divot there, in the middle of the hallway."

I unfolded the paper and began scanning headlines.

"Every time we step on it, we're going to think of them. We're going to name it. It will be The B&K Divot." The kids had ceased whatever it was they had been doing. "What are you looking at?" I said, and they returned to their morning explorations of the new space.

"Can we have them fix it?"

"How?" I asked. "Tear up the carpeting? Cut open the carpeting? No. It's a permanent situation—until we recarpet, and we're not going to do that anytime soon."

Donna put her arms around my neck from behind and kissed my scratchy cheek. "Good *morning,*" she said.

I turned and said, "Good morning, darling. How are you?"

"Excited," she said. "I slept great."

We were in a sea of boxes, but we also had our old couch, the beloved kitchen table, the bed all familiar and rumpled. I set up the TV and the VCR in order to throw in some Bugs Bunny cartoons, classics, for the kids ("An innnnn-teresing monster, needs an innnn-teresting hairdo—bobby pins, please"), and Donna and I sat at the table. It was both exciting in its strangeness and deeply familiar.

At eight, shortly before Donna left to take A. to school, J. wanted more juice, which we didn't have in the cooler here. This would require a trip down three flights of stairs to the basement, where a secondhand refrigerator whirred away, and back up again. Descending to the second floor of our house, I heard a radio. I smelled cigarette smoke. I turned the corner into the dining room—kitchen area, and there was John and his assistant, Mone, stalwart employees of B&K. John, Dunkin' Donuts coffee in hand, dragged on a Kool. They stopped talking. I stood there in my new house at 8:00 A.M. wearing my bathrobe. John, in torn jeans, work boots and Carhartt jacket, stared sleepily back. I don't think either of us, for different reasons, wanted to see the other. A paint-spattered radio was tuned to WMMS, a station specializing in late-seventies rock-and-roll.

John blew a cloud of smoke and said, "Good morning, Mr. Ruhlman." He was as tall as I was and about a decade fitter.

"Good morning," I said. Then, taking just a moment to get used to people surprising me in my own house and unconscious of the fact that it's all but impossible to be commanding in a bathrobe, I said, "John, you didn't fix the floor upstairs."

"Yeah I did."

"No you didn't."

"I fixed that board two days ago."

"There were two places where boards were broken."

He lifted his eyebrows. "I only fixed one."

"I know."

He pulled on his cigarette, then ground it out on the plywood floor, exhaling a plume of smoke.

I heard movement on the stairs above. "Donna's got to take A. to school—do you mind moving your van?"

"No problem," he said.

I carried on toward the basement, steadying myself against the wall as I stepped carefully down the ladder propped over where the missing stairs had been. John followed, making the same precarious descent with no hands, as it was something he'd been doing many times a day now. When I came back up, A., in her big orange winter coat, dark shoes, navy stockings, and dress, backed down the ladder, staring at the terrifying drop below, as Donna steadied her and held the ladder.

"We've got to get some stairs in here," she said. Getting A. out of the house was often exasperating for one reason or another, and this didn't help.

"I told Carl," I said.

"And?"

"He did what he always does—he nodded emphatically and said 'I know,' but then he scratched the back of his head and winced. So who knows?"

Donna steadied herself as she stepped down toward the back door. "And John never hooked up the washer and dryer. I explicitly told them I wanted it working when we were in. It's not hooked up. A., stay out of those puddles!"

This was a serious matter. Several days ago I'd made a special trip to Sears to get the set of tubing and brackets to attach the washing machine to the plumbing and the dryer to the vent outside. The items remained on the floor of what had previously been a bedroom at the rear of the house, in front of the new machines. Donna caught John before he backed out, and I saw her mouth moving quite a bit, and every now and then she'd point up at the room in question, marked on the outside by a small plastic vent, two stories up, very white and flimsy looking against the stodgy old brick. John was nodding, and I could see him saying, "No problem." Which he'd said several days ago.

We liked John. And John tolerated us, the griping homeowners, because he had to. He managed all the various tradesmen at work on our place—heating guys, flooring guys, plumber, mason, even the painters whom we'd hired independently—and almost always took care of what we'd asked and did so with alacrity. The upstairs floorboard was a regrettable lapse, and the washer and dryer hookup was an oversight, given all that was going on in this house, especially yesterday, with five guys trudging through John's workplace like ants under their loads, filling up the house with boxes and furniture.

What John didn't understand, why our irritation sounded like rich-folk whining, was the extent to which the ability to do laundry affected Donna's psyche. From the time A. was a couple of months old and weather required clothing, laundry took on an increasing urgency, and now, with two kids, the ability to dump an armload of dirty clothes into a washing machine and an hour and a half later to be folding warm, fragrant cotton was fundamental to Donna's sense of stability and well-being. For me, something like roasting a chicken gave me a sense of stability and well-being. The inability to do laundry made Donna cranky. She didn't love to do it—it was just as much of a drag for her as for everyone else, the mindless, forever folding, as much fun as bill paying, which Donna also did, but laundry was more relentless. It just kept coming. Laundry had to be done, she knew that no one else (meaning me) was going to do it, and if she was prevented from doing this chore, she couldn't relax. Having clean clothes for everyone was important to her.

Because we had so much space in this house, we could use an upstairs room for doing laundry. It would be one of the many small-seeming but in fact extraordinary ways life would improve for Donna.

I didn't want to tabulate the number of days Donna's laundry hours would add up to—the sorting, washing, drying but mainly folding of our clothes—because it would probably be a mortifying figure that would embarrass and shame me, since I did so little to help. To situate this necessity up here, in a bright, freshly painted room with two large windows, altered in a substantial way the tone of Donna's days. She wouldn't be folding, folding, folding beside a puddle and a filthy, turn-of-the-century stone laundry sink by the light of a bare bulb. She would be in a bright, warm, dry room on the second floor, a room flooded only with sunlight. Her thoughts would be different up here than they would be if this time were spent underground. The things you look at get into your head. She wouldn't stare at cobwebs netting the dirty, ground-level windows. J. could play in the new laundry room unattended while she folded, hiding under the plastic laundry basket or making a boat out of it in a bed of the fresh folded cotton. Laundry was not the way anyone wanted to be defined unless he or she actually did it for money, but the fact was, Donna did laundry almost every day, and everyone depended on her to do it. To be able to situate the laundry room in this old Cleveland Heights house on the second floor was a big deal.

The machines had to be hooked up for this substantial intent to take effect. They weren't. The tires of the Jeep kicked up gravel and mud as Donna backed fast down the drive. Moments later John's gray van moved into the Jeep's place.

Plenty of work lay ahead just to create room to move around in. We set up a makeshift food area. Our appliances for the next weeks and months would be a toaster oven, a microwave, and an electric frypan. For refrigeration we'd rely on a large cooler. The kids' stuff could be unpacked, but Donna and I would live mainly out of boxes till the master bedroom was done months from now (I needed to redo the crown molding, build a headboard, patch and repair walls and windows, prime and paint). Most of the house below our attic nest remained a shell.

What were we striving for? Packing our lives into boxes, changing dwellings yet again. Why were we going to all this trouble?

We wanted more, obviously, than to do laundry on the same floor where we put on and took off that laundry, but not much more. We intended a series of small changes just like that. All great accomplishments are composed entirely of interlocking details. A second-floor laundry room was a good example of the kind of detail we wanted to provide throughout the house.

We hoped to stop leaving homes, and in order to do this, we needed a home we *couldn't* leave. We wanted the perfect house in which to make the perfect home. Part of what defines the perfect home is the elegance with which the house contributes to the work of your particular life and spirit, the actions and emotions of each of your days, a structure complex enough in its design and details that it will always engage you while remaining a comfortable, sensible structure that is pleasing to look at and even better to look out from.

In order to be perfect, a home has to be the proper scale for your particular life. I don't understand the need of the superrich to buy or build thirty-thousand-square-foot houses. My mother, a real estate agent, sells these things in Florida, and they're beautiful, some truly spectacular to behold; they please aesthetically, and I'm sure they do what they're supposed to for the ego of the owner, reflecting financial success and personal worth and power in a big way. But you can't possibly live a normal life in them, because they're completely out of scale with normal life. A $20 million monster of luxury would belittle you at every turn. How can you eat a bowl of cereal in a kitchen the size of the Ritz? I'd want to hide. Also, they're impractical. If I go to my office and then remember I've left my reading glasses by the bed, I don't want a fifteen-minute walk there and back to get them. Multiply that by the number of times you change rooms by the number of years you live there, and pretty soon you realize you're not living in your house, you're commuting within it.

Some of today's McMansions have great rooms, in which you can do dishes at a kitchen island watching a big-screen TV fifty feet away in a bookcase that suggests a den or living room, with nothing but space in between, or maybe a distant couch or easy chair. A room like that is out of scale with the actions of the room—you get lost; it's uncomfortably spacious. Our former kitchen was too small—our table barely fit in it; we were always squeezing through it—out of scale.

Scale is critical. This house of ours, though ugly and disgusting according to my daughter, is the perfect scale for a husband and wife who do much of their work at home and two children who will quickly grow to adult proportions. Provided that neither of the kids decide they want a drum set for Christmas, it will be completely comfortable, a little on the roomy side, which is just right. Roomy is comfortable. Miles of wide-open indoor space are not.

Efficiency of action, which is related to scale but not the same, is another main component of the perfect home. My daily actions are writing and cooking, Donna's are photography, child rearing, bill paying, and laundry. The rooms, the space, are themselves tools. I needed a spacious kitchen and a comfortable office. Donna needed comfortable rooms that would enhance the work she did—a laundry room, a darkroom, and a large dining table that most days of the year served as an enormous in-box. This is more precisely how a house displays who you are, rather than the status objects you might fill it with. The way you use a house is the true reflection of your psyche.

Donna, who liked to think about houses, mused, "I wonder if you can really grow up if you never leave the house you were raised in."

While there are generations of people, no doubt, who live their lives in one structure and manage to grow up, it was an interesting thought. As we grow, becoming inevitably more and more the people that we are, our dwellings, as we move from one to the next, usually grow increasingly complex, more and more reflect the increasing complexity of our lives. If you lived as an adult in the same space you did as a boy, how could that structure fulfill your very different adult life? The scale and comfort and efficiency that were perfect for you as a fourteen-year-old couldn't possibly be perfect for you as a fifty-year-old, could they? For most people these days, living their whole lives in the same house isn't an option, but even if you had the choice, is it a good thing?

"I was talking with Ray," I said to Donna across our kitchen table. "He said, 'Houses are victimized or idolized by the people who walk through them.' We're idolizing this house."

"Remember your house at Duke?" she responded.

"I do, 814 Onslow Street."

"You trashed it, didn't you?"

"If it had been a living thing," I said, "it would have died a horrible death."

"I don't think of our response to a house as victimizing or idolizing," she said. "It's a two-way interaction. Some houses serve their owners, some owners serve their houses."

We sought the perfect house and also the perfect home. Here we were, installed in the attic of our house. Not yet "home"—the heavily freighted word, sentimentalized with notions of warmth, protection, well-being, the loved and denigrated word. We wanted not just to own the perfect house, we wanted to *be* home. We wanted to hang our jackets on a hook and take a load off, permanently. We'd been moving forever. How many days or weeks of our lives had been devoted solely to filling boxes, filling trucks, and then unfilling them again, achieving nothing but literal movement, nothing permanent? Had either of our adult selves existed in such a place, a true home? I didn't know many friends who had either. I'd grown up in one—and I became increasingly aware of what good luck it had been to spend my first eighteen years of life in the same place. I'd left that home two decades before. Donna's first two decades of life were rent in the middle when her mom left her dad (and the house he'd grown up in), uprooting the five kids from Queens to Port Washington, Long Island, so she'd parted with her original home longer ago than I. And we'd kept moving. Even when we *owned* a house, we'd lived in different states, turning ourselves into renters and land-lords in one shot. Homeownership was not the key that freed us from our vagabondage.

In every home and apartment, we never thought of it as the final place.

Now, well past the halfway mark of our allotted threescore and ten, it was time to settle down. Here we would stay. It sounds almost un-American to admit it. We would be itinerants no longer.

"We're a land of vagabonds," Reynolds Price had said to our class my sophomore year at Duke University. He was the one who'd got me thinking about Americans' wanderlust. He also passed along this: "A need to tell and hear stories is essential to the species *Homo sapiens*—second in necessity apparently after nourishment and before love and shelter." Many have lived without love or shelter, he reasoned. No one survives in silence. Stories—from the literature of our culture to descriptions of our days to the lunatic's ravings—appear to be hard-wired into us. Even in sleep we tell ourselves stories through dreams, and it's been shown that those who are prevented from doing so cease to function. These two ideas were news to me, then, and they were linked somehow. Price had collected them back-to-back, coincidentally, in a big book of essays called *A Common Room*, and for me, as in that book, one idea followed the other.

Price's was not an ordinary classroom, rows of desks beneath fluorescent lights. His was a small, dark study atop a stone tower, filled with ancient artifacts (rocks, bones), art, and books. Narrow leaded windows looked down through tree branches to the expansive corridor of grass that stretched from one end of Duke's campus to the other. At the far side of the room was a red leather chair, a table and lamp beside it, for Price to sit in as he rendered his judgment of you at the end of term; at the other, a small bookcase. In the center of this room was a seminar table around which nine or ten of us sat comfortably discussing each other's work with the ham-handed ruthlessness of the young and untalented.

Price, then fifty-three, had named this course Writing Longer Narrative Fiction. I wrote about a house then, too—it has just now occurred to me—a memory twenty years dormant . . . how interesting. A house was one of three main characters in my first try at a story that could last more than twenty pages without crumbling under its own weight. A man is breaking into a house. A man breaks into the house to punish the owner. The man breaking into the house and the house's owner are in fact the same person, so the house is intended to be in part a metaphor for the psyche. Houses certainly can be that, a metaphor. Psychoanalysts have observed that in our dreams houses are the one symbol that can represent an entire psyche.

The words of a writer are spun in large measure by unconscious forces, Price said—certainly those of a novelist, who creates material out of nothing more than what's already in his or her mind. But I believe this is true for any writer of book-length narratives, any kind of story created over months or years, and these unconscious forces can be trained to do the work of generating story.

We are not inclined to remember most of our dreams, our sleep stories, and often when we do, they disappear as we try to shape them with words. But keep a dream log, pursue the remembrance, and you'll find yourself with increasing amounts of vivid, incomprehensible story on a daily basis. You can train your mind to do this. So, too, can a writer train his or her mind to offer up the goods on a daily basis by initiating and maintaining a routine.

Therefore, if I wanted to write, I'd do so at the same hour each day for the same length of time. It was good also, I learned, to have a goal in mind. This would prevent me from simply staring at what was now a computer screen with time-destroying e-mail and Internet services. On a good day, how much could I get done—a page, two, three? Whatever my rate of word metabolism, I'd choose an amount and make that my goal. Always have a goal.

So I learned that the work must be willed, that I might be able to will it if I tried this way, learned to *manage* my time in a serious and committed manner. I would sit each morning for a minimum of two hours and sweat out 350 words of my house story within a little house in Durham rented with several friends. During that time I found I could perform this physical act, not worrying much about the ultimate value of those words. And I'd wager that anyone who wanted to become a writer and had the basic intellectual equipment, but failed, did so because he or she couldn't sit down and *stay down* for those consecutive hours day after day for however many years it took to figure out what worked (for me it took ten years). It's a physical act, holding still like that, and it's especially difficult at first. It's easier instead to get up, to get something to eat, to look out the window, to check e-mail, to listen to music, compared with *choosing* to sit still and squeeze your fist over a blank piece of paper until blood at last starts to drip out.

This act happens best and easiest, for me, within a house. Some writers prefer to write in public, at a café, where they can be alone without being alone—writing is fundamentally solitary work, so if you don't like being alone, you'll find something else to do quickly. Writers in cities have writing rooms or rent offices. Raymond Carver wrote in his car out of necessity, driven from his house by noise and children. Who knows how James Joyce managed to write? He created one of the masterworks of modern English literature while moving almost daily from rented room to rented room, everywhere throughout Europe, it seems, but his homeland, leaving his wife to raise their firstborn in the parks and cafés of whatever city they happened to be in. Perhaps Joyce could do it because his vagabondage paralleled his fiction, which he named after Western lit's most famous wanderer and home seeker, Ulysses, Odysseus.

I don't think it's completely coincidental that I wrote the story about a house for and with a teacher who gave me the tools to continue writing. House and work are connected for me. Writing every day is bound up in my understanding of what a house is; in a house the writing, the life of a marriage and a family, entwine.

So what this writer impressed on me was the fundamental importance of time management, of routine in the life of a writer, that you had to use routine like a tool, like a fulcrum and lever for heavy lifting. And I came to realize that a house didn't simply facilitate a routine, it propelled routine, deepened and enhanced it through the shape and use of its rooms and halls, the perfect physical landscape for the physical and psychical work of a writer, as well as for the time away from work.

In a house you could have a room to yourself. You needed not a room with a view but a room with a door. A door made the device of a room work, was its critical moving part. Outside this room, somewhere, was a kitchen that needed visiting every so often for a coffee refill. The coffee would require the use of a bathroom across a hall. Just enough distraction for rest after bursts of words, just enough distance to travel—out of the hot center but not out of its orbit; step outside into the sunlight and you might lose your day's work. When you finished work, you could turn off the light and go somewhere else, not have to look at the site of the work, let it cool down, but not have to leave the vicinity altogether either. You might relax by preparing a meal. You were home.

Soon I would have exactly this. The new house would have an envy-inspiring office. Two walls of ceiling-high bookshelves, a bay window with a view to the street, and not one but two doors, one conventional door leading to the dining room, paneled and with a knob, and an enormous paneled door with the same luxurious darkly stained wood that slid into a pocket in the wall. In addition to this pocket door's Victorian elegance was the benefit of its weight: It was too heavy for the kids to slide open. A radiator would hiss and clank in the winter, keeping the room toasty; in the summer four separate windows could be opened to let a breeze through. It was just a few steps from the kitchen and the coffee that percolated there. The scale of it was perfection.

And the house provided the same for Donna. Later, when the big work was done, she would choose a basement room to seal off from the light in which to set up her equipment. The long, open expanse of the new kitchen allowed her to feed the kids, say, while she worked on the mountain of paperwork that arrived as relentlessly as the morning papers. Outside, there was lawn to cut, flower beds to turn over; this was her exercise. She loved to work outside. And she loved to make the house beautiful on the inside. She called herself a nester, and took to that work with zeal.

Of course, where this house was, was as much part of the house as its windows and doors and massive brick sides and cozy front porch. A house alone on a prairie is different from that very same structure squeezed between brownstones in Brooklyn. The same house is a different home depending where it is. Terrain matters.

Houses, in *my* experience, came in groups separated from each other by driveways, trees and grass; I liked trees and grass and, if they were paved, driveways. This house had a spacious front lawn with a walk running straight up its center, a lawn that spread out about thirty feet east of the house to the driveway. Many minor trees and saplings surrounded the house, but three major ones anchored the house in its place. Off the front corner was a thick, tall sycamore; its broad, knotty trunk, with the smooth, ever-peeling bark, had been for years strangled by vines of poison ivy reaching twenty feet up to its first branches. In back an ancient silver maple that had divided into four adult trunks spread out high over our roof, our neighbor's roof, and our back-door neighbor's garage. Between the driveway and the house stood a stately ash.

The place we had chosen, created many decades ago, had, like the house, a scale of its own. How big were the houses? How close together? What was the neighborhood's population? How dense? How wide were the streets? How far from the commercial centers were the residences? How far from the city center? How far from the highway? The answers to these questions described the nature of the place.

Houses here were spread out—set back on deep lawns divided by a broad street, the spaces between roomy. This house had been created in the heyday of public transportation. Its streets were drawn on maps before cars were invented. Not only were the streets formed around a streetcar line, but commercial districts were built within walking distance. Here Donna had been prescient in what she demanded from a house. "I want to be able to walk places," she said.

We wanted a street where the kids could run around without our feeling the urge to check on them every five minutes, a street that was pleasant to walk along. Donna especially wanted a house near some sort of town center, and we had two, both built before the Depression, rows of two-story buildings that could accommodate a shop at ground level and an apartment above (a design now typically outlawed by zoning laws separating residences and business). We could actually walk to the grocery store, to the library, to the video store, to three playgrounds, to an ice cream parlor, to a half dozen nice restaurants or a half dozen chain restaurants—every route defined by wide sandstone sidewalks, tall trees, and houses of diverse, intriguing styles. This was part of the house's scale as well. It had to be the right-size house in the right-size community. We didn't want to have to drive twenty minutes for milk, nor did we want the store directly across the street.

This ability to walk to virtually all the places we could need in our daily life—the only service not within walking distance was a post office—is a circumstance that's almost unheard of in contemporary American suburbia. Unheard of at least in part because it's unnecessary—we drive everywhere. As others have noted, America is now scaled for cars, not humans. For humans, America is out of scale.

We, too, would continue to drive to the grocery store even though we could walk (to avoid lugging all those groceries home on foot). But the option to walk to get an ice cream cone with the kids on a summer evening, or to get some new books at the library, Donna knew, was fundamental to her ideal home. And of course every now and then we wanted a Wal-Mart, but these places and every place we needed was a quick drive away. The grocery store, the post office, Home Depot and Wal-Mart, and Donna's lab. Many of them could be found in the same gigantic expanse of blacktop and concrete, modern monstrosities of convenience bearable to me because of the convenience and the fact that I didn't work there. You could get your errands done in those soulless places efficiently and return to the soulful quiet of your house beneath shady maples and oaks.

Donna couldn't articulate it, but being able to walk places, she believed, was more than just a pleasant benefit. It connected you to something bigger, something nourishing. The idea of living in a McMansion suburb, on the other hand, was like living in a bubble—they didn't even make sidewalks anymore, because people no longer walked. This was page-one news in *USA Today,* and our neighboring county, Geauga, was picked out as an example, the quintessence of suburban sprawl containing, not coincidentally, more fatties than anywhere in America. When there was nowhere to walk to, and nothing to walk on, you were cut off from your neighbors and your neighborhood. Our neighborhood in Cleveland Heights had been shaped on a scale relative to foot traffic and the electric streetcar. We didn't think deeply about this at the time. Donna simply insisted, "I want to be able to walk places," and I felt the same way.

In a book called *How Cities Work,* journalist Alex Marshall describes how spaces become places. The three main forces that determine the nature of a place in America are transportation, the exchange of money, and politics, and the most powerful of those by far is transportation.

When the car supplanted public transportation, it changed the way we shaped the space that this country has in such abundance. And the shape of a place in turn shapes the way we interact with one another and within a community. We've separated ourselves from each other almost absolutely. We have cut off commerce from community. Bookstores are dying because we can buy books and CDs and DVDs from Amazon without leaving the house; we can buy nearly anything at all on eBay and have it delivered to our doorstep—doesn't get more convenient than that. We do our daily shopping at big superstores surrounded by big parking lots. Community is based on foot traffic, but in subdivisions with no sidewalks, we have houses but not communities. Who needs sidewalks? *There's nothing to walk to.* You've got to drive. For exercise you order a StairMaster and do your walking in place, going nowhere.

"How we get around," Marshall writes, "determines how we live. . . . Different transportation systems produce different types of cities. . . . This dynamic is almost impossible to change.

"It was not until the introduction of the raised, limited-access freeway after World War II," he continues, "that the era of place, of urbanity and cities was truly swept away. An interstate highway is incompatible with any form of street-based activity. This postwar invention swept away streets and the need for them. We enter a world of pods placed off freeway ramps, the pods ranging from subdivisions to shopping malls and office parks."

Among the many actual and figurative deaths brought about by these highways is the death of community. The way we've shaped our places has in fact given us isolated, fragmented lives. We are liberated by the car and the Internet, we own a series of increasingly larger homes with bigger bathrooms and swankier kitchens, but we don't know our neighbors, and this, writes Marshall, is a "brutal situation."

"I speak without any sentimentality or nostalgia for the past," he says. "I believe, however, that the generally fragmented lives so many of us lead break up marriages, disturb childhoods, isolate people when they most need help, and make life not as much fun."

In the book Marshall talks about where he lives, in Norfolk, Virginia, the place where he was born, with his wife, also born there. Here was a writer who was doing exactly what I was doing, actively choosing to remain in the city where he grew up, even though it wasn't a cosmopolitan center of energy and ideas—wasn't New York City, that is, where a writer and journalist, able to hobnob with editors and agents and prominent colleagues, might advance his career to the fullest. He was doing his work from his hometown because he could; he valued this choice and advocated it to others. Here was a kindred spirit. It's no wonder, I suppose, that I found his voice to be elegant and straightforward, his blend of personal convictions and objective reportage well balanced. He lived in a good city where he could get places on foot and knew who he was.

Given his dire descriptions of place in American, though, I should probably cast a wary glance at that convenient, soul-killing, Home Depot–Wal-Mart complex that I was happy to have near me. But all grim forecasts about the way America was changing aside, there seemed little for us, personally, to worry about. We were lucky: Our house and our place had formed before the car and the highway took over as the determiners of place, and it was not likely to change, because the houses themselves were valuable and cared for. Ours was being cared for in a very expensive way, but soon that would end; soon the shell below would fill with usable rooms. We were on a street where we could walk everywhere we needed routinely or simply take a walk for some fresh air. We could do our work in our house, and we could relax after work in our house, the structure facilitating all the things we cared about. Soon it would be the perfect house.

10

The Routine of Domesticity

D onna needed only a couple of days to bed the nest up here—
organize the boxes, find the kids' clothes and get them into drawers, set up a food station, make life more or less efficient. Yes, we
had to scuttle ratlike across a ladder to get from the back door onto the
solid floor of the kitchen and climb two flights through a still-demoed
house, often passing strangers at work on our dwelling, but when we
did, we arrived in the haven of the freshly painted, carpeted, tiled,
plumbed, fully lighted, warmly heated third floor that would be our
home for the winter.

The playroom, eighteen by twenty feet, now functioned as master
bedroom, kitchen, and living room, and it was big enough to handle all
of those duties more or less comfortably for a family of four, plenty big
enough to live in permanently, that floor alone. A thousand square feet
including what we called the train room, a long, narrow space that was
too small to be a room and too big to be called a closet, now packed with
boxes. This was a two-bedroom apartment up here—we'd pay $3,000 a
month for this same space in Manhattan, double our monthly mortgage
for the entire house. We were self-contained above the house, cozy, dry,
and well supplied. It was like living on a boat and gave us the sense of
being on a journey, or maybe just caught in a storm, trapped in a mountain grotto but warm.

And we soon found a routine. At 8:10 every morning, A. and I would be in the car waiting for John, who always arrived between 8:00 and 8:05, to move his van. I'd drop her at school at 8:17, then head to my father's house and my old desk to begin tapping out the daily work. Donna would labor on the house itself and look after the kids, taking J. to his toddler class and then picking both kids up. I'd stop by Lemongrass on the way home for some takeout, arriving not long after six o'clock, and there we would remain for the evening. It was a lovely winter routine.

By nine o'clock I was reading from a Little House on the Prairie book to A., who listened so attentively as to seem utterly disengaged and oblivious. When I stopped, she would jolt her head toward the page, see that I'd reached the end of a chapter and say, "Noooo, pleeeeeeeze, *mooooorrre.*" But she'd be tired and, in moments, calm enough to let sleep take her. I'd next kiss J.'s fat cheek, and he'd answer with a cartoonish snore and a smack of his lips—out cold.

The kitchen table now sat on an area rug in the main room, giving the impression that it was an intended space, separate from the living room, which was demarcated by the back of the ratty old Jennifer convertible, and the bedroom, demarcated by the bed. School papers, bills for two structures (for ten weeks we owned both houses), folders containing paperwork for the work on this house—contractor estimates, receipts, more bills, faxes featuring pictures of an array of faucets and knobs and sconces for the three bathrooms and kitchen below—piled on this table, as well as plain old mail, magazines we had no time to read, the first of the holiday's cards bearing pictures of friends' kids, catalogs, and more catalogs. Donna stood at this table, kind of playing it, a complex form of solitaire, hindered somewhat by the cartons of Thai takeout still there.

Without lifting her eyes from the board, Donna said, "Is she asleep?"

"No, but you'd better say good night now if you want a response."

It was already Thursday, a week since moving day, and our routine was set. Donna laid the stack in hand on a second stack and left to have a few moments with her daughter. I opened the cooler, which pressed against the back of the couch, and removed two large, squishy cold packs that needed to be exchanged for frozen ones from the refrigerator

in the basement. The trip there required shoes, and I sat on the hall landing, where carpeting ended, to put them on. It was quite warm up here
with the ceiling newly insulated, and the murmurings of mother and
daughter enhanced the warmth. I stood to begin my descent—at night
this trip felt like actually going down into the earth, sinking through
layers of preserved time, forgotten and decayed eras of domesticity. A
time when servants in skirt and apron trod these same stairs, a time
when men used safety razors and deposited the used blades in a slot in
the wall (John had uncovered hundreds of rusty old blades in the wall of
the second bathroom here). The stairs creaked as I stepped, the naked
bulbs of the second floor throwing harsh light onto bare walls, empty
windows, primer- and mud-spattered floors. Mud from a dozen pairs of
work boots was everywhere. The gravel in the drive was mainly gone,
replaced by ruts—you couldn't avoid tracking mud in.

The ground floor was dark, only silhouettes of sawhorses and miter
saws visible by streetlamp, lumber propped against walls. John had
clamped a utility light to a stud in the middle of the kitchen. The cord
dangled down to an extension outlet on the floor, which connected to
the main panel in the basement. I felt around in the dark for it, hit the
switch. There was no heat down here, and my breath glowed like smoke
in the dim light. The empty spaces amplified the scraping of my shoes
on the nail-littered plywood floor. I stepped carefully down the ladder
that leaned between the kitchen floor and the back-door landing, several feet lower, holding on to the floor as I stepped, then descended the
last of the way, belowground.

Here I exchanged warm cold packs for frozen ones, then thought
carefully whether there was anything more from down here that we
would need for the rest of this night and tomorrow morning. Juice? I
had brought up milk for cereal and coffee, hadn't I? Yes, I remembered
seeing it. I shut off the basement lights and began my ascent, rising like a
mole out of the earth, shutting off the utility light and feeling my way in
the dark to the back staircase and straight up to the warm, carpeted hallway of our third floor. It was a long way up. I placed the cold packs
snugly in the cooler. I was still breathing hard when I sat.

"Did you remember milk?" Donna asked as she came into the room.

"There's milk in there."

Donna pulled the half-gallon jug and shook it. "Just a drop."

Best not to think about it, best just to accept the fact and think of something else while you're retying your shoes to repeat the trip, fifty-four stairs down and fifty-four back up. This wouldn't have happened had I still been a cook—you simply didn't have time to waste like that. But here we did. This was colossally inefficient apartment living, a necessary phase in our quest for perfect domesticity.

"Domestic well-being is a fundamental human need that is deeply rooted in us and that must be satisfied," writes Witold Rybczynski in his book *Home: The Short History of an Idea*. Domesticity is a broad cultural idea, not a fashion like décor or the way we use our living rooms, and such ideas tend to have staying power. "Domesticity, for example," Rybczynski writes, "has existed for more than three centuries."

The perfect domesticity was also a part of the perfect home, and Rybczynski's words gave me a sense of comfort in this quest. It would be all too easy for me to acknowledge what, on the surface, this crazy houselust home quest amounted to—the ultimate act of consumerism, purchasing a bigger house than you need and filling it up with all manner of stuff you never use. Were we simply two more vacuous members of the bourgeoisie, grossly indulging in comfort rather than putting our money toward something either useful (our kids' education comes to mind) or charitable? I needed to face the grim possibility head-on: Had we become superficial sybarites, vainly struggling with the meaninglessness of our empty suburban lives by wallowing in an equally meaningless material world, one filled with Ralph Lauren faux furniture and Jeep Grand Cherokees and overpriced Williams-Sonoma terrine molds? I mean, really, what were we doing, and why were we doing it? Was it all for shallow comfort? Given that we already had an acceptable house, shouldn't we be putting our time and resources toward something more meaningful than a larger, more comfortable one on a lovelier street? What were we doing with our lives that made this big gamble, this extraordinary upheaval, a good decision? Was this domesticity that we craved a romantic lie? Nostalgic? Sentimental? Was it always in the searching rather than the having—would we always crave more goods, bigger houses to fill the existential void?

I had no desire to flay myself unnecessarily. I'd give myself every benefit of the doubt, but I also didn't want to live in delusions. What did I really want, and was it a good thing or bad?

Only this: to roast a chicken in my nifty thirty-six-inch Viking oven after a productive day of work, a big Boos cutting board on the spacious island, a fire crackling, Donna spotting her black-and-white prints at the table, and the kids either at my ankles or nearby playing. If it was Sunday, with the Cleveland Browns on in the background, losing, I'd know that all was right with the universe, the planets were aligned. I wanted that, and I wanted at least the hope of seeing grandchildren visit the very same kitchen and to roast a chicken for them as well. I wanted what Rybczynski refers to as domestic comfort, and I wanted it absolutely.

In his book *Home,* this architect and professor who turned to writing in middle age takes the reader through a history of how we in the Western world have used our homes and how we feel about them, a fascinating study that's useful in understanding how and why we live as we do.

He traces the seed of domesticity to the Middle Ages and opens the book by describing a European home of the 1500s. Homes were completely open then, with the space used for every manner of activity by numerous family members—cooking, eating, working, bathing, and sleeping—none of it done in private. It was unusual for anyone in a sixteenth-century family to have his own room, Rybczynski writes. To be comfortable was not an issue—it wasn't even a concept. Comfort was a verb only: to strengthen, shore up, console. Chairs were a concept lost in the murk of the Dark Ages. "In the Middle Ages people didn't so much live in their houses as camp in them," he writes.

The change that Rybczynski first notes, then, citing the work of the historian John Lukacs, is the fruition "of something new in human consciousness: the appearance of the internal world of the individual, of the self, and of the family.

"[The evolution of domestic comfort] is more than a simple search for physical well-being; it begins in the appreciation of the house as a set-ting for an emerging interior life."

Here is house not as a metaphor for the psyche but as direct projec-tion of it. A change in personality, in our consciousness, then, caused a change in domestic architecture. There were no technological break-throughs required to divide the house into separate spaces. But in order for this interior life to emerge freely, the notion of privacy had to be physically built in to the home itself, an actual separation between the various members of an extended family living under the same roof—privacy, which began in the late sixteenth and early seventeenth cen-turies. Here home begins to change: We shape the house to accommodate our changing selves; the shape of the house facilitates and propels that change.

With a division of rooms comes the division of domestic arrange-ments. Children have their room, and the husband and wife, with the children separated, Rybczynski notes, "have begun to think of them-selves—perhaps for the first time—as a couple."

Formal schools for children replaced apprenticeships. For the first time in centuries, parents watched their children grow up. These domestic changes reinforced "the growing self-awareness of the family," writes Rybczynski, and a deepening sense of domestic intimacy.

It was the beginning of domesticity as we know it today, and it came to full flower, Rybczynski explains, in the seventeenth-century Nether-lands, the Dutch golden age.

"The Dutch were bourgeois by inclination," Rybczynski writes, not-ing that even at a time of extraordinary military, economic, and intel-lectual might, a middle-class ethic that valued moderation, hard work, and financial prudence predominated. And they loved their houses—unpretentious brick and wood affairs with gabled facades and plenty of large windows. Houses held small families, one couple and their chil-dren, not big ones. Few people had servants, as was the custom else-where throughout Europe; even the most privileged women hung their own laundry, swept their own stoops. Houses here stopped doubling as workplaces.

"The emergence of the family home reflected the growing importance of the family in Dutch society," Rybczynski writes. Children were held in higher regard than anywhere else on the continent, with relationships characterized more by affection than by discipline. Children were raised by their mother, not a nurse. They went to school from an early age, were not shipped off to apprentice in a trade, and this surely contributed to the fact that the Netherlands registered the highest literacy in Europe. It was here—in a small home with separate rooms, a place to which children returned after school and to which the man returned after work, where the family ate together and where a husband and wife watched the infant-child-adult transformation close up—that the notion of "childhood" came into being. In France the concept did not exist, says Rybczynski. To a Frenchman, children were no more than miniature, troublesome adults. It was in the Netherlands that a "rapprochement between parents and family, and between the concept of family and the concept of childhood" occurred.

The house was the physical center and the spiritual embodiment of what the Dutch cherished. They loved their homes so much that it was common for people to commission the building of elaborate scale models of them. The interior décor and furnishings were spare but comfortable. The layouts divided activities into day and night, formal and informal, the spaces snug but efficient.

The large windows not only decreased the weight of the narrow cross walls of the house (houses built on pilings in this sea-level land) but gave actual brightness to their deep interiors. Residents controlled the light with shutters and curtains. As windows grew large, opening them inward or outward, like doors, became inconvenient; thus was engineered the double-hung or sash window, which could be opened without taking up more space.

Women kept their houses "spotlessly, immaculately, unbelievably clean," extending their cleaning to the front stoop, the sidewalk, and even the street in front of the house. For the first time, women came to dominate the household. "The feminization of the home in seventeenth-century Holland was one of the most important events in the evolution of the domestic interior," writes Rybczynski. They did the work, and because they did the work, as opposed to directing servants to do the work, household amenities began to appear, with the kitchen as the templelike center of the home. The cupboard was a family's most prized possession, holding treasured items such as fine china and linens. Highly polished copper pots hung from the walls; washing was done in copper or marble sinks, sometimes fed by a continuous supply of hot water. For the first time, the person who did the housework controlled family purchases and domestic arrangements. And here were the earliest seeds of convenience planted.

Not only did the home grow "more intimate, it was also, in the process, acquiring a special atmosphere," Rybczynski writes, "becoming a feminine place, or at least a place under feminine control. This control was tangible and real. It resulted in cleanliness, and in enforced rules, but it also introduced something to the house which had not existed before: domesticity."

Rybczynski defines domesticity not as a single attitude but rather as a "set of felt emotions" comprising intimacy, devotion to the home, a sense of the home's containing and embodying those values that help a family to flourish. It depended on a rich interior awareness and was fundamentally the achievement of the women of this society. Domesticity was not inevitable, says Rybczynski. Indeed, it might have remained a hundred years away were it not for this society's general atmosphere of egalitarianism and the independence of its women.

Future comfort and domestic pursuits were partly why we were now enduring the discomfort of living in an attic. Slowly the rooms below took their shape. The new bathroom fixtures went in. John framed off the new shower area in the master bath. The final studs came down in the kitchen, drywall went up in a blink, a new oak floor went in, and the kitchen cabinetry lay in the living room waiting for the finish carpenters to attach each to its wall. On weekends, when the crews were gone, Donna would prime the new kitchen walls, the new bathroom walls, snow outside slanting across black trees and gray sky. And I would work on the bedroom molding or building bathroom shelves in cold, empty rooms. The kitchen and the master bedroom and bath felt like the main thrust of our work. When these two parts of the house were done, we could move out of the attic and begin a life that approximated what one expects when one lives in a house; we could separate ourselves and our routines within the house. This was one of the great features of a house: various spaces for specific activities. In the attic we did everything in one room; we camped there. So the goal was clear: get out of the Middle Ages. To cook in a kitchen and sleep in our own bedroom, that would signal we'd crested the top of the hill, and the downward roll toward a finished house would begin.

11

The Problem with Contractors

They keep asking for money.

That's not damning in itself, I guess, but when the contractor delivers yet another "payment request" and the work you paid for a couple weeks ago still isn't done—there are still holes in the walls, missing light switches, missing floor molding, charges for goods you didn't want, stuff you once had that's disappeared, you're still living in the attic, and the B&K divot in the carpet is already beginning to sag visibly—it can make you cranky.

Perhaps it's all these relative strangers working on an object that's increasingly personal to you, indeed so personal that it comes to feel like a part of your own body and hurts when it's mistreated. Perhaps, too, you're just tired of the sight of dirty dishes in the bathroom sink or making jelly sandwiches on a cutting board on the floor. Or perhaps there's simply antagonism built in to the contractor-homeowner relationship— anger, suspicion, and resentment flow just below the surface, ever threatening to erupt. And when they do, it's over something so nugatory as to make the one who's mad seem a little bit insane. A wobbly cold-water handle in the new bathroom that's apparently "good enough" or a bit of missing floor molding.

I got out of the house every day—"John, could you please move your van, please?"—deposited A. at school, and headed to my father's to write, while Donna remained in "the project" to paint rooms and to take care of J.

Donna had seemingly endless jobs ahead of her. Every old surface—walls and ceilings—needed to be painted. She was like Mary Bailey fixing up the old Granville place, except this was real life, not *It's a Wonderful Life*. Mary Bailey didn't have to deal with contractors. There were many new surfaces, too, like those in the two upstairs bathrooms, the downstairs bathroom or half bath, but really she was responsible for painting the entire interior of a big old house—five upstairs rooms, numerous closets, a substantial hallway, a back staircase, a downstairs hall, a living room, my office, the dining room, the kitchen, the bathroom. The sheer square-yardage of what she intended to cover with one, two, in some places three coats of finished paint was staggering.

Crews of workers filled the house: the painting crew we'd hired to remove wallpaper and take everything down to bare surfaces, which were then to be primed either by them or by Donna; John and the B&K workers; the drywallers; the heating-and-cooling crew; John the mason; Jim the plumber; Dennis the tile guy and his assistant. The house was packed with people all day long. It was like employing a small city in here.

For Donna—"Bye-bye, sweetheart, have a good day," I'd say, trundling off to a warm, complete, quiet house to write in peace—managing the housework was full-time in the best-case scenario. Taking care of J. in an unfinished house—filled with work crews and rusted nails and discarded box-cutter blades and open drums of primer, amid walls that had holes in them with wire sticking out—created additional stress. Her dual role of mother and house renovator against the backdrop of an overflowing Dumpster and the deadly cold gray of a Cleveland winter, it all pressed down on her. Add to this some contractor mistakes, such as a working garbage disposal that went missing, the delivery of the wrong bathroom tile, miscommunications that translated to even more work for her, stir in a some PMS, and you have a volatile little cocktail on your hands.

As was typical of those winter days, I'd finish up the current pages on a child's missing left ventricle, a surgical error, a heroic nurse, a family hovering over their unconscious baby in the pediatric ICU praying for a heart to arrive, and then I would shut off my laptop, phone in an order at Lemongrass for coconut shrimp soup, beef satay, the fried rice that Donna loved, which would be ready for pickup in the time it took me to clean the coffeepot, pack my briefcase, and drive through the snowy darkness to the restaurant. Dinner in hand, I headed home, parked in the mud puddles of our drive (now treacherously frozen), climbed the ladder over the basement hole between the back-door landing and the kitchen, and trudged up the two flights of stairs to our attic apartment. It was like a Himalayan cave up there.

I arrived into comfort and warmth and exclamations from the kids, who lit up and threw their arms around me. But Donna had been here the whole day, *dealing*. And, without any satisfactory vent, it would all bubble over by the time dinner was done, the kids were in bed, and she'd had a couple glasses of wine. Only then, when the kids were finally down, could we allow ourselves to relax. And where Donna was concerned, relaxing simply meant unscrewing the release valves on the pressure cooker of her mind to talk about the house. It took energy, real psychic energy, to contain the steam, and by the end of the day, that energy was gone.

"*Jim*," it might begin, the name spoken with the emphasis of a curse. Or "Dennis—what is his problem?" Or simply, "Carl." We sat at the kitchen table in a room that contained most of our living room furniture, bedroom furniture, and minor kitchen appliances, the table itself stacked with faxes from the tile company, from plumbing supply, bills, mail.

"Did you call Carl?"

"Yes, I called—I talked with Dave."

"What did he say?"

"He said he'd leave a message for Carl," Donna continued. "When I asked him what was going on, told him we needed the steps—we need to get rid of that hole before one of the kids falls through it—he said, 'I understand.' I said, 'Do you know how frustrating it is?' 'I do, I understand,' he says. I tell him, 'We're paying you a lot of money, and I can't even get Carl to return a call.' 'I understand,' he says. I wonder how many people he's got to say that to? And where is Rob? What happened to him?"

The problem with Jim was classic—an apparently minor, honest mistake, was in fact the embodiment of a pattern of little mistakes that are not dealt with but instead denied, and thus mount into something more substantial. The one paying the contractor and ultimately over-seeing the work (Donna) perceives these mistakes, but none are large enough to require an argument beyond a sentence of correction; how-ever, a calm sentence is not enough force to get the glitch corrected, so many such glitches accumulate and fester. Soon they amount to some-thing like a spiritual boil that one of these days will simply get too big, and when it blows, it's going to be a surprise and it's gonna be messy.

As Donna explained it, she just happened to be passing the down-stairs bath as Jim the plumber was hooking up the toilet there. Jim was our age, handsome guy with dark curly hair, usually in T-shirt and jeans with something a little sad about him, even when he smiled. He was a very good guy, thoughtful, articulate, and yet everything seemed to be a struggle for Jim; everything seemed to be just a little more difficult than he'd expected. Donna knew to look at what he was doing.

"Jim," she said, "that's the wrong toilet."

"What? No it's not."

"Jim, I bought the toilets—I know."

"But it said on the box."

"Jim, I chose everything for a specific reason," Donna said patiently. "This is a tiny bathroom. Why would I put this big, elongated toilet into a tiny half bath?"

The room, beneath the back staircase, measured four by five feet with a very high ceiling, and Donna had been struggling with sink and toilet styles that would fit the space without making its intended use awkward and uncomfortable. We'd been in those half baths squeezed beneath a staircase in old suburban homes not initially designed with a downstairs bathroom, in which you could scarcely turn around without knocking something over, where you couldn't use the commode without banging your head on a door or a towel bar. She'd found a rectangular sink that was long side to side but shallow front to back, with a narrow basin with-out handles and faucet, one that came out of the wall, saving several inches of depth. (This sink had arrived several weeks ago and had yet to be installed, another point that would become significant.) The toilet she'd chosen had a more or less round basin. For the spacious upstairs baths, she'd chosen bowls that were more elongated.

Donna worked through the reasoning with him. Jim's response was, "But the box said." Which, translated, is the subcontractor's maxim: *not my fault.*

Of course, as this was far from the first such instance, the frustration of it pressed her into more than simply fixing the problem. Angered, she dug at him a little bit. "What if I hadn't walked by just now?"

There was nothing to say. Both knew the answer—Donna in her anger wanted Jim to think about it. The box with the placement written on it was in the Dumpster, so the point was moot. Donna had found the error; now Jim had to haul this one upstairs, then go out to the garage, hunt around for the right toilet, and hook that one up where this one now sat. A week ago it had been a loose handle in the master bath. Donna had to haul Jim *and* Carl in there and ask Carl, "Is it *really* supposed to jiggle like this?" "No, it's not," Carl admitted.

"The thing is," Donna told me, pacing now, "Jim's response is to exhale and roll his eyes. As if it's *my* fault. As if *I'm* being a pain in the ass."

Donna bared her teeth, pushed out her formidable chin, neck turning red, arteries visibly pulsing, and she actually growled: *Errrrrrrrrrr!* "It makes me so *mad.*"

"Where is Carl?" I asked.

"I don't know! *I don't know!* He won't return calls!"

This kind of noncommunication between her and Carl, between Carl and his crew, resulted in the fact that there was not an extra outlet in this downstairs bath where Donna had specifically requested one. She knew she wanted a lamp in this bathroom to avoid relying on a bright overhead fixture. City code demands a ground fault circuit interrupter outlet, one with a breaker, above sink level. Donna didn't want a cord hanging out of the wall above the sink. She noticed during the toilet brouhaha that there was no discrete outlet above the floor molding, only the GFCI outlet. Where is Carl?

"Dave," she said into the phone, "do you know how frustrating it is to find these mistakes and not be able to fix them because Carl won't return a call?"

"I understand, Mrs. Ruhlman."

"Will you please give Carl the message?"

"Absolutely."

"And where is Rob, *Dave*? We had talked about all of this—the outlet, the tile situation in the master bath. All these things Rob knows, we discussed them for hours—doesn't he talk to Carl? This is costing me my *time*."

"I understand."

Of course, all this would be sorted out, and there would come a day when Donna and Carl, semireconciled out of necessity, stood in the doorway of this bathroom talking. Carl had got Vern back to put in the new outlet—something of a pain for everyone, given that the toilet was now installed and drywall had been put up in the kitchen on the other side of this wall. Vern had to cut holes in two walls, holes John would have to patch and sand smooth, work that wouldn't have been necessary had Vern put the outlet in with the other wiring as Donna had requested of Rob at the start. Donna then got out the primer and primed it. She seethed as she worked because she'd already primed this bathroom once, goddamn it; there was too much to do to waste her time like this, not only forcing her to watch the crews like a hawk, argue with them when they fucked up ("he rolled his eyes, as if *I'm* causing the problem"), but also forcing her to do extra painting, which she needed like a hole in the head (I seethed with her on these nights as she vented rage). But ultimately—time healing all wounds, yes?—there the two of them stood, she and Carl, everything at last right, the toilet, the sink, the outlet—the molding . . . something was off. It didn't look right.

Donna stepped back. Throughout the entire house, the floor molding was the same: toe molding, a wide baseboard below a narrow one, and an ornamental strip on top. John had done a good job of matching baseboards on new walls with the existing ones.

"What happened here?" she said, as if to herself, noticing for the first time that the molding in the bathroom was missing one of the two baseboards, making it half as high as the rest of the floor molding throughout the entire house. "Why is it shorter than the rest? It's missing one of the baseboards." She looked at Carl. She'd asked it as if she were clearly not seeing something obvious and Carl would fill her in.

Carl nodded and scratched the back of his head. "I don't know, John must have run out."

Long pause. "Run out?" Another long pause, to let the steam build up some pressure. "What do you mean 'run out'?" she asked. This would be when Carl began to get the sense that he'd like to be elsewhere. The pitch of her voice rose: "Run out?" Certainly he could detect a slight quiver of her head, a twitch. "Run out?! Carl! If he runs out, he needs to . . . *get more! Doesn't he? Isn't that how it works?*"

Carl admitted that that would have been the appropriate response. But the thing is—and this was what would come out at night, not there in the hall—it wasn't the mistake itself, which would become a permanent part of the house (few would notice it, but for Donna it would be a defect). What drove her bananas was that she had to *tell* him. He was the man in charge, and to let it go at that—*I guess he ran out*—was acceptable? Why did she have to work so damn hard for this, when there was other stuff that *really* needed the work, that really required her efforts? Like, maybe spend time with the son she felt she was ignoring.

This kind of thing happened continually. Every now and then, I'd have a fantasy of Donna turning into the killer bunny rabbit from *Monty Python and the Holy Grail,* where I'd arrive home and find carnage, stepping over workmen sprawled in puddles on the floor, gore and limbs everywhere, Donna amid it all, bouncing J. on her knee, anxiety-free at last, completely and sweetly content.

My wife is beautiful in a no-makeup way, just sort of naturally athletic and good-looking, but when she'd tell me these stories, and growl uncontrollably and turn red, her throat's blood vessels visibly pulsing, she could scare the shit out me. She was a force.

What *should* she do then when Carl delivered another bill and in this bill was buried a rush-delivery charge for that narrow downstairs-bath sink, which, after being rushed to our address for an additional expense of something like sixty bucks, then sat in the box for weeks? This principle infuriated her and me: *They stick us with too many nickel-and-dime charges as it is. Don't pile your mistakes on us, too!* she wanted to scream. Donna popped gaskets daily.

"Mrs. Ruhlman?" Dennis said. "Before I put this tile in, I just want to check, just want to *make sure* it's the right tile." They'd already tangled, Dennis the tile guy and Donna, about the third-floor kids' shower. She'd wanted to include a band of four-inch blue tiles standing on end like diamonds, but Dennis said that involved a lot of extra cutting and would probably be reflected on the next B&K payment request. So she'd given in and agreed to a simple band of straight four-inch tiles around the top. When she next saw the shower, Dennis had put in a band of six-inch tiles. Not the size she'd wanted—her intent had been to at least vary the size if not the pattern—and it looked a little clunky. This was annoying, but what was she going to do, make Dennis rip it all out, order the right tile, and put that in at a time when we were on a deadline? Then, in going over the invoices, she saw that the box of six-inch tile was twice as expensive as the four-inch tile. She was paying *extra* for the compromise and mistake. Where does one put the, uh, energy this discovery creates?

This is why she'd asked Dennis to please holler for her before he put in something permanent, just to check. And so he did.

Donna left what she was doing and went to the master bath, where Dennis and his assistant were about to lay tile. They had everything ready to go.

"No!" Donna said. "That's *not* right."

Dennis couldn't believe it. He rolled his eyes, as if to say, *You have to be kidding me.*

"This is *not* the tile. This is the wrong tile."

"It's what they sent."

"I don't care that it's what they sent. It's not what I ordered. It's wrong."

Dennis threw up his hands; his angry look fell on Donna. This ended work for the day for him, meaning he couldn't finish the job and so wouldn't get paid. Many boxes of tile, several hundred dollars' worth, would have to be returned and replaced, and when the correct tiles did finally come, there was several hundred dollars' worth of extra tile, for which we were charged, seven boxes in all, at more than fifty bucks a box. B&K had ordered this excess of tile and had put it in their payment request. Along with a charge for hanging a new back door, which we had requested and then decided, with Carl's help, that we didn't need after all—$250. Small error, honest mistake, nobody's fault, you can see how it would happen with all the stuff going on.

"Dave, I'm leaving another message for Carl."

"I'll make sure he gets it."

"You say that every time, Dave. This is getting old."

"I understand."

"I'm very frustrated."

"I don't blame you, Mrs. Ruhlman. I completely understand."

Donna took a slug of wine as we went over the day's events. "God, why couldn't B&K be like the drywall guys? The drywall guys blew everyone away," she said, leaning back in her chair. We conversed over a table piled with bills and cartons from Lemongrass, the kids snoozing deeply. It was only once they were asleep that we could have an unbroken conversation. With kids in that small space, we were lucky to get in a single back-and-forth volley. At the end of the day, Donna could talk like a normal adult. "Blew *everyone* away," she said admiringly.

"Yeah, they were great weren't they? Granted, drywalling doesn't require the skill of a finish carpenter, but, in and out in three days—no talking, no errors; they walked into a room of brick wall and studs and bare light fixtures, and when they were gone, everything was perfectly smooth. That was nice."

"Why can't everyone work that way? Why isn't it just a matter of course?" she asked. "Oh, and you know what I found out today? Carl's been on *vacation* for three weeks. He hasn't even been in town. So obviously he wasn't returning our calls."

"Why didn't they just tell us that? Is there something wrong with being on vacation?"

Donna looked at me hard. "You know what 'I understand' means? I finally realized."

"What?"

"'You're talking to a wall.'"

Donna stood and paced, playing both parts, until she simply recited it over and over in a variety of inflections.

Straightforward: You're talking to a wall.

Breezy conversational: You're talking to a wall.

Mild compassion: *You* are talking to a *wall.*

A little defiant, but cordial: You are talking to a *waaall.*

Genuine compassion: You, oh, you are *talking* to a *wall.*

I laughed, but she was really pissed, and I'm sure I didn't completely appreciate the extent of it, even when she stopped and said, "*I am on a rampage.* Where is Rob?"

Ultimately we'd move the conversation back to the kids or my work, anything not related to the contractors, so that she could calm herself enough for sleep. She'd brush her teeth and wash her face and pull a brush through her shoulder-length hair till it was smooth and straight and the brush moved through it with little resistance. She'd say good night to me, climb into bed, and fall asleep before she'd read five pages, physically and emotionally spent.

What was perhaps the most troubling aspect of the contractor situation was the fact that B&K was a good company, generally, with many happy customers and a thriving business in this little land of houses. The majority of their work was decent. Overall, they were doing a good job on our house. We liked the crew, who were conscientious and enormously agreeable. It's a complex job involving many people, and we were tense, but they were honest and fair, and when they made a mistake, they did what they could to correct it.

Our contractor problems didn't approach the cliché level most did as far shoddy work and unreturned phone calls went. One didn't need to go far to hear stories—just ask practically anyone who's hired a contractor, and you'll soon be listening to a laundry list of astonishing stories. My cousin complained to his contractor about bad work, demanded that they do it right, and the contractor *sued him.* This apparently intimidates people who decide to eat the cost rather than call a lawyer and begin an involved legal process (though not my cousin). One of the docs I was writing about, she and her husband had bought a house nearby, and after a horrific experience of missed deadlines and sloppy work, they fired the guy, though they'd already paid him in full, plus thousands in extra charges. This would be bad enough, of course, but shortly thereafter they began getting harassing phone calls in the middle of the night from their contractor's subcontractors. Apparently the main contractor hadn't paid them, saying he'd been stiffed. Our friends had to make copies of the canceled checks to the contractor before the harassing calls would stop.

So we should feel lucky, right? What's the deal with contractors and the tradesmen who work on domestic structures? They looked normal, no outward signs of serious mutations, handicaps, learning disabilities, psychoses—and yet something was not right. I couldn't help but begin to think of contractors generally as healthy and normal in every way, except they were missing one little important part, one small link of DNA, and while this missing piece didn't keep them from working, something was a bit off. They didn't run smoothly; they backfired at odd intervals. They functioned, but they were defective. So yes, I did feel lucky that John was a decent, dependable worker and ran the crew well and that Carl was honest and ultimately responsive.

It must be admitted, of course, that I was a little defective, too, if only for having realized too late how the situation had to be handled. It took me three and a half months to realize that an excellent way to encourage Carl to return phone calls, to get work done lickety-split, was to delay payment. I don't know why it took me so long. Our harassed friends had made the error of paying according to the contract schedule, even though the work wasn't getting done—now they know better. How silly of me. I'd always thought that to get work done, you *paid* for it; that was how the transaction worked. In fact, the fastest way to get something done, we quickly and happily discovered, was *not* to pay. Amazingly, the faster you didn't pay, the faster the work got done.

The winter proceeded thus. January rolled into February, February into March, our heads down and focused on work, the kids in their stable school routine. On cold, snowy weekends, I got the molding done in the second-floor bedrooms, using the dining room as a workroom, sawdust and wood scraps everywhere. Donna finished all the painting in those rooms, and soon afterward, almost unbeknownst to me, since I spent all day elsewhere, she got carpeting in—I didn't even have to see it, didn't have a chance to jinx it with my bad carpet karma. As far as I know, it all went smoothly.

Piece by piece, carpenters installed the kitchen cabinets and the island; a template was made for the granite countertop, and that was soon cut. Jim hooked up pipes to two sinks, the dishwasher, the pot filler, and the complicated foot pedals to the island sink. The swank stainless-steel appliances went in. The floors were sanded and varnished.

With Donna asleep, I'd turn off the lights and go out into the hallway and sit on the stairs to read. I'd put on my glasses—a new acquisition that underscored my sense of the inevitable decay—lean against the wall, one foot on the top step, and read in complete peace. Life was good, wasn't it? We were at last getting somewhere.

12

Return Pain

The kitchen was not done. The walls were primed but not painted. GFCI plugs dangled out of walls and out of the island. But I could no longer resist it. The kitchen called to me, like the voice in Costner's baseball field. This room had its critical working parts. The cabinets, a handsome blue-green-gray, had gone in over the past few weeks. A template of the island, the countertops, and sinks had been made so that the slab of granite Donna had chosen months earlier could be cut. There was now a single sink basin—a foot deep and more than two feet wide—beside a dishwasher. Surely we'd one day appreciate the nuances of the choice of sink, the placement of the dishwasher, but what they meant that weekend in March, when the countertops at last went in and Jim had hooked up the faucets and drains, was no more washing dishes in a small bathroom sink. We were liberated.

I stocked the shelves with plates and glasses—the cabinet doors above the sink had glass panels, as did a cabinet at the dining room end of the island—unpacking the boxes we'd filled long ago in our old house. It's difficult to convey completely the euphoria of the task, of thinking, Hmm, coffee mugs here, drinking glasses here? It was like a narcotic.

Where am I? Look at that stainless stove—it looked to me like a sports car. I retrieved a box of pans from the basement, many of which I could dangle from a bar along high shelves on either side of the range hood. We'd designed open, below-counter cupboards on either side of the stove, with pull-out drawers. I'd made one low drawer big enough to hold the Kitchen Aid mixer and the food processor—they wouldn't take up valuable counter space. I hauled these up as well and stored them. There would be plenty of room here.

I made a shopping list. I leaned on the amazing rock, shining green granite veined gray like marble, and wrote basic food items. I looked across the island's length, a field two feet wide and seven feet long with a central sink whose hot- and cold-water faucets were connected to foot pedals. This would provide plenty of room to work. And, like an island rising out of a calm sea, it was three inches higher than the counters on either side, at thirty-nine inches. The counters gleamed, and my shopping list lengthened. The thought of simply walking into the back door, taking stairs up, and setting bags of groceries on this island in front of the built-in refrigerator seemed a small miracle to me. What astonishing efficiency. A refrigerator, not a cooler. I could buy several days' worth of food and store it in a refrigerator in a kitchen. I marveled at the thought. Dishwasher beside sink, the refrigerator-countertop combo, I recognized now, were masterworks of ingenuity. My God, how convenient this was going to be. We were moving to civilization from the Third World of our attic; we were time-traveling from the sixteenth century to the present.

When I returned from the store, sure enough, theory bore out elegantly. The island held the bag of groceries. The refrigerator door cleared the overhanging granite of the island by a quarter inch—a remarkable feat of planning and installation by the cabinet guys. I filled the refrigerator, and it was so neat and organized it looked like an advertisement for this very refrigerator.

I turned on the oven. I took a cast iron pan off its hook. I set a fresh chicken in it and salted the bird well.

There was never a doubt what the first meal in the new kitchen would be. Roast chicken, baked potatoes, green beans with lemon and butter. Roast chicken is to me the iconic meal of the home. Many pleasures attended its cooking; in a way it seasoned the kitchen, the way you'd season a pan. Its smell filled the room, the house. I like to baste a chicken, to hear the crackling juices from the cavity spill into the fat, to spoon hot, clear fat over the darkening skin. A perfectly roasted bird is a beautiful sight.

And it worked. The kids appeared, lured by the unfamiliar smell that had been sucked up the stairs along with all the downstairs heat. Donna came in to see, then got her camera. When the cabinets were in, we'd brought the kitchen table and area rug down here. The table fit. No more squeezing around it. It looked perfect against the brick of the fire-place. A. sat by the fire, which was about a foot and a half off the floor, right at chair height. J. immediately found the toe-kick heaters Carl and Rob had suggested since we'd gotten rid of the radiator in this room. He lolled at my feet in the warm current.

Nothing much else was down here. On the other side of the island from the kitchen table and fireplace was the dining room, which had a carpet of sawdust on it, scraps of wood, and a compound miter saw. The bookshelves on either side of the fireplace were empty. Paint cans and can-vas tarps filled the office; the living room was stacked with furniture beneath sheets and plastic tarps. But the kitchen had opened, and it made the whole house feel alive for the first time since we'd moved in. Anyone passing the house on this chilly March evening might have seen smoke rising out of the rear chimney and maybe smelled the fire, might notice the warm yellow glow in kitchen windows that had been dark all winter.

Donna leaned on the island and said, "How do you like your new kitchen?"

I stood across from her and said, "I don't know whose kitchen this is, but I think it's fantastic."

"It's your kitchen."

"I don't deserve a kitchen like this," I said, and I meant it.

She said, "I don't know anyone who deserves it more."

Donna set the table. She put another log on the fire. I pulled the chicken and lifted it onto the cutting board to rest while I made a quick *jus* from the skin stuck to the pan and the roasted wing tips and roasted neck, heart and gizzard, with some chopped onion, carrot, wine, and water. Juices from the resting bird dripped off the cutting board and onto the floor, which I noticed only when Donna noticed it; she sighed

and rolled her eyes. I now had a lot more room to make a mess in. I
spread four plates across the island when I was ready to serve the food—
the space was unbelievable. I hoped the novelty would never wear off.
We sat. Donna raised her glass to the kitchen. We touched glasses.

"Cheers," she said.

I said it, too, but I was focused more on her, on the look in her eyes;
the eyes sparkled, and she grinned.

We felt unspeakably lucky. It was still pulling teeth to get the kids to
eat, but at least the effort was now being exerted in a proper kitchen
with good fresh food. And yes, we'd soon leave this unfinished kitchen
and hike up through the shell of a house to our cozy grotto, but until
then we had our eating place, our four corners where we sat for pleasure
and nourishment, facing one another, and then the incredible luxury of
a large sink beside a modern appliance for cleaning up, an activity with
its own routine and import in the life of a family. Our kitchen was both
grand and homey at the same time, in the perfect scale, of the perfect materials and texture—wood floors and cabinets, a brick fireplace,
polished granite, steel. Roasted chicken at our kitchen table on a late-
winter evening, the four of us together, a fire crackling in the background.
It was like heaven.

When spring arrived, Carl delivered the final bill. The work was done.
The house had emptied of workers. The interior remained in various
stages of completion, but the rest was up to us. It still felt like an unfinished house. I'd swept up the sawdust in the dining room, stored wood
and molding scraps in the basement, but it was empty and unpainted.
The office was a hardware storeroom. The living room, more storage.
Our focus on master bedroom and bath was soon to pay off. We were
ready to paint and then carpet, and before it was truly finished, Donna
was struggling to get the mattress down the stairs. She couldn't wait to
have the bedroom, to separate ourselves from the children—we were
enacting the medieval moment when the family ceased to camp in their
dwelling and begin living in it, when a husband and wife again became a
couple and happily might make a verb of that hopeful word in a closed

room. We unloaded all our clothes into separate long closets. We set up the bathroom. One day we'd retile the fireplace and get it working, create a cozy sitting and reading area on the far side of the room, but for now it was enough to have a beautifully made bed, carpet, freshly painted walls.

A cold, rainy April followed a cold, snowy March (Donna reminded me that April in Cleveland is still winter; she doesn't care what the natives say). We cleaned out the dining room, Donna painted it, and with the furniture already here, this room was in use. And then, at last, May arrived and the outdoors beckoned.

The air grew fresh, and as the sun warmed the grass and new leaves, I could move through the house opening windows, sliding the storm up and the screen down to let new air into the stale, sawdusty rooms, really for the first time ever for us. Boxed in, enclosed in an attic cave for four months of cold, deep gray interrupted only by darkness, we were eager to be outside in the fragrant warmth.

We'd dug up the concrete walk in back and needed soon to replace what was a mud-slopped path with brick. Another brick walk along the front was needed, as was a brick patio on the side of the house, along with another very small patio in back, in our oddly shaped, cramped backyard. And a new driveway. Our last house had had a gravel drive, and so did this one, though most of the gravel was gone now, and it was deeply rutted—inconvenient and a code violation. We could regrade and regravel, but I'd had enough of gravel. I spent most of the summer in bare feet. I was tired of walking like a cripple every time I hit our driveway. I wanted to walk on smooth blacktop. On summer evenings at the house I grew up in, when the air had cooled but the driveway was still warm, I'd walked barefoot with thoughtless pleasure on that smooth drive. I wanted A. and J., both of whom were shoeless May through September, to share this luxury. It made a difference all summer long.

Last fall Donna had ripped out the vivid blue Astroturf carpeting that had covered the floorboards of the front-porch floor; one of the central boards here was broken, and others were cracked badly enough to represent a potential hazard to the kids. We'd have to rip out the floor and put in a new one.

I'd read a while back a comment by a husband writing about his new home and all the work he and his wife had done—mainly cosmetic, it sounded like, interior decorating and minor repairs. He noted how they'd taken a break from the work, and that was it, they'd never really started again. The writer wanted us to know a fundamental truth about houses: Once you stop working on a house, that's it; you never again return to it in the same way. From there on out, only maintenance is possible. I took this warning to heart. Part of the difficulty here, I knew, was that when you live in a place, you stop seeing it as you once did. Already, for instance, I'd stopped thinking about that rusted chain-link fence separating us from the neighbors, the one that was six feet high and topped with barbed wire. When I first saw that fence, I wanted it out like I wanted the carpeting out. And yet now I scarcely thought of it.

We would have to be diligent about the way we thought of this house. It would have to be a way of life. To be at work on this house was not simply to complete a punch list, a finite set of items to be ticked off one after the other until there were no more left; it was a fact of our day, each day, for the foreseeable future. To do it right, and to do right by the house, repair and improvement would have to become a part of the fabric of our lives, like grocery shopping and laundry. It was forever. Because it was a cool old house, this was not a bad thing.

What was so strange about work on the house once the contractors were gone was how unpredictable it became. We have far more to do in our lives than there's time for. I will never be able to read all the books I want to, write all the stories, cook all the dishes, see all the movies I want to see, let alone have enough time with my children and wife, not to mention the places we might go, new work we might pursue. So, given limited time, I determined to be organized about life, always to have a plan, always to be accomplishing something. What drove me crazy was that it was impossible to plan on this house. The house did it for you— suddenly it ate your weekend. It demanded your attention, as if it were a living creature, as if it had a plan of its own.

I'd be enjoying my morning coffee at the kitchen island, the kids star- ing at SpongeBob on the TV, Donna more or less putzing, fussing with that broken board on the front porch that had been nagging at her. One of the kids was sure to step through it one of these days, so, crowbar in hand, Donna yanked it out like a rotten tooth.

Of course, there was now not the *threat* of a hole in the center of the front porch, there was an *actual* hole—something had to be done before something or someone fell into it. This was a much-traveled area. The kids played on the porch. The mail carrier deposited our bills and catalogs here. And with luck the paper landed here each morning. Before I knew it, it was late afternoon Sunday, and I'd spent all weekend ripping out the boards and clawing out hundreds of three-inch nails that remained corroded into the floor joists. All the while balancing on the joists themselves above a three-foot drop into the rubble and dirt below (where, given my overactive imagination and the peculiar karma of the house, I was certain I'd spot a skeleton's hand sticking up or the joint end of a human femur). Donna ran several trips to and from Home Depot picking up more twelve-foot tongue-and-groove floorboards.

I was glad to get it done, better now than later, but what astonished me always was that when I'd awakened yesterday morning, I'd had not the least intention of spending the weekend ripping out a porch floor. It was a complete surprise. I had no control over anything—the house was in charge.

I'd lift a stone, big as a sidewalk slab, to see if I could get it on a dolly to move it from the side of the house, where it had been part of a path, to the back of the house, where I hoped one day to put in a small patio. Dan, my stalwart neighbor, having noticed my struggle, would appear, and say, "Need a hand?"

Within the hour Dan and I somehow began digging the patio area, and Thomas from across the street rolled his rototiller over and brought a mattock to make the digging go faster. With no plan whatever, a back patio was irrevocably begun, neighbors sucked into it as well, as if the house had somehow determined it. *Some* force did; I sure didn't.

The warmth brought everyone out—people emerged like moving buds from a hibernation mandated by Cleveland winter. It was almost a surprise to find that we had not just any neighbors but just-like-us neighbors. We had timed our move perfectly in the life of this street. During the past several years, the three houses to our east had been bought by families with young kids. Across the street there were not only kids but baby-sitters for those kids. When Jack and Karen had moved in fifteen years before with two offspring and three more to come, the block still contained the previous generation, empty-nesters. We had moved in and were immediately part of a community of adults with children. Donna grew up on a street in Flushing with more than seventy kids and recalled with deep pleasure the endless fun she'd had, her dread of nightfall when the gaming had to end. Always more or less loners by nature, joiners of nothing, Donna and I were by accident part of a neighborhood, and it gave us unexpected delight.

I loved what might become of us as we engaged with the neighborhood. This was more than I'd been after in a house, and I embraced it. Neighbors we liked with kids our kids liked proved to be a part of the domesticity I'd never thought of because I'd never known it, nor was it something you could go out and choose, a house with perfect neighbors.

As I thought about this house and why we'd pursued it as we had, it became clear to me that I wanted it even more for my kids than for Donna and myself. I wanted them to have a single place to grow up in, one spot they could count on, didn't even have to think about it—like breathing, vital but thoughtless. I'd had one, a single place, and I knew now how lucky a circumstance that was.

Also, I wanted for me and Donna an unmoving vantage from which to watch their transformation. In the tumult of adolescence—sexuality stirring, hormones roiling—in the inevitable confusion and complexity of the transformation from child to adolescent to young woman and young man, having a single home that was always there, that never changed, was *useful,* a terrific advantage, real ballast during stormy adolescence. Even times of exasperating boredom for me in the suburbs—another Saturday afternoon watching a baseball game, eating potato chips, and drinking Pepsi Light in the den—were experiences you had to endure periodically, like the flu. A small price to pay for the stability of years there.

Home continued to be useful to me, made the work possible. A home was the structure of routine, and routine was my oxygen. A home could be that unmoving center for my kids and for me and Donna, the still spot in a world spinning ever faster. I had roots here already. Donna, uprooted from Flushing to Port Washington on the early edge of her adolescence, with clear good memories of both places, departed that second hometown as soon after her high-school graduation as I had mine. I wondered what her attachment to these two places were; was the intensity and future pull of her sense of home place diminished by the rift? Was it possible for her to take some root here?

Why hadn't she? She said she loved suburban Cleveland, loved the houses and the streets and the environment in which we'd placed ourselves. It was the diminished industrial city of Cleveland as a whole that was not beautiful, nor did it support her work, nor was it a place she, who'd grown up so close to Manhatttan, could remotely identify with.

Was there anything real in my feeling such a powerful attachment to suburban Cleveland? Was it actually feeding me, or was I indulgently bathing in sentimentality? If it was only sentimentality, a primary motor of self-delusion, then I had better know it; otherwise it would become clear as our children went slowly bad on us, then up and left, and Donna and I grew angrier and more bitter each day, until we fell apart.

How easily that could happen! Wasn't that the main story of the suburbs since each of their postwar booms? The lie of house and home. The inevitable descent into provincialism, conformity, abandoned ambition, as a married couple (via sentimentality) refuses to admit their fundamental mediocrity; unhappiness followed by bitterness followed by emptiness and loneliness (both daily and existential). In a *best*-case scenario. The worst case stirred in alcoholism, mental illness, abandonment, and premature death. Marriage was, after all, as much an invention as the suburb in which it fell apart, and fell apart because it was a sentimental lie.

I didn't have to be in Cleveland, I reasoned. If my affection for the place was composed of sentiment and nostalgia, that might be reason to visit, but not reason to pursue a home here. And yet I had pursued it vigorously, despite a resisting Donna, who had regularly voiced a desire to find a place to live closer to the East Coast. If I'd acted on sentimentality alone, to stake her down in a city she had neither feeling for nor practical need of, that would be harmful to her.

Was that it? Was I rotten with sentimentality? Should I have recognized that my nostalgia for home *place* was phony, given that I was right where my nostalgia told me to be and yet I was still nostalgic, longing for what I had? How can you long for what you have?

The word "nostalgia," as writers about home often note, originally meant "homesickness." *Nost-algia*—literally, "return pain"—was coined by a Swiss medical student in the seventeenth century to translate the German *heimweh*—a romantic word for a German, combining "home" with an old-fashioned, even precious, term for pain/sorrow. The student who translated it did so because the condition seemed to include physical symptoms (fever, sleeplessness, heart palpitations). At the time and for centuries after, it was believed that people afflicted with the disease, if untreated, could die from nostalgia; they *had* to go home. "Nostalgia demonstrates that the importance of attachment to place was once well recognized," writes Edward Relph in *Place and Placelessness,* recounting this etymology in a book that explores why and how places have or do not have meaning for us. In our rootless culture, the attachment to place described by nostalgia seems to be forgotten, or perhaps it simply seems less important, given that we've turned our places into, as Kunstler puts it, "a joyless junk habitat."

Scott Russell Sanders, an essayist and literature professor at Indiana University, describes this very common form of pain in a book of essays called *Staying Put.* "A footloose people, we find it difficult to honor the lifelong, bone-deep attachment to place. We are slow to acknowledge the pain in yearning for one's native ground, the deep anguish in not being able, ever, to return."

He's speaking on the occasion of stopping by the land where he'd grown up (not an hour's drive from my own home, as it happens—perhaps there's something homey in the Ohio soil). Upon his return, he can only stand at a guardrail and look out over a body of water where his home had been, because in the 1960s town officials dammed a river to make a recreational lake. That's a physical example of the *You Can't Go Home Again*-ness that characterizes the country. Entire populations throughout Europe have been forced from their homes because of ethnic and religious horrors—those people never looked at flight as an opportunity; it was a nightmare. This country was once largely composed of such people.

Nostalgia, the pain of not being able to return or the pain of returning to a home that is gone, is so common that the title of the novel bearing this sentiment has become a cliché. A culture composed of immigrants, we are quick to denigrate the importance of return pain. Indeed, H. W. Fowler, in his dictionary, notes that the word "nostalgia" began to be debased as early as 1926. Now, of course, it's for sale with a designer label.

However we may acknowledge this form of pain—by denigrating it or by trying to understand it—even if we don't have a respectable word for it anymore, we all share the experience, because just about all of us in this country do seem to leave where we are or have arrived from somewhere else; it may be the commonest attribute among Americans, nostalgia, for immigrants and natives alike, given the fact that few people now live where they grew up, that almost everyone has a home he or she can't return to. Nostalgia, in the sense of return pain, may be one of the few shared notions in this complex, rapidly changing, multicultural society.

Another novel, considered by some to be the greatest novel of the twentieth century, *Remembrance of Things Past,* begins with and takes as its subject nostalgia. Vladimir Nabokov wished to retranslate the name of Marcel Proust's novel, *À la Recherche du Temps Perdu,* literally, to make it a more meaningful and apt title than the Shakespearean syrup attached to Proust's work by the original translator. Far better, thought Nabokov, as did later translators who actually made the change, far more powerful and poignant to call it by the name Proust intended: *In Search of Lost Time.* That certainly is the kind of return pain that defines true nostalgia. And Nabokov, whose cherished father was assassinated, who was flushed from his beloved Russian estate by the revolution, all before he was out of his teens—he knew the catastrophic loss of home place.

We search for what can never be found; we know that it can never be found, and yet we are doomed to carry on searching, forever searching for what we know does not exist. My lost city, the archetypal romantic, F. Scott Fitzgerald, laments, the promise of Manhattan and fame of his youth, gone gone gone, replaced by shaky alcoholism and visits to his wife in the asylum, every one of his books out of print. The romantic madeleine eater becomes the ultimate existential hero; nostalgia becomes the rock that Sisyphus pushes ever upward in his search for lost time.

I believed it might be a part of our makeup as humans, this search response, might be so deeply rooted in us that even I, who live and work among the detritus of my own lost time, feel this acute return pain. For it's not really a *place* I'm searching for; it is *time* I've been after all along. I've been searching for the childhood and the youth that recedes before me, instant by instant, lost, gone.

I could see this now. I was watching it from the shallow square I'd dug in the backyard where I spread a thick layer of crushed sandstone; I'd level this crushed rock, pack it down, and place the slabs of sandstone here for the patio begun this weekend. I could stop, though, and rest, breathing heavily in the heat, watch all the kids in the drive next to ours, just across the low hedge. A band of them screaming and cavorting, chasing each other, playing with balls, with kites, with foam-rocket launchers, on bikes, on skates—kids from four different households early on a Saturday evening. My daughter, rummaging in Dan and Betsy's garage, had found a pogo stick and was quickly becoming expert enough to bounce without hands. I used to bounce in my driveway for an imagined world record when I was her age.

The sight of the kids in the low evening sun, in their own time, made me so happy I became sad.

This was a good place to be from—I'd been lucky—and it was a place to which we could return after two decades of wandering, and stay. We'd found a grand old house. There would always be work to do on it. But tonight, after I put the tools in the garage, I could step inside the back door, walk up steps into the clean kitchen, take a glass from the cupboard, fill it with cold water, head upstairs to a comfortable shower, then return to the kitchen to begin dinner.

13

A House with Good Bones

The tearing out and repouring of the living room fireplace hearth began as all significant projects on the house had—without a plan, without even a moment of forethought. Donna pulled something out, turning an imperfection into a hole.

It's easy to live with imperfections. The light-switch plate that's not returned. The strip of frame in the window beside my bed that was never replaced, leaving the lower sash loose, letting in cold air. Each fall as the wind starts to blow, I will determine to fix it, but I won't, because it requires disassembling the entire window. How could I do that but ignore the half-inch gap between the bedroom fireplace mantel and the wall, which still bugged me every time I saw it? The brickwork of the fireplace had been crumbling, so we'd taken the mantel off the wall; John the mason had rebuilt it, leaving a facade that stuck out about a half inch beyond the original; when John put the mantel back, it was no longer flush with the wall. I'm still not sure how I should fix it. This house has countless glaring imperfections. I could make a hobby of quirky repair jobs. There's probably three seasons' worth of a half-hour home-repair show in this house.

One of the biggest imperfections, biggest in terms of being emotionally grating, and one that's difficult for an amateur carpenter to fix, is the doorframe and door to my daughter's room. The door can't be fully closed because the frame is broken out where the latch would normally catch. The door, too, is damaged. Someone tried to repair the frame with wood patch and didn't do a good job of it. An awkward hardware-store handle has replaced the original iron fixture that the other doors have. The way the frame is broken is particularly vivid; it appears to be stretched, then cracked from the pressure, the crack running two feet up and down the frame in the shape of a shark fin. This door was so obviously broken down—somebody kicking it or smashing it until finally the wood gave and the door burst open—that when you look at it, it all but screams at you. It's such a powerful emblem of violence that I want it removed. But this would require dismantling the doorframe, refitting two of its pieces, and either replacing the door or replacing the post that houses the handle and latch. A big project.

This is the nature of a house that has been lived in by people, by families, for a hundred years.

As far as repairs, I'm content to get a few big ones done each year and, with any luck, get them done fast enough to stay ahead of the things falling apart. We would damage our psyches if we ever believed that the house would be *done*. That Sunday in the future when we could get up and read the paper for three uninterrupted hours because there was nothing more to do on the house, not a thing, because it was exactly the way we wanted it? Not going to happen. The only way to finish this house is to walk away from it, with luck leaving it in the hands of some youthful couple clever with tools and possessed of some skill and taste appropriate to the structure.

I tried not to pull things out, but Donna couldn't resist. In the same way she yanked up the broken board on the front porch that kept bugging her, she pulled a brick out of the living room hearth. The hearth was composed of thin bricks, laid on their sides so that their narrowest length faced up. Part of this brick hearth had buckled as if pushed up from below, cracked, the mortar crumbling, leaving the bricks as loose as bad teeth. When Donna pulled the loosest one, it freed the others. She pulled those as well. Soon there were stacks of these bricks on the living room floor and a big hole where the hearth had been. The bricks had been laid upon a poured-concrete bed, now likewise cracked and crumbling.

Here was the next project, no choice. I'd have to clean it out, pour a new hearth, and Donna would take care of tiling it. Generally I do the stuff that suits me, hammering out chunks of concrete, mixing big batches of cement in a wheelbarrow, and Donna does what pleases her, tiling and painting. We're in the conventional gender roles of home improvement. Donna had already painted the ceiling, picture-frame molding, floor molding, window frames and trim, walls, and the wood mantel. The brick section of the mantel had various splotches on it where she'd tried to rub the red and white paint away to see if stripping was an option (it wasn't). She'd placed a wide mirror above the mantel, between the two handsome sconces. In the corner of the room was a large square of carpeting loaded with paint cans, a stepladder, some scraps of wood. That was it. It was a long way from being the kind of place where you'd stand a Christmas tree or invite urbane dinner guests, martini glasses in hand, to join in conversation.

Wearing torn jeans and a T-shirt in the cool, empty living room, I stacked the old bricks, then began to remove the moldering concrete bed. It came out in chunks. When I would pull another chunk, dust and rubble would fall onto the boiler in the basement below. The boiler was tied in to this chimney.

I pulled another chunk out, and there it was. The hairs on my neck and shins pricked up. I gripped the end of the bone with my fingers and wiggled it loose from the concrete. More chunks fell onto the boiler and the floor in the basement below. A thick bone three or four inches long was embedded in the concrete. It wasn't a chicken bone. It looked like the clavicle of a small animal, had the gentle curve of a collarbone. It was pale and smooth and clean. As I broke away more of the concrete in this spot of the hearth, I found another bone; this one was larger, seven inches long, a leg bone, a tibia. This bone was also darker than the clavicle, almost amber.

"Donna," I called. "C'mere!"

She was working in the kitchen and came. She held the bones. Her eyes went wide with the creeps. Then she shook her head. "No. These are chicken bones or something."

"This is *not* a chicken bone," I said, holding the long one.

"What do you think? You think they're human bones?"

"*No*," I said, but thinking, *Maybe.* An infant's tibia would be smaller than this. "Of course not. But what are they? They're not chicken bones. And why are they in all this concrete?"

Donna nodded. She didn't really like this, but soon she got into the spirit of things. She saw all the rubble dropping onto the boiler and took it upon herself to clean it up down there. I'd hear her call out in high spirits, "Found more bones!" And I'd rush to see.

In total, we found about seven bones. We didn't pulverize all the concrete looking for more. We left the bigger blocks of it intact. I showed the bones to Dan and Betsy and across the street to Thomas—good house show-and-tell. Everyone appreciated it. I gave the bones to my father, who said that an amateur bone sleuth worked in his office. He returned them saying his colleague wasn't sure. Some of the lighter ones seem to be bird bones. The long leg bone, she couldn't tell, a small animal; she guessed a goat. A goat sounded good to me, conjuring images of blood sacrifice and dark offerings on this land where Gypsies were said once to have lived. Betsy's father is a retired orthopedic surgeon. I mentioned the bones to him when he and his wife visited.

"I can't tell you what they are necessarily," he said, "but I can tell you whether they're human." I brought him the bones. He held the large leg bone, turning it over in his hands for several moments. "Definitely not human," he said.

There had always been something grave about our house. Its severe brick sides, dingy with a century of soot. The creepy karma I'd always felt here. The vermin nests, the neglect, the ghost footsteps. The buried bones were less a surprise than a reiteration, an underscoring of a theme of our house. You find things in an old house. They've become a part of it. In high school I got stuck in the leg, deep, with a graphite pencil; the graphite is still there, part of me. The bones would be shapely, intriguing mementos on a shelf in my future office, permanent artifacts. But we're unlikely to know who buried them in the concrete hearth foundation or why anyone would. They will always be fundamentally a mystery.

The newspaper clipping about the murder had been unearthed like the bones, was another part of the house we'd bought. Steve, our real estate agent, had known the family that had lived in the house and had told us that one of the kids who'd lived here was on Ohio's death row. All he'd said was that it had been drug-related and ugly. And for us that was appropriately vague. Grisly murder by a kid who'd lived in this house. It didn't really *mean* anything; it just became part of the aura of the place.

Things. They leave the how and why behind as they endure to become pure objects. And as pure objects they somehow become insistent. When you renovate a house, they make themselves known. They seem to me charged with a force, a current within the concrete that cracks it, lifts up the bricks to be acknowledged, pushes the mantelpiece away from the wall to be found.

The grisly murder—at first darkly romantic in a tabloid way; in its vagueness the story felt not quite real—became clearer with the newspaper clipping. A physical description of the victim and the clothes. The names of the detectives in the case, an enticing detail: "killed elsewhere and dumped in the creek." The location itself, Doan Creek, was named for Nathaniel Doan who'd opened a tavern and a store not far from there; it ran along Martin Luther King Jr. Boulevard, a street originally called Liberty Boulevard, that wove through the parkland John Rockefeller had donated to the city. Part of Doan Creek gurgled a block up from our house, through a neighbor's front yard and down the hill. These details brought the story from tabloid fiction and rumor to fact, like documentary footage, real but past. And more: It showed someone's personal stake in the story, cutting this small article out of the paper and writing on it significant phone numbers of relatives.

Soon, unbidden by us, the complete story was tossed onto the new floor of our front porch. The complete story, page one so we wouldn't miss it. The victim, according to the article in the *Plain Dealer,* had been a teenager who'd supposedly known the whereabouts of some drugs stolen from one of the convicted killers. Three men were charged with murder. One squealed to avoid a long prison sentence, and his two accomplices—who'd wielded a hunting knife and cut the young man's throat—were sentenced to death.

But new evidence had recently come to light twelve years after the crime. A lawyer-priest who spends time with inmates on Ohio's death row as part of his efforts to stop the death penalty heard one of the convicted men's stories and took an interest in him and the case. The priest's detective work uncovered a significant piece of information: The victim, this teenager supposedly killed over some drugs he hadn't stolen, had in fact been the sole witness called to testify in a homosexual-rape trial. The man accused of the rape just happened to be the man who first identified the body.

A new scenario was obvious: The kid might not have been killed over missing drugs but rather to prevent his testimony in the rape trial; this threw the murder convictions and death sentences into serious question. Many inconsistencies in the squealer's story turned up upon reevaluation. A lot of it didn't add up. The two men now on death row, one of whom had grown up in our house, might have been scapegoats, might be sitting in jail innocent while the squealer, who had family in Chicago—the numbers on the clipping had Chicago area codes—walked free. The man charged with rape was never prosecuted and eventually left town. Everyone knew each other.

How can the innocent land in jail, we always want to know, we who hold jobs, maintain bank accounts and homes, pay taxes?

Earlier in the year, a different *Plain Dealer* reporter had been a Pulitzer finalist for her story about a man wrongly incarcerated for rape for thirteen years, a story that resulted in the real rapist's confession—from guilt, after he read the story. Thirteen years. It's a living nightmare, to be wrongly imprisoned. How does it happen? A variety of reasons, but a critical one is simply that the people who are unjustly imprisoned have almost invariably lived lives that make them vulnerable to unjust convictions. As is the case here. One man was a former army mechanic who after two years of odd jobs had no bank account and no driver's license and was about to be evicted from his apartment; the other, the one who'd grown up in this house, in this well-to-do and civic-minded community, had a string of convictions behind him for drug possession, drug trafficking, grand theft, rape, and kidnapping. Clearly not Eagle Scout material. That's the kind of stuff that leaves a guy vulnerable.

And yet the other side of the story—the law-enforcement side—is equally sordid. What if these guys didn't do it? They'd been aggressively prosecuted. The woman who reported the story for the *Plain Dealer* confessed to getting a "creepy political sense" of the motives of some of the county lawyers and judges involved, and she noted the difficulty of addressing such a phenomenal wrong, let alone overturning it. "Boggles the mind," she told me. "The whole system is set up to prevent it." She noted how vigorously the county prosecutor intends to fight such an overturning in this case, a county prosecutor who, the reporter noted *by the way,* intends to run for attorney general in a county whose voters like their law enforcers to go for blood.

I cut thin sheet metal to the dimensions of the hearth. I mixed a few bags of concrete in a wheelbarrow in the living room. I poured a layer over the sheet metal, threw down some metal mesh for increased support, then filled up the hole with the remaining mud just below floor level, so that when Donna laid the tile, it would be flush, and then I troweled it smooth.

This was a good project to get done over a weekend. When Donna was finished with the tile, the room would be good to go. Area rug, couch, chairs, coffee table, side tables. The room would soon come together. The bones, the ghosts not withstanding.

The memory of the footsteps I'd heard the first time I entered the house alone endured. I had heard them. A lot of people don't think it's crazy to believe in ghosts and devote serious chunks of their lives to exploring the possibilities. A couple of groups in Ohio are devoted to it, as is one committed Clevelander (they have Web sites, even: spiritseekersofohio.net and maryannghostbuster.com). One of the surgeons I'd written about visited our house not long ago. I showed him the bones, and he seemed impressed. "Tibia," he said. I told him about the ghost. He said, "We had a ghost in our house when we were growing up." Matter-of-factly he said it, a man of science. His ghost, he offered, was a real mischief maker, pushing over bookshelves, cutting through electrical cords. Even for me this seemed a bit much. The surgeon's fiancée went on to tell her own ghost stories. Neither of them offered any qualifications or doubt.

Donna woke in the middle of the night—we'd been well installed in our own bedroom by then—and nudged me awake. "I feel someone's presence," she whispered. "Listen."

I listened.

"It sounds like someone trying to be quiet," she said. I looked up to see that the alarm was on, then drifted back into sleep. "There," she said, bringing me back to alertness.

I then stayed half awake listening for the next two hours, before drifting into actual sleep. Donna said the next morning that she must have been dreaming. I knew otherwise. Obviously the ghost had been out. Donna does not believe in ghosts.

Today I hear the ghost. A typical instance is this. It's 6:00 A.M., still dark, I'm at the kitchen table reading. Weekdays I get up early to read books because it's the only quiet time to get concentrated reading done. I will hear, *"Dad!"* and I'll know from the way the voice echoes that J. is in the hallway, he's gotten up, gone to the top of the stairs, and called for me. This shoots any serious reading for that morning. I sigh, put the book down, and walk to the stairs, but no one is there. The house is quiet. My heart starts to beat a little faster and I find that J. is in bed, deep asleep, completely peaceful; he no more called for me than did Donna, also dead to the world. The sound had come from the hallway. Sometimes all I hear is a cry, but it's enough to make me get out of bed and walk around the house looking, making sure that, yes, everyone is sound asleep. Donna grows annoyed when I talk about this. She does not believe in ghosts. I don't either, except every now and then.

J. has actually seen the ghost. One evening just before dinner, he came down the stairs and, with a tone of mature helpfulness, said that he'd seen a ghost. I asked him, by then age three, to show me where he'd seen the ghost. He brought me to the third-floor playroom and pointed to the doorway. It closed the door, he said.

"Is it a bad ghost?" I asked.

J. shook his head.

"Do you want to see the ghost again?"

"No," he said, shaking his head.

"Is it a scary ghost?" I asked.

"Yes," he said, nodding.

"What does it look like?"

"It looks like a dirty bubble," he said.

I mentioned the incident to Chef Eric when I spoke with him next. He wasn't surprised. "Children see much better than adults," he said.

While the existence of the ghost may simply be one facet of a complex house that I like to believe in, a different possibility nagged at me—that something actively evil was in this place. Most of us know *The Shining,* Stephen King's book, or at least remember how Jack Nicholson in the film version goes crazy in that great big deserted hotel and becomes a homicidal maniac. That story is successful because it's got a mythlike truth about it: The place isn't haunted, it's evil, and the evil gets inside you. It's part of the power of a structure. We sense it. A place shapes who you are.

The family who lived here before us—some bad things had happened in that family. We'd been told a daughter had died in young middle age and a son was now incarcerated on death row, perhaps unjustly, and we happened to share their given names.

My daughter had abhorred the house when we were looking at it, with a passion that seemed out of all proportion. She continued her dislike of it after we moved in. I wondered, of course, if she could "see" it better, if she was responding more purely to its particular karma. I'd set some flour and water in a juice glass to see what would happen. In a few days, it was bubbling and frothy from the yeast that had got in there. The yeast made excellent bread. A food-scientist friend was surprised by how easy it had been for me, told me I must just have been lucky. But I knew the air here was teeming with hungry microflora. Couldn't see them, but I had proof they were there. Maybe it was something *in the house.*

As part of the new season's landscaping efforts, we bought a maple tree to replace some gnarly trees we'd taken down. Aaron, the landscaper, who put it into the front lawn in the spot where an old oak had once grown, dug deep and found several enormous larvae, truly scary-looking creatures about three inches long and an inch fat, miniature monsters whose pincers and legs clawed wildly in the air. The kids circled around, enthralled, poking them with a stick. "Never seen those before," Aaron had said, staring closely at one of them rolling and curling in his shovel. The forces were in the soil itself. The tree died. It's the kind of idea that can take over your thoughts late at night, as you lie awake listening for somebody who's trying not to be noticed. People used to call this land Heathen Ridge. Gypsies used to live here. It was a heath. It's an old house on old land, that's a fact.

14

Unstoppable Houses
on Changeless Terrain

I accelerated over the arc of the Lorain-Carnegie Bridge and turned right at the yellow brick clock tower of the West Side Market toward the Cuyahoga County archives, a Victorian Italianate brick mansion built in 1874, two blocks up from the bland urban thoroughfare of West Twenty-fifth Street. I parked and followed a strange-looking man up the walk and steps, in through the doorway, paused behind him as he signed his name at the front desk. Long red hair hung in loose curls down the back of his black T-shirt, sleeves cut off to reveal the totality of his hairy arms, one of which cradled a soft leather briefcase. He disappeared into the recesses of the house. I noted the name, "Craig Bobby," before signing my own, writing the time and the reason for my visit: "Research."

The house now holding the county's archives had a traditional Colonial layout, with a grand entry hall and two large rooms on each side now reserved for public research. The ceilings must have been fifteen feet. The tops of the broad doorways leading into either room were too high for me to reach.

Glenda, an athletically built African-American easily six feet tall, waited impatiently through my elaborate mumbled explanation of what I wanted, then asked, "Do you have the permanent parcel number?" I dug through some sheets I'd gotten from the Cleveland Heights City Hall till she saw what she needed. She conveyed the number to another worker, who left and returned with a folder containing the real estate reappraisal card, recording several appraisals beginning in 1944 and including a 1958 photograph of the house, which I marveled at. Our lawn had been fenced off from the sidewalk by waist-high shrubbery, and the May foliage obscured all but the front steps and half the front gable; it looked like a movie set in the 1920s suburbs. The card listed our house's date of construction as 1902, eight years previous to a date we'd been told by one of our city's house sleuths and twenty-three years earlier than what was listed on the official real estate record.

I had these photocopied and went to the front room of the house, once a dining room or living room, now unoccupied but for a woman a generation older than myself, seated at a long table scrutinizing some old maps of streets a few minutes' walk from my own. It's part of the smallness of Cleveland that I didn't think it a coincidence that we knew of each other. Her name was Marian Morton, and I had written about her ex-husband, a career-long school man, in my first book. I had in fact read and liked her recent book, a highly readable history of Cleveland Heights, subtitled *The Making of an Urban Suburb,* the first I'd read about my section of the city once referred to as the Euclid Heights Allotment.

We exchanged a few words, and I explained to her that I was looking into the history of my house and neighborhood—certainly, as a historian, she'd be able to help. I had the name of the original owner but not a date of construction. "I've got three different years, and I don't know which, if any, is right."

A voice behind me said, "I can probably find out when your house was built in two minutes."

It was Craig Bobby. He stood about five-ten in white sneakers, wore tight-fitting jeans, and the sleeveless T-shirt fitted his compact torso snugly. Much of his heavy-metal hair hung down the front of his shirt on either side, still wet as if he'd raced from the shower straight here, water marks spreading out on the shirt fabric. His head was large and strongly featured: sharp cheekbones, powerful nose and jaw, and lashes so distinct they circumscribed the clear blue eyes in an unbroken line. His gaze was intense, almost angry.

"I know the area," he said when I told him the street name.

"I believe that Frank and Grace Harding were the first owners and lived there in 1910," I added.

"I said I could *probably* find it," he repeated. "If you have the old lot number." I opened a folder with a map of the area that included the old lot numbers. Craig touched the outlined lot on the street map and said, "Three eighty-seven." He vanished.

As I recall, Marian and I couldn't have chatted for more than two minutes before Craig returned. "Your house was built in 1901. I can say that fairly certainly."

"How do you know?"

"City tax records. They show a jump in value of that lot from three hundred dollars to three thousand in 1902."

"Really? So can we find out if Mr. and Mrs. Harding were living there then?"

"I don't know. I said there was jump in the value of the land. We can check quickly." He strode to the far wall, lined with city directories, and pulled one from 1903.

"Frank I. Harding," I said.

He found the page and said, "Frank Harding here lives on Windsor Avenue." Craig found a 1910 city directory, thumbed it fast, and said, "Here he's in your house, Frank Harding."

"So what was going on with the house if it was built in 1901, as you say, but he's not living there?"

"I can't answer that," Craig said, deadly serious.

Marian and I stood still as Craig went on talking. He talked and talked, and after a half hour it dawned on me—distracted by his appearance and the sheer volume of words issuing from his mouth—that I hadn't a clue what he was saying beyond the fact that it centered on what he called "common architecture," which so often meant the domestic dwellings we're quick to dismiss or tear down.

"I study structures, not neighborhoods, not people," he said. "I often study structures that aren't even *there* anymore." And he chuckled without losing any of his angry intensity. He didn't seem crazy, but there was clearly a mania that propelled him. After perhaps forty-five minutes, he said, "I'll show you."

I hustled behind him up back stairways into the realm of musty old books, tax-collector records, plat maps, allotment drawings. He had narrow hips and took short strides as he bobbed down the hallways, but he flew up the stairs swiftly, clearly in active good health—at age fifty, he later told me. He brought me to the tax records, put his hand on the 1902 volume of the area of the county that contained my lot, and found the page. Sliding his finger down a column of lots valued at $300, he stopped at one in which $3,000 had been written in above the $300, then slid his finger to the left of the page to the lot number, 387. "In 1902 recorders say this property jumped in value by three *thousand* dollars. You *know* a house went up here. This is 1902, reflecting what would have . . . *happened* . . . in 1901."

The century-old book, Volume 33, was a beautiful object. About two feet high and a foot and a half wide, its hard cover bound in gray canvas, the ledger held about two hundred pages, and each of the thousands of entries was written in very fine pale black ink, in script of extraordinary uniformity. Its lined pages were tinted brown and speckled with age but still supple. These ledgers, hundreds of them squeezed onto metal shelving, filled this silent storage room.

"But the property wasn't owned by your Mr. Harding. It was owned by the Euclid Realty Company." He flipped pages. "All those lots were owned by Euclid Realty. Look at that. He flipped page after page, counting not the lots but the pages. "Thirteen *pages,*" he said.

"The Euclid Heights Allotment," I said. Three hundred acres of land, developed by a man named Calhoun, that would become my neighborhood.

Craig Bobby talked as he led me up and down stairways to various rooms, "There's one more thing I want to check," he would say, and off he'd go. He'd run his hand along even larger books, huge map books, two by four feet and a couple of inches thick. He opened one of these to what is now Cleveland Heights, to my street, a large hand-drawn map with big lots numbered 405 and 406 and the name "W. S. Streator" written on it.

"Streator, I know that name," I said.

"Sure," Craig said, "Dr. Streator. This is what he owned."

Streator's name had a line through it, and his lot 406 was divided into many lots along what are now the neighborhood's streets, with various names written in each of them and a date. Grace Harding had purchased our lot on October 9, 1909, and across the street, where Thomas and Heather live, J. G. W. Cowles—another name I knew, a prominent banker and Rockefeller's Cleveland real estate guy—was crossed out and the name of the new owner of the lot, Harriet Oakes, Heather's great-grandmother, written in beside the date, 1919. This enormous map was an extraordinary historical document, certainly, but to my eyes, and my hands, also intimate, my neighbors' names written here with dates of purchase, the Cowleses and Oakeses and Coakleys and Pecks and Hickoxes. Like a kid in an imaginary game, I wanted to fall into it and go back in time.

But Craig was off through the cavernous archives. "Usually the one I want has thirty other volumes leaning against it," he said, grunting like a lineman to tilt a row of enormous volumes the other way, hefting out the volume he was after. "You've got to be in good shape to do this work. I mean it."

He set the book on the floor and got down on his knees. This one was much smaller, two and a half feet tall and half as wide, but must have weighed twenty pounds. "This is where I do all my work. Right here on the floor."

He had checked a thick white spiral notebook, jammed with penciled notes, some of them scarcely legible. "I can't believe I didn't write that volume number down." Then, to me, "If you don't write these things down, what use is it? It doesn't mean anything. You've got to write this stuff down."

He had found Volume 19 of the Cuyahoga County plat maps. The large pages were like thin cardboard, perhaps actual manila board, browning now around the edges, very smooth, and filled with streets writ so large in india ink that each broad sheet contained only sections of a few streets. I recognized the street names of my neighborhood. Craig flipped the pages, the first nine of which concerned the sections of street in the Euclid Heights Allotment. "There's your street," he said, pointing.

"Land of the Railway Security Company," read the titles on these pages in thick, ornate ink letters, handwritten in 1892. And below, the names of people I'd read about: Ernest Bowditch, the landscape designer hired to draw the neighborhood; William L. Rice, a lawyer and one of the first residents of the neighborhood who would be murdered there; the Parmalees; the Browns; Mr. John G. W. Cowles. I found myself reaching out to touch the smooth page as if to touch the time, a record of men and their wives entering into a speculative real estate deal that would become one of the country's first streetcar suburbs.

"This was just a plan," Craig said. "You see here, Franklin Street and Columbia Street, they don't exist. They were designing the neighborhood at this point. It wasn't even Euclid Heights Realty Company yet, which it would be ten years later, as we saw in the tax duplicates."

These objects had a powerful physical appeal, actual documents beautifully handwritten. But Craig closed the book and was off searching more. I followed him, his long red hair trailing him like banner. He had other buildings to search for and not enough time, so many buildings. He was hunting the date of two houses on the near West Side that no longer existed, scanning his notebook and talking to himself and chuckling like a man possessed as he knelt on the archive floor between rows of books, a map book open before him. "It would have been right about here," he said aloud.

I was just beginning this work, this search, and Mr. Bobby had saved me at least eight hours of hunting; but I didn't really understand why I was interested, why I cared. What did it mean, finding the origins of the house, when and why it was built? A new kitchen with a long granite-topped island, a new old-looking fireplace just beyond the kitchen table—that meant something. What would this mean? Craig had hefted one of the massive tax ledgers back onto the shelf and shoved it back into place with his shoulder, having found the information he'd sought. *"Whatever that means,"* he had said, issuing his nervous, intense chuckle. "I don't know *what* it means!" This fact seemed hardly to bother him, though; he was compelled to hunt down the information like a woodsman after prey.

I soon learned that he'd amassed voluminous documentation of houses in my neighborhood—which included a photograph of our house that he himself had taken, after we'd bought it but before we'd painted it—that were but a fraction of his own personal archives, numbering in the many hundreds of structures. "It would be impossible to give you anything but a ballpark figure," he said when I asked how many buildings he had a file on. "Hundreds. I don't count them. That would be of no use to me. Why would I count them?"

There were half a dozen people expert in my neighborhood whom I *knew* about; I supposed that neighborhoods throughout the city each had their own followers, and neighboring Shaker Heights, one of the most successful and wealthiest suburban developments in the country, had professional historians writing about it.

But it was Craig Bobby who personified both the eccentricity of my city and the mania of the exploration of historical common architecture, so much so that I began to think that it was not coincidental that I'd arrived for the first time at those archives, the county attic, on his heels, that I'd signed my name below his.

Craig was unconventional in appearance, certainly, and that made him vivid. Kara O'Donnell, in the preservation office at City Hall, knew him and was grateful for the information he dug up for her. When I asked her about him, she said, "Did you know he's a mailman living in Lakewood?" He had mentioned that in our first meeting, though technically he's called a letter carrier—"which is kind of goofy, because we carry a *lot* more than letters," he'd said—and is a member of the National Association of Letter Carriers, founded in 1889. Judy Cetina, who had run these county archives for twenty-six years, said she'd found Craig a little off-putting at first because of his appearance, what with the long hair and cutoff T-shirts, but she got to know him during his habitual visits to the archives and was ultimately won over by his intelligence ("He's so smart," she said), as well as his help in unearthing information pertinent to the archives. He had become part of their small "family," as she called it, and he had free run of the place. He was also so well known at Cleveland's City Hall that he had free run there as well.

I arranged to meet him at the archives again. I was as curious about him as about my house. We spoke on the phone, exchanged e-mail.

"You spend . . . a *lot* of time doing this, researching structures, many of which don't even exist," I said.

"Almost every waking moment," he replied. "If it wasn't for the other things I need to do—you know, to have food, making sure there's gas in the car, this kind of a thing—it would be almost all the time I have other than sleeping. And I don't get enough sleep, because I'm choosing to stay up late. Not because I'm watching TV. It's because of what you might call research."

"How do you describe your research?"

"What do you mean by that?" he asked, edgily, maybe warily. I stammered a bit before he went on: "I'm interested in the buildings. Usually Victorian-era buildings. I'm interested in them, and primarily what I *usually* find out that I'm *usually* satisfied with and *usually* don't go any further is just when they were built and whom they were built for, though that's secondary.

"I'm interested in Victorian. Victorian buildings are very artistic. . . . Most architecture isn't. Previous to Victorian and certainly after Victorian. They didn't go out of their way to do that type of thing, the embellishments, the decorative elements. Victorian—they treated it as if it weren't an architect at work but an artist and that the building was some sort of canvas. It was very much like that.

"I'm trying to teach myself something, I suppose," he went on. "It has to do with architecture, it has to do with the evolution of architecture, it has to do with the specific evolution of architecture in the city of Cleveland as formulated, if that's the right word, by our local architects."

"How long have you been doing this?" I asked.

He wasn't sure, he said. It seemed to coincide with his work for the postal service, which began in 1989. But then he noted that it really began in his twenties. "I was just out having fun for a long, long time, and somewhere in my twenties I suddenly, *seemingly* suddenly, realized I had this interest in Victorian-era buildings, and it was so overwhelming that it didn't matter how much fun I wanted to have—I also was making sure I had some amount of time to do this as well."

"Do you ever worry that you'll run out of buildings to research?" I asked.

"Oh, that'll never happen, because of all the buildings that were demolished."

"How do you know about them?

"Because of pictures. I find the pictures. The Cleveland Public Library has a good collection of pictures of all kinds."

"What do you do with all this stuff?"

"I have these images," he said, images of the structures, at the bottom of which he writes the date of construction, the builder, and any other pertinent information. "Then it goes into the sheet protector and the binder."

"And what happens to it?"

"Right now nothing's happening to it," he said, chuckling. "Right now it's sitting in my living room, and I'm the only person looking at it. That's really the way it is."

"Is that OK with you?"

"Maybe that's not OK with me, but what difference does it make if it's not OK with me? Can I force people to be interested in a subject they're not interested in? Of course I cannot. The average Clevelander doesn't give a damn about old buildings. Whatever. That's their right. But I do, and I'm glad that I have found out whatever I've found out about every one of these buildings."

Buildings matter. And the terrain on which those buildings rise matters. The shape of the terrain, unlike razable buildings, doesn't change. The slope of the land helps one to understand a city's development. I can begin to walk, for instance, at the northernmost oxbow of the crooked river, near where the boy John Rockefeller had his first offices, on Superior in the Flats. It's a hill. You have to lean forward to climb it, but it's short, and as the land levels out, it's a few minutes' walk straight ahead to the town center, called, earnestly, Public Square, anchored by the Terminal Tower. There's a reason for its distance from the river. You wouldn't build a square on the river or on a hill; a good square needs plenty of space all around it, but you'd also want it not too far from the river. It had been placed just right, a quarter mile or so from the bustling river commerce, and it had been especially accommodating when its pastoral warmth had a community feel to it, a wide dirt road surrounding four grassy, stump- and tree-filled quadrants. I'd have paid as much attention then to a wild swine crossing my path as I would a squirrel today. Cows got in there to graze, which annoyed people. In the summertime the air would be redolent of horse manure and dirt; in the winter you'd want a really good pair of boots just to cross the street.

As I approach, the massive brick monolith built by Standard Oil of Ohio—now owned by the British Petroleum Company and referred to as the BP Building—looms over the square, but the square's oldest buildings remain, hinting at its original grandeur. On the north side is the Old Stone Church, dedicated there in 1834, razed and rebuilt in 1853 in Romanesque Revival style; its blackened stones are a pleasure to behold. The building across the street, the Society for Savings Building, completed in 1890, is composed of huge blocks of red sandstone, more gorgeous today than they would have been then, when such material was commonplace.

I could walk east from the foot of the British Petroleum Building along Euclid Avenue to East Fortieth Street to know just how long Flagler and Rockefeller would have had to plan and plot their rebate deal and their Standard Oil trust as they walked to and from work, a route they traveled four times daily, a distance less than two miles.

Rockefeller's house had been torn down decades ago, and a gas station, appropriately enough, went up in its place, though even that's gone now. The last Millionaires' Row mansion, now a CSU administrative building, sits above an overpass, endless cars zipping by on Interstate 90—a dowager looking down upon the future.

Euclid Avenue itself was likely created by the tread of the feet of Native Americans, a path once called the Buffalo Road because that was how you got to Buffalo, New York, 180 miles away. The path became a dirt road. It widened, and people built houses on it. They put planks down on it to make travel in wet seasons easier. They had sleigh races during the winter, the competitors bundled in coats made from buffalo hides. Soon the city paved the street.

Foot tread had designed the main transportation route east out of the city, the route along which John Hartness Brown, a Cleveland businessman, took Patrick Calhoun during the summer of 1890, an event that began the neighborhood in which our house sits. Mr. Brown would have used an actual carriage hitched to a couple of horses and likely picked up Calhoun in the hot, dusty bustle of Public Square, industrial smoke rising out of the Flats and into the sky. The day was likely warm, and the city's center teemed with horses and bicycles and horse-drawn streetcars kicking up dust. Shoppers along Superior tied their mounts to wooden posts outside stores. Ladies wore bustles and kept the sun off their pale necks with parasols. Men wore collars and hats despite the heat of a clear summer day.

Calhoun, the grandson of statesman and politician John Calhoun, was a tall, commanding, and self-assured railroad lawyer and entrepreneur from South Carolina. He had short fair hair and vivid blue eyes in a round face. He read the Stoic philosophers and took icy baths in the morning. He had a temper, was stern and aggressive to the point of arrogance, but also charismatic. A year before this trip, he'd challenged to a duel a fellow Atlanta lawyer who'd impugned his character; both men emerged unscathed and good friends. He was devoted to his wife and eight children.

Having concluded his railroad business—he'd traveled here to increase railroad commerce between the busy center of Cleveland and South Carolina—and with his own train not departing till evening, Calhoun took a ride east with Mr. Brown to see the Garfield Monument, a 180-foot Byzantine-Gothic structure, apparently the first true American mausoleum, serving as both tomb and memorial for the country's twentieth president, and dedicated just a few months earlier.

In a few minutes' time, Brown could have pointed to his right at Rockefeller's understated Euclid Avenue house. Rockefeller was in town that month enjoying Forest Hill (he wouldn't buy his Pocantico Hills estate in New York for three more years). Indeed, Rockefeller may well have been the one who put Calhoun up to this in the first place. Brown might then have noted that there, on their left as they approached the bustling Doan's Corners, was the residence of Dr. Worthy Streator, a landowner active in many of the city's industries and railroads.

While along Millionaires' Row, they would have enjoyed a peaceful ride on this fine summer day, but after Doan's Corners, a thriving commercial center, Brown and Calhoun would have crossed a streetcar line at Wade Park.

According to Calhoun's son-in-law, Warren Wick, who'd grown up on Millionaires' Row, the member of a prominent banking family, Calhoun at this point said to Brown, "Where does Cleveland grow from here? I haven't seen a vacant property all the way out Euclid Avenue."

Brown intended to show Calhoun and took him the back way, up a winding dirt road called Cedar Glen. The horse and carriage and the summer birdsong would have been the only sounds, along with perhaps the gobbling of turkeys crossing the road or the cart of one of the Gypsies who squatted around here heading down to trade at Doan's Corners. Cedar Glen was heavily forested with alder, oak, maple, and elm, and so they rode in shade. The going would have been relatively smooth on a dry day along this half-mile bend, a bank rising to 275 feet above lake level.

When they crested the top of the hill, Calhoun beheld a rolling plateau of cleared land, used now for cattle and horses, and, farther east, vineyards and rock quarries. It was a lovely pastoral vista, refreshing after the hot, dusty Public Square, where his journey began.

They proceeded north toward the monument, its spire visible in the distance below. Calhoun and Brown gazed at Lake Erie spreading out, three miles off and in clear view. Turning to their left, they could see oil-refinery and steel-mill smoke. Rising out of the city to these heights to behold this vista clearly had a dramatic effect on Calhoun. He must have sensed he'd arrived on this plateau at an unusually auspicious moment. He had just come from Richmond, Virginia, where innovative city developers were for the first time linking electric street railways, new technology, with residential real estate development. The United States was flush with cash, industry thrived. Here he saw undeveloped land near a booming industrial city, tenth biggest in the country and growing. He sensed that day unlimited business opportunities by combining real estate speculation with the new streetcar development he'd been watching in Richmond. This was prime land, too; all it needed was a streetcar to get people easily up and down that hill and into the city.

Calhoun said, "Who owns this land?"

"Dr. Streator," Brown replied.

According to local legend and the few published accounts of this meeting, Calhoun made an offer on the spot. Calhoun was the sort of maverick who would eventually brag about the number of fortunes he'd lost. Brown found Streator immediately, and by the time Calhoun had boarded his evening train, the story goes, he'd agreed to pay $50,000 for approximately three hundred acres of this land.

"Electric cars, East Cleveland Railway Company, East End Development, nothing going on in the heights," said Bill Barrow, special-collections librarian at Cleveland State, who'd written his master's thesis on the Euclid Heights Allotment. "Then what happened? A railroad lawyer with experience in electric-streetcar real estate development dropped into town one day in a parachute, and the next thing you know, he crested the heights and built a luxury subdivision at the end of a streetcar line.

"It's a fortuitous grouping of elements that his arrival here brings together."

Calhoun is representative of his time, the old order on the cusp of the new, a man who has arrived just a decade or so too early to profit from his own forward-thinking ideas because he is unable to predict the awesome changes about to sweep the country when the automobile arrives.

Calhoun will serve the land well, but the reverse will not be true. He will be the force behind the paving of its curving streets, the delivery of water and sewage lines, the man who manipulates the street railways to crest the hill, thus creating at great but necessary expense the infrastructure that will ensure the establishment and permanence of a fine residential streetcar suburb. The neighborhood will be his home and his family's, but it will bankrupt him. It is land marked by continual strife. The suburb is a force of nature, like a fire.

It was the beginning of the era of the electric streetcar. With the increased speed and efficiency of cars powered by electricity rather than by horses, cars that could travel greater distances and scale steep hills dependably year-round, suburbs blossomed throughout the country during this decade, but the movement would quickly end as the automobile and the country's exploding population obliterated the city on which the streetcar suburb thrived.

Calhoun and his associates in Cleveland intended not simply a residential neighborhood for the merchant class but rather one for the city's elite, an aristocratic Anglo village. They hired the Boston landscape architect Ernest Bowditch, who designed the streets based on the work of Olmsted, who had recommended "gracefully-curved lines, generous spaces, and the absence of sharp corners, the idea being to suggest and imply contemplativeness and happy tranquility."

In the first years of the Euclid Heights Allotment, a handful of prominent families bought property and built fine houses on the treeless plateau overlooking lake and city, in addition to those of its developers, Calhoun, Brown, Cowles, and the president of the company, Rice, who had one of the grandest mansions on the hill. The Euclid Heights Realty Company spent hundreds of thousands of dollars to put in sewers and water mains and electricity, paved graceful streets then called the Overlook and Edge Hill. On weekends city folks came to walk or bicycle its smooth streets and breathe fresh air. The company advertised the healthful location and easy commute in the *Plain Dealer,* noting Euclid Heights' many utilities, and assuring all interested home buyers of long-term property values, its location smack in the center of the path of city growth. As Barrow noted, Euclid Heights "epitomized the planning of residential communities at the end of the nineteenth century"—that is, it featured clean air and a rural setting with easy access to the city's center by electric rail.

Houses went up a few a year, here and there, first on the streets north of Euclid Heights Boulevard, commanding the prime views of city and lake. Newspapers and magazines printed photographs of the houses built in the final years of the century. Ours was among the first four to be built on our street, on the south side of the boulevard that bisected

Calhoun's purchase, two broad, one-way streets on either side of street-car rails; across from ours a gorgeous Victorian had been completed just before construction on ours began.

As long ago as the earliest of these house constructions were, 1895, they were remarkably similar to what we expect today in terms of convenience, fitted out with all the luxuries of the day that would quickly become automatic in all the houses that followed. Running water, electricity and gas, indoor bathrooms, central heating—the core systems of a house—were largely in place in American house construction by the century's end. Inspector Archer would have been at home here at the neighborhood's inception.

These amenities had existed in various forms throughout the past century, but they still felt relatively new. A toilet was created in England in 1776 that used an ingeniously simple S-shaped curve below the basin that prevented sewer gases from rising and expelled water with siphon pressure, but flush toilets did not become common until the last decades of the nineteenth century.

At about the same time that the electric streetcar spurred house construction outside the city, the electric motor became applicable to the interior household life. Telephone subscriptions, begun in 1880 in Cleveland, had risen to three thousand in a decade.

As Rybczynski notes in *Home,* the "'modern' devices that contribute to our domestic comfort—central heating, indoor plumbing, running hot and cold water, electric light and power and elevators—were unavailable before 1890, and were well known by 1920."

In August 1901 the Euclid Club opened, a grand Tudor mansion that *Town Topics,* a society magazine of the time, called "the prettiest and most complete home of its kind outside Chicago and Europe." Designed by the prominent architects responsible for many of the neighborhood's homes, Frank Meade and Abram Garfield, the late president's son, it offered apartments, fine dining, golf, weekend dances. Japanese immigrants served its guests. The back nine holes of its links were on land donated by Rockefeller; as avid a Baptist as he was a golfer, his only stipulation upon giving the land was that no golf be played on those holes on the holy day of the week.

Calhoun, who'd moved his family to Edge Hill Road in 1896, built a mansion a few hundred yards east of the club. After water mains and a sewage system had been put in, trees were planted on this land that ten years earlier had grazed horses and cattle. The turn-of-the-century residential neighborhood slowly took shape. Newspaper accounts at the time described that the aim of the Euclid Heights Realty Company was "to establish a suburban residence district second to none in this country."

As there weren't many such garden villages served by electric rail then, that goal doesn't seem outlandish. Seven years later the same newspaper wrote an article titled "Aristocratic Little Village," taking note of those "fleeing the dust and soot" of the city and an area where "an astonishing number of houses" had been built over the past few years.

Unfortunately, the lots of Euclid Heights didn't sell quickly enough for the developers who were sinking so much cash into infrastructure. Our house, for instance, remained the property of the company for several years. The company's coupon bonds, a thousand of them for a total loan of $1.1 million, came due in 1907, and they couldn't pay up. The Euclid Realty Company was soon in default. Cleveland Trust took over the properties until the company resumed control three years later, but it was a dying effort.

Meanwhile, Calhoun had got tied up in a San Francisco corruption trial, accused of bribing city officials who'd given him the city's "traction franchise," that city's lucrative streetcar business. Back in the Euclid Heights Allotment, company president William Rice left the lavish Euclid Club after dinner on a midsummer night in 1910 and proceeded by foot to his home a half mile north of the club. At the corner of Euclid Heights Boulevard and Derbyshire, Rice was jumped, beaten, his throat fatally cut. The subsequent inquest into the murder of so prominent a citizen drew extraordinary media attention, but no one was convicted. The most intriguing theory held that John Hartness Brown, the man who'd first brought Calhoun up this hill, had murdered Rice. Brown had left the realty company for other real estate ventures in the city, and Rice had reputedly swindled him out of a building. Brown had "mysteriously" been the first person to arrive at the scene where Rice lay dying. After the inquest Brown left the city, never to return.

Disappointing sales, the unreturned investment in infrastructure, Calhoun's West Coast imbroglios, Rice's murder, and the company's failure to develop a convenient commercial center nearby all contributed to Calhoun's never realizing his vision of an elite English village. But a force beyond his control may have been the ultimate obstacle.

Between 1890 and the 1914 sheriff's sale, which officially marks Calhoun's bankruptcy and the end of his involvement in the Euclid Heights Allotment, the automobile arrived to obliterate the relationship between the suburban dweller and the city. One historian likens the impact of the automobile on suburbia to the big bang's impact on the universe. By the 1920s the crest of Cedar Glen, which thirty years earlier had been a dirt-and-mud ascent populated by turkeys and Gypsies, had become the most congested traffic spot in the city, a squeezed entrance to all the neighborhoods of the heights now booming and expanding at this prosperous moment in the country's history.

Those who followed Calhoun would see considerably more success using the very methods he'd introduced into the Heights: the integration of planned neighborhoods with graceful streets, deeds dictating minimum construction costs, and strict architectural design requirements. The most famous of these was Shaker Heights, created by Otis and Mantis van Sweringen on land abutting Cleveland Heights. In 1905 the eccentric brothers bought the first parcels of what had been a community of Shakers, a group of Christian communards who actually did "shake" as part of their worship. By 1916 the van Sweringen brothers had opened Shaker Heights lots for sale. They built their own railway from Public Square to their community, service that would augment rather than compete with the growing use of motorcars. The houses they built all shared a Georgian-Colonial style, though none were identical. The first of their houses were grand structures, but between 1919 and 1929, they built three hundred houses a year, most of them the four-bedroom, two-and-a-half-bath Colonials that would become the staple dwelling of the middle-class burb.

Domestic technology began in earnest in the late 1700s and developed rapidly during the 1800s, but it wasn't until 1890 through the 1920s that home efficiency as we know it today flourished, an era shared by the streetcar, logically enough. Electricity and the electric motor supplied power for all kinds of comfort-making and laborsaving devices in the home—fans and water heaters, toasters, hot plates and coffee percolators, electric irons and vacuum cleaners. Because more women of the house, and not servants, were doing the work, they could and would demand comfort in their housework.

Shaker Heights became one of the country's most durable suburbs, and famous, too, especially after the 1960 census declared it the wealthiest community in America. As one writer noted at the time, what had been begun by the Shakers as a spiritualist utopia had become a house-filled paradise for the well-to-do, "a communistic experiment turned into a capitalistic triumph."

The fifteen-year difference in timing between the van Sweringens' fantastically successful development and Calhoun's failed one illustrates more than anything else the speed with which America was changing because of advances in technology, transportation, and explosive population growth. All of which would grind to a halt in October 1929.

The ease with which the early suburb fell into bankruptcy, and its remarkable resilience, is a hallmark of the area once called Euclid Heights. Calhoun presided over a map of his lots at the sheriff's sale in 1914, noting each property as it sold. Born before the Civil War, a drastically different era from the year 1914, with the world on the brink of the bloodiest war ever, Calhoun would cast about for his next fortune, eventually winding up in Pasadena, California, where he would be killed in 1943—run down, in a bit of cosmic symbolism, by a car.

But the streets of the neighborhood—Derbyshire, Berkshire, Edgehill, Overlook, Kenilworth, Norfolk, Kent, and the eponymous main boulevard—continued to fill up with houses in the teens and twenties, even after Calhoun left the area for good. Calhoun could go bankrupt, and his partner in the company could meet a sudden violent end, but the houses kept rising despite circumstances. The houses were unstoppable.

15

The Secret Nature of the Suburban Marriage

Donna and I were loners by nature, liked a solitary life, but this also made us doting parents, intensely involving the kids in our lives. We marveled at friends who could fly to Italy for two weeks, leaving youngsters with a nanny—for us that was unthinkable, and even were it financially possible, we'd be miserable with worry and longing. I don't think that's noble or foolish; it's just the way we were. But it meant that for eight years we'd scarcely had any time for the two of us, certainly no extended periods by ourselves to really talk, to let things come out, no more animated, passionate conversations ending when the morning paper smacked the front door.

Nor did Donna join a clutch of girls to vent about the thoughtlessness of husbands, the crushing weight of raising kids twenty-four hours a day for years on end, the city her husband had brought her to, or simply to talk about aging bodies or aspirations after forty.

The psychological world of women requires voluminous expression to attentive friends. Women, generally, need to be around other women for reasons unique to their sex. Men, generally, do not need to be together in groups to talk. I've never heard of a guys' book club, but women gather in great numbers to discuss books and talk. Guys simply are not that complex. We have fewer working parts, which means we're easily satisfied by televised sports and we break less frequently. What outlets I needed, I found in my writing. Donna had had no outlet other than me, and we'd been so caught up in house and kids that I no longer functioned as an outlet.

We aimed to fix this. We planned a three-day trip at a mountain resort. We would go out more, the two of us. We would simply walk to a place in our neighborhood. This was part of our reason for choosing our place—it was scaled for walking. With the air warm and fragrant from abundant lilac and black locust blooms, we would stroll to Nighttown for a bite to eat. My generous dad would stay with the kids.

Nighttown had a good bar and standard careless American bistro food (onion soup and Caesar salad, an overpriced steak, an uninspired, clean-out-the-fridge pasta dish). Food was not the point, though; the point was to walk to a neighborhood spot, to sit at an elegant bar and enjoy one another. We saw Heather and Thomas from across the street and waved to them at the end of the bar as we sat to order. He was an artist of impressionistic landscapes that combined Renaissance style with what he called naive Americana, and she was a jewelry maker with a thriving business—they both had studios in their sprawling attic, which we could see from our sprawling attic.

Our old neighbor and real estate agent Steve—all of us more or less reconciled now—touched me on the shoulder to say hello; he was here with his wife, whom we hadn't seen in ages. How old-fashioned, how small-townish this was. Donna was still pissed at Steve over his handling of the house sale and the chattel issues, but she was prepared to be quiet in the interests of neighborly harmony and the good spirit of the evening. We talked easily about our kids.

When Steve and Julie had left to find their table, I asked Donna, "What are you thinking about in terms of getting back to work?" Now that the major renovations on the house were complete and the kids were on their way in school, I wanted to do everything I could to encourage her return to work, to the photography she loved and was good at. She was a working girl who'd been too long a mom only. Work was how one found oneself and *where* one found oneself. I was certain that Donna needed to return to this part of her psyche, so long dormant she may have wondered if its rejuvenation would even happen.

"When J. is in kindergarten," she said. "We've talked about this."

"What if I took care of the kids in the afternoon?" I said.

"What are you talking about?" Donna said.

"After the current projects are finished, I could work in the morning, take care of J. in the afternoon, and get back to work at three-thirty. That would give you nearly the whole day."

Donna said, "Please don't tell me what to do. Don't pressure me."

"OK," I said. "I'm just trying to help."

The waitress paused, and I nodded for another drink. The desired effect—excitement at a new and unforeseen possibility and gratitude to Donna's thoughtful, generous husband—had not been achieved.

"I was just *thinking*," I said quietly. "I want to help."

Is conflagration inevitable and even necessary, initially damaging though it may seem? Or is there a moment in a conversation with your wife when you can stop, halt before a line crossed, a point at which you might simply say, "Honey, God, I love you. I am so lucky," then tell the bartender you've decided on the burger medium rare, and change the fate of the evening?

"I don't know why I couldn't do it," I said.

"Michael," she said, "tell me what I do. Can you?" She was exasperated with me, but I didn't understand why. I was inept.

I didn't know how to answer, didn't want to cross the minefield. "Laundry" was one possible response, and it was so depressing I didn't want to hear myself say it. Volatile fumes, I realized right then, were rising off my wife, waiting for a spark. I'd been reading a friend's biography of the novelist Richard Yates at the time, and I was mortified when I read a line written by Yates's first wife about tabulating the amount of laundry and cleaning her life amounted to during the years her husband sat in a shed in the suburbs swilling bourbon and writing his masterpiece about suburban tragedy. This woman would come to think very little of her ex in the end, and consider the marriage to be a lot of wasted time cleaning. Donna was doing just that, I thought, and I wasn't even The

Artist, as Yates had been in the truest sense. I was just a basic nonfiction guy who got to do cool things like learn to cook and hang out in boat-yards and operating rooms taking notes. Sheila Yates was at least serving Art. Donna was serving Michael.

"I know what *you* do," she said. "Tell me what I do."

"Laundry," I said, asking for it, wanting now to wallow and thus avoid any truly crushing blow she might deliver. "Laundry and bills." But then, thinking more seriously, I said, "And you're raising our chil-dren."

I tried to sound grave and meaningful, but this, too, was another minefield.

"Michael, you have no idea what I do, do you?" she said tilting her empty glass to look down into it. "How about our taxes? How about dealing with the *mountain* of paperwork we generate?" She looked away and exhaled. "How about all the work I did on our first house? How about the photography—the editorial stuff, what little there is here? I worked for American Greetings, for Progressive Insurance, I shot trucks and sewer pipe, remember? How about moving us to New York and back home? How about moving us to Massachusetts and back home? How about all the work I've done on the house? Do you have any idea how hard I've worked on this house and still managed to get all the rest done? *Laundry?*"

Thomas and Heather were on their way out. "Hi, guys," Thomas said, passing behind our stools. He made some further remark I didn't hear. Thomas was funny, and ordinarily we liked them both, but they evi-dently saw our thin-lipped smiles and quickly departed. The jazz singer had arrived—while the food here couldn't have been more pedestrian, the jazz was superb—and the volume level of the place picked up, forc-ing ours to do the same.

"How can you say that—you'll take care of the kids? Just like that. What am I supposed to make of that? Do you think that's all I'm con-tending with? Do you think it's simply a matter of taking care of the kids for two hours in the middle of the day?"

I noticed that the second martini of mine had kicked in quite hard, and I said nothing.

"I don't know what I'm going to do. Do I want photography? Yes. Am I excited about it?"

"I don't understand how you can say you're not excited about photography."

The tears that rose up in her eyes indicated that I'd again said exactly the wrong thing, had completely missed the point, hadn't a clue as to the emotional welter beneath my lovely wife's patient, understanding facade. I had pushed a needle precisely into the already open cut.

"I *tried* that here," she said. "Don't you remember? When we arrived in Cleveland, I was excited. I tried, but this place beat me down. This is a manufacturing town. That's not what I do. They photograph nuts and bolts and sewer pipe here, not people. This is not where I should be. You say you'd be happy to die here in Cleveland? Well, I wouldn't be, and I won't. You may love it here, but for me, as a photographer, I couldn't be in a *worse* place. We can live anywhere. And you insist on living in the worst place possible for me—how do you think that makes me feel? What does that say about us?" Donna squinted, her face pinched up to keep the tears from spilling in this public place.

I felt like I'd been hit on the head with a bat. My wife was in love with a person who'd done the worst thing possible for her. Did we eat dinner that night? I don't recall. I do recall that I ordered a third martini, knowing that it was a bad idea but reasoning that I needed it to pass the time and to dull the pain of Donna's words, which only continued, escalating in volume with the clatter and conversation and music in the room. It was no use trying to halt her—once she got rolling, best to let her roll until she ran out of gas.

We walked home, one of us in mute regret, a confused mix of self-pity and self-hatred, the other continuing the conversation, digging it in, on the attack. We arrived home and pretended for my eagerly smiling father to have had a great dinner. Donna went upstairs quickly to check on the kids and kiss their sleeping faces, while I smiled and waved good-bye to my father from the driveway.

Later, downstairs, pouring herself a glass of ice water, emotionally spent, looking forward to sleep, Donna paused. The water pitcher hovered above the half-full glass, and then she finished pouring. She wasn't thinking about me or us. She returned the pitcher to the refrigerator. It was as if I weren't even there. She spoke to the beautiful granite island countertop she'd picked out for my kitchen: "Where did my *confidence* go? I used to be so sure of myself. I'm the shell of who I was. What *happened*?"

"I need time to myself. I need to be myself," Donna said.

We'd traveled to a fancy resort, our first consecutive two nights away from the kids. My mom had flown up from Florida; July was hot there, and the house business was slow. Our midweek getaway was to be a marriage idyll. I began to get sick on the drive down. During our first day, midday at the pool the chill hit, there in the hot sun. By late afternoon I was under the covers with the shakes, a fever, and a killer headache. I was determined not to ruin it completely for Donna and rallied for dinner.

I ate a dainty salad, and she had big fat chop. By the time the waitress appeared to ask if we wanted dessert, Donna's face was stained with tears.

"I asked you years ago to give me time alone, and you haven't. You never did."

I wanted desperately for her to believe what I believed. "Yes, anytime, I want you to take time."

"No, you never did," she said.

I couldn't argue further.

"I am losing myself, Michael. Do you know how scary that is? And you are not helping me. I need time alone. I need to be by myself."

"You've got it. I can't tell you when or how or make you take it, but whenever you want it, say so, and we'll make sure it happens."

I made a fan of the sheet to create a little breeze in bed on this still night in the dead of summer. That had not been a bad one, that fight at the resort. I really had been sick, from an infected bug bite, we later discovered, and Donna was sympathetic and stayed with me in the resort's clinic while they took blood and did lung X-rays and performed unpleasant examinations. But her tearful plea was yet another sign of the depths of her unhappiness, which I ignored at our peril. She went out of her way after these events to say she didn't know where they came from or why, but the emotions were real, and so was the problem.

"Michael," she would say, "please know how lucky I feel. I am so lucky. To have you, to have our children. We are so lucky. I know I've said things that have hurt you, and I'm sorry. But we have to address my problems or we're not going to make it, and that is unthinkable to me."

When she'd say those things, it was like daylight arriving after I'd spent an ominous, creepy night, not knowing what was waiting around the corner. It was equally unthinkable to me. She'd been my closest friend for more than a decade, an eventful decade—having and raising children, writing numerous books, living on Martha's Vineyard and in the Hudson Valley, writing about and working with some of the country's best chefs, buying and renovating an old house. And at last we were in that house; this was to be our anchor. The decade of our thirties had been *good*. We'd worked hard and well, and the fruits were real to enjoy. What is going on here? This is like a bad accident happening, I thought.

Especially now. Lying here, Donna asleep beside me, and I have no idea where she is, in her own head, in her own life. I am alone, and the house is empty. An ominous vision of the future. Our worst possible end, right here.

We had again returned from the restaurant early, had enjoyed the meal my father had insisted on buying us for my fortieth birthday, and even had an easy after-dinner drink at the bar, saw an old friend, sous-chef Frank from Lola, the restaurant across the street, who introduced us to his wife with the news that they were expecting. Our route home took us across the crooked Cuyahoga River and the Industrial Flats; past the grim, stately Terminal Tower; past the splendid Jacobs field, where the Tribe had returned to their losing ways; then up Carnegie to Cedar Hill and into the leafy burbs, rolling to a stop on our smooth, blacktopped drive.

"I understand what it means to you," Donna said. "I *understand* why you want to be here. But you have to understand that it doesn't mean that to me. Cleveland is the last place in the world I want to be. It's important for you to understand that. Do you understand that?"

We left the car, then knocked softly on Dan and Betsy's door. Betsy, who'd offered to take care of the kids till we got home, had called us at the restaurant to say that the kids would sleep at their house tonight— "enjoy your birthday." Betsy and Dan appeared at the door, and Betsy smiled at the gift they were giving us on my fortieth, a whole night alone, without the kids, no J. in our bed, a quiet morning. "They're sound asleep—*go,*" she said with a grin.

Why didn't we simply shut the hell up, go upstairs, and have sex? Instead I drank and Donna fought, and I did my best to sit there and eat it, but I was tired. I was so damn tired of this I wanted to scream.

"You said to me, 'We are going to live in Cleveland, and if you don't want to, you can leave.'"

"I never said that."

"Did I have a choice?" she countered. "I feel bullied. That is not a fifty-fifty marriage. I expect it to be, but you are telling me how I'm going to live my life."

"I'm sorry, Donna."

"I have *cleaned* for you," she went on, ignoring my nonstatement. "And you know when people have told you how productive you've been—'Look at all you've done in so short a time,' they say. And you nod in that humble, work-ethic way. I know how *pleased* you are when they say that. And you *should* be proud of what you've done. But what about me? I take some pride when they say that, too. I take some *credit* for that, for making your life orderly and clean and taking care of the daily business so that you can get your work done. I deal with the *mess* so you don't have to. Face it, day-to-day living with kids is a mess I'm forever cleaning up. Do you ever say that to the people who praise you? No, you accept their praise as yours alone. It's the same thing when we have a dinner party. I clean all day, I make this place beautiful, I make the table beautiful, you serve an incredible meal, and everybody swoons and thanks *you* for all *your* amazing efforts." In a bitter, mocking voice: "Such *talent.*"

She rolled on. "I clean. I've given in and accepted we're living in Cleveland for the foreseeable future, even though it's not where I want to be. Tell me, Michael, what sacrifices have you made for me?" She paused, folded her arms, and rested her hip against the island counter. "Name them."

I couldn't name one, other than doing work that I loved, which was anything but a sacrifice. She was right: I'd gotten everything I'd wanted without giving anything back. This hurt me, and she knew it.

"So," I said, "what do we do?"

"You tell me, Michael."

"You're unhappy," I said.

"That's right, it's *my* fault. We're fighting because it's my fault. It's always *my* fault."

"You're the one who's *always unhappy!*"

"Why is that, Michael? *Why do you think that is?!*" she said, beyond anger now, tears welling from the intensity of emotion.

"I don't know," I said.

I'm so damn tired of this, I'm so tired. I glanced at the clock above the fireplace, and she *saw* me glance at the clock. I've got to work tomorrow, I've got to stick to my routine. If I lost a day's work for every late-night fight we've had, I'd still be on my second book. Why do we always fight at night?

"I want you to *think* about it," she said, smearing tears off her face.

"I will." I'm ready to end this dead-end conversation, so I ask, "When do you want to talk again about this?"

"When," she said—not a question.

"You say."

"Nine-ten tomorrow morning, after I drop the kids at camp."

"Fine," I said.

"Really?"

"Anytime you want—this is more important than work."

"Is that what you want?"

"I want to figure this out," I said.

"You want to get it *over* with, so you can get on with your *routine.*"

"That's right. I don't like this. This is unpleasant. I'm tired of it."

"You can't just shove it away and forget about it, Michael, don't you see?"

"I don't want to, I don't want to sweep it under the rug, where it will fester and come back again. I want to deal with it. I'm tired of this. I want to resolve it."

"Do you?"

"Yes."

"You're not exactly convincing."

"Donna, I don't like this. I don't like that you're unhappy or that you feel I've forced you to live a life you didn't intend and don't want."

"Michael, I love our children, and I love you."

"I'm not saying you don't. But *you* are telling me I haven't given you any say in the matter, I've bullied you to where you are. I resent that."

"We need to address it."

"And I want to. That's why I want to talk about it. Tomorrow morning, right?"

"Is that what you want?"

"No, frankly. I've got *work* to do."

"So do I."

"But if it's what we need, it's what I want."

"We need to talk more, Michael."

"I'm tired of talking. That's all we do. I don't want to talk just to *talk.* I want talk to result in action."

"This isn't a board meeting. This is not a business trying to increase productivity. This is our marriage."

"Oh, OK, fine, then let's . . . *share* our *feelings* with each other."

"That's *not* what I'm saying!"

"I want to do what it takes."

"You don't sound very sincere."

"What do you want, you want me on my on my knees, begging you, weeping? You want me to cry?"

She departed without a word, almost breezily, just walked off as though she realized she'd been talking to the wrong person this whole time. And now she was beside me, her back to me, and I didn't know where she was or where we were or how we'd got here. I'd thought we were doing really well. I'd thought we were great. But in fact my love is lost and we're falling apart. I'd thought we had everything.

Before going to bed myself, I went to check on the kids out of habit. Their vacant places were the saddest sight. God, I missed them. The house was deathly empty without them. When I walked the halls turning out lights, they were so echoey and deserted-sounding. A hollow house. God, I wanted to kiss their cheeks and just look at them. Instead I stared at unmade beds.

Outside my daughter's room hangs a photograph from the summer of 1968, and I stopped to look at it. My friend Kley and I sit in lounge chairs, his grandma's swimming pool and lush foliage behind us. We're smiling huge, kid smiles. I'm eating a red-white-and-blue Popsicle, Kley an ice cream sandwich. Our hair is wet from swimming. It's a moment of pure, don't-know-anything-else-but happiness.

I remember the feeling today. All happiness and fun at his grandma's pool, all summer. Sometimes I wish I could know that kind of happiness again, the unalloyed happiness of a cared-for child. Kley lived seven or eight houses up the street from me. I called his mom and dad "aunt" and "uncle." I walked nearly a mile to school with Kley every day of kindergarten, first, and second grade. We swam and ate grilled-cheese sandwiches and ice cream in the summer. Then Kley's family moved away from Cleveland. Things went sour in the family. His mom and dad split up. His younger sister developed some serious problems of her own.

Somehow Kley and I stayed in touch. He was now married with three kids, in a suburb outside D.C. He came to our wedding and gave me this poolside picture of the two of us as kids, as a gift. A picture of happiness in time. My son was now almost the age I am in the picture. Kley's kids were similar ages.

In the winter when we'd lived in the attic and I'd been writing the surgeon book at my father's, Kley had come to town for the funeral of a family friend. He had a late flight out, and he'd called and asked to get together. He met me at my father's after I finished work. We picked up some Indian takeout on the way home and had dinner at the kitchen table in the attic above two empty, demoed floors of house, and talked easily. Kley is serious and wry, tall, with big feet in business shoes like his dad and, also like his dad, a large oval head that is a part of my memories from the very beginning—he'd always looked this way. He can be funny or very critical, but he has an expression I've never seen on anyone else. He looks always to be trying to withhold a smile.

Kley said that on the way to meet me at my father's house, he'd stopped by his old house. He always did this. He once knocked on its door and was invited inside. Today he'd just sat in his car and looked at the house he'd lived in till he was eight.

"Why do you do that, Kley?" I asked. "Stare at the house."

He wore that familiar expression but said nothing.

"I mean, do you know why? You left when we were in the middle of third grade. It's been a long time."

After several moments he said, "It was the last place my parents were happy."

He paused.

"I guess I wonder how it might have been different if they'd stayed."

Kley was my age, a husband to a wonderful wife, father to three perfect kids, gainfully employed, a solid man in all those roles, had avoided the hazards that broke up his parents. He and his parents moved away more than thirty years ago, thirty years have passed, and he longs for that time when his *parents* were happy. For himself. His parents are remarried and, so far as I know, are happy in their separate lives. They were both good people. My dad and his dad were a year apart at the same high school. Kley probably didn't even know that his dad had grown up just down the street from where we now sat, used to play in the basement that now belongs to Heather and Thomas. All of that's gone, though, doesn't really matter. For Kley, his boyhood house was the focus of his lost time. He was now the age his parents were when they fell apart, and our children the age he and I had been when he left town and everything changed. If they'd stayed in that house, maybe things would have been different, Kley thought. Every time he was in town, he drove by his old house and stared at it.

It was an era I recall with deep affection. Children were usually immune to the woes of middle-class life going on then just above us, our parents in their early thirties as the 1960s turned to the 1970s, the alcoholism that awaited, the divorce, the troubled kids who smoked pot and ate quaaludes out of boredom, not to mention the travesties of style and design that were inescapable in the 1970s, in everything from clothes to cars to houses.

I became self-aware in the 1970s, a decade I think about with a mixture of sentimentality and embarrassment. But mostly embarrassment, because there is so much to be embarrassed about from the 1970s. Certainly some political and social justice continued to happen for women and black Americans, but it's hard to think of much good during the 1970s, and little of value that endures from that decade, except for great movies, books not really of their time, and one TV show very much of its time, *Saturday Night Live,* which could only have been born of such a decade and could not survive meaningfully without it. I felt pretty lucky to have been a suburban dunderhead in jean cutoffs and tube socks, an oversize T-shirt that read ZONK! and disguised my pasty, well-fed belly— a powerless kid, luckily inert, rather than an adult rejoicing in the inane new "freedoms" and acting on them.

I am not nostalgic for Nixon, or Ford, or Ford Thunderbirds, "gourmet" recipes using canned soup and grapes, the kitchen gadgets sold on TV, or furniture design or clothes—all the stuff cluttering Middle American home life. God, the clothes and hairstyles. Look at movies or photographs or illustrations of middle-class culture from any decade in human history—only the 1970s will produce outright embarrassment. In all of human history. The seventies were a travesty, the Ugliest Decade, and also the time when things fell apart. Cities, such as New York and Cleveland, went into default, my dear, rusted-out city. And the suburb died because it was no longer fundamental to the dying city it sat apart from. The city was no longer what it had been, and we'd polluted the waters around it till they were poisonous. We built malls on the other side of the suburbs and did our shopping there, and then we rented offices where we did our shopping, and built more freeways to give us easy access to work and the department store.

I had no idea the suburb was dying when I became conscious of my own love of suburbia, but living amid the thriving shopping and business complexes rising outside the city, I felt it and saw it: ugly, cold, soulless, but very convenient. Convenience may now be the driving force of American development and progress. Having taken care of comfort, we strive to refine an element of that comfort. Convenient food, convenient parking, easy access. A quest for convenience has built these new cities, the name for which has not yet become part of our common lexicon— "exurbia," "technoburb," "edge cities" have been posited—perhaps because no one likes them, perhaps because they're so hard to define. But certainly they're antiurban, whereas the suburb was historically good for the city, strengthened it. The death of Euclid Avenue in Cleveland, Millionaires' Row, was less the result of white flight to the suburbs than the fact of a diminished urban center and the rise of the office complex at highway intersections made possible by the automobile.

The suburbs died, and the force of the technoburb, the exurb, the edge city lumbered through America, a mindless giant squatting down over broad swaths of land and dropping enormous turds called office parks and subdivisions and shopping malls, malls filled with numerous stores that quickly became a few gigantic ones, Wal-Mart and Home Depot and Office Max.

At the time I was growing up, swimming and eating Popsicles and walking to school, much fell apart in places like Cleveland. It became a confused, fractured place. Like other places across the country, Cleveland had made a mess of itself.

"It's tempting to ponder whether the Death of Place is linked with some general withering away of coherency and structure in nearly every field of artistic endeavor," writes Alex Marshall in *How Cities Work.* "Poems no longer rhyme. Sonnets are a dead art form. Representational painting is one small side road in contemporary painting, rather than a central avenue. Architecture, as we have been told so many times, has dropped any sort of rules or structure. Contemporary classical music jettisons melody, harmony, rhythm, and sometimes even the standard fifteen-note chromatic scale.

"In the same way, the narrative line of cities has broken down. . . . The incoherence of our places matches the incoherence of our lives."

This from a kindred spirit living in his hometown of Norfolk, Virginia, with his hometown wife. I think he's right, and I don't want that—a fractured place or a fractured marriage—and I think I can prevent it at least in my own life, because I'm lucky enough to be able to buy a 100-year-old house in a 110-year-old neighborhood that hasn't changed a whole lot since the 1920s. It's a center that could hold, because its location was a house built well with durable materials, on a street in a neighborhood that was so elegantly designed no one wanted to change it, near two small commercial centers both of which have enough architectural appeal that no one wants to destroy them and put up something new; people spend money in these small stores and restaurants; people here like their houses and so spend time and money to keep them from falling apart, and they like their neighborhood and so put care and money into it to prevent change. Called an inner suburb with a population of about fifty thousand, Cleveland Heights remains desirable today, as the rising house values, as the $70 million of new construction now under way, almost all of it residential, indicate.

We bought an old house and fixed it, pumped more money than we had into what isn't visible but will give it integrity for at least a generation, if not more; we gave it the respect it deserved, intending to stay. Our lives are not incoherent, in large part because of this house.

I was so impressed with Marshall's clear, sensible voice that I searched Google to see if there were some way to contact him. Sure enough, he had a site with an e-mail address. I wrote to tell him how much I'd enjoyed his book, how we were kindred spirits defending our hometowns with our lives.

He wrote back that day to say thanks for the e-mail, then added this:

"Tellingly, since I wrote *How Cities Work,* I have gotten divorced and moved away from Norfolk to New York City where I have remarried just a few months ago. A lot of change in a short time. I have mixed feelings about it all. Most of the thoughts I wrote in the chapter 'Community' still apply, even though I am now in a different place. I am interested in how people make connections with each other in an economy and society that pushes people apart, physically and otherwise. I'm finding New York an incredibly soulless place."

New York, he continued, wasn't all bad, but he missed his friends, missed being involved in his community, missed taking a walk on Saturday mornings, recognizing and saying hello to the people he passed.

"When I lived in Norfolk, my wife and I became very close friends with two couples who lived on the same street. It was really wonderful. Such close friendships would not have been possible without physical proximity. I think that is what I mull over. We are becoming less physically based in so many ways, from the Internet to television to telephones, etc. But for much of life, having things together in one place is necessary. I would like a close friend who lives around the corner. . . . I would like to belong to a community, but still the wider world beckons. I used to get upset when friends moved away and didn't stay in one place, yet I ended up doing the same thing."

I wrote back telling him to move to my neighborhood.

I thought this an excellent idea, but I know it's not the answer, because he's not *from* here. He's got no deposits of time spent, of family, of friends, no accounts to draw from, no dividends to enjoy, and, not unimportantly, no debt, the payment of which (in some form of offering to the community that feeds you) is part of the spiritual dynamic of returning to where you were born. His deposits, his dividends and debts, are in Norfolk, a city he says he's unlikely ever to return to. We leave that form of currency, both income and debit, behind when we uproot, can't take it with us. When we pursue the American dream of flight, we wander with empty pockets, but owing no one. I'm curious to know where Marshall will be living in twenty years and what in the long run he sacrificed and gained by leaving his hometown.

I also wonder if he noted, in his stated interest in how people connect, our connection. We were connected briefly and it was a good connection that wouldn't have happened ten years ago. I am in touch with legions of people because of the Internet, maintain contact with friends and readers that would have been impossible before this nonphysical vehicle of the information highway became available to everyone. The Internet is, as its metaphorical name implies, a form of transportation, and transportation, Alex argues, is the main force that shapes place.

And of course I couldn't think about the spiritual currency of returning to your hometown without acknowledging the fact that my wife wandered here with empty pockets of her own, had her own currency from another place that wasn't accepted here. How did this affect her? She is a very intuitive person. I wondered if she sensed but did not articulate this form of debt. Could this be part of her gathering disenchantment?

I looked a while longer at the picture of me and Kley by the pool, age five, happy, never happier, in fact—in all of life, so purely happy. I turned out the lights up there and went down to bed, crawled in next to Donna, who did not stir.

On August 14, Donna had the kids and I'd returned from my father's early and so was alone when I heard the house shut down with a *thunk*. The whole house, out. Minutes later Donna pulled up and the kids stormed the house, my daughter informing me that power was out all the way to the East Coast.

We had a few hours to evaluate the situation and get organized before darkness fell. Donna filled the tub in case we lost water, as most neighborhoods had, there being no electricity to run the pumps at the city's water plants. We had an oversupply of food, as usual, and a gas stove.

While Donna organized the homestead, I took the kids across the street. I was a little spooked by the unprecedented interstate blackout—everyone's first thought was terrorism—and wanted to be around people. Heather was outside, and her three kids were climbing all over the play set in back. I told her we were blacked out all the way to Manhattan, and she said, "Wow, I just got home from there. Just now." Thomas was still emptying their suburban vehicle, grumbling abstractedly about something unrelated to the blackout, which didn't appear to concern him. Heather immediately tried to reach her sister, who lived in New York.

We chatted a while longer, and the kids played. Gorgeous August afternoon. When we headed home, Betsy had just arrived with her kids. Work having ended, I suggested I do a barbecue for both our families. Betsy's husband, Dan, would soon be home, the kids were hungry, and we had all kinds of raw meat to throw on the fire. Betsy brought their goods over in a brown paper grocery bag and set them on the island in the kitchen.

Betsy picked up the book I'd been reading while I ate lunch and had failed to put away. She read the spine. *"Relationship Rescue,"* she said. "Is this any good?"

Embarrassment was my immediate and visceral response. I thought, Oh, Christ, how could you leave that thing sitting out on the counter? What are you trying to do, advertise your fights? I cringed at the thought that our neighbor, with whom we'd grown close, would be let in on our problems. I don't want her or anyone to know about this. I'm sure we *seemed* perfectly wonderful, and I wanted to keep the blinds closed. Betsy hadn't even thought before speaking. If she had, she'd never have embarrassed me that way, I'm sure. Betsy was good and thoughtful to a fault. She just picked it up and said the first thing that came to mind because that's how she is—"Is this any good?" As if it were a novel. On the other hand, maybe saying nothing would have made me feel worse. I'd watched her pick it up. If she'd said nothing—*ooops*—we'd both have known what she was thinking.

Wanting to assure her that Donna and I were perfectly fine, for chris-sake, completely fine, couldn't be better, but also fess up to the presence of the book (not say, "Someone must have left it there I never saw it before where the hell did that thing come from?"), I said, "Donna and I have been fighting about the same things over and over, and we needed to do something. Yeah, it's a good book."

"Huh," Betsy said, and continued to unload food, perhaps realizing then from my awkwardness exactly what it meant to find a book in your neighbor's kitchen called Relationship Rescue, a book obviously being thoroughly read, cover dispensed with, dog-eared pages, coffee stains, under-lining going on. I'm sure I said something like, "I hope we have enough charcoal," but the shame lingered.

Getting that book had actually been fun and had turned out to be a fruitful way to begin conversations with my wife. Every morning after we'd fought that summer, we talked by phone, I at my father's. They were amazing, cathartic conversations, extremely tender because of the damage and fear, but neither of us believed that sweet phone calls would solve anything. As we were not the therapy sort, we decided to find a book and fix ourselves ourselves. It was one of the happiest moments of the summer, in fact, clicking through Amazon's bestselling relationship books with Donna—doing something together in a way we hadn't in months. Odd but true. At any rate it was how we chose to deal with a problem that wasn't going away.

It was going to work, but I didn't want anyone else to *know* about it. Only after I stopped being ashamed at Betsy's having seen the book, did I think, Why did Betsy ask if it was any good? I hope *they're* OK. Not that I'd know if they weren't, because it's not something you advertise. It's something you urgently hide. But why? Was marriage supposed to be a breeze?

A short time later, I learned of the separation of friends we hadn't seen in a while, with kids our kids' ages. How sad that we had *no* idea. And then *another* couple who lived around the corner from us—they were divorcing, too, selling the house they'd bought shortly after we'd bought ours, no kids, and she'd taken a job in New York City.

The fact is, we have no idea what our married friends say to one another when the kids are asleep, when real stresses of life bubble up to take the place of all the busyness of the day.

In the fall, on the way home from a school function, a skating party at our community center, Donna said, "Sally and Bill are separated."

"You're kidding," I said.

"I have never once asked how they're doing," Donna went on. "I don't know why I did then. I just said, 'How are you and Bill?' She looked at me angrily. She said, 'Not good.' Then, 'We're separated.' When she realized that I hadn't known, she felt relieved. It was comforting to think that she and Bill weren't being gossiped about, she said."

I don't say to close friends, "How is your marriage working out?" any more than I ask to talk about a wife's sexual proclivities or how well they're making ends meet. Maybe that's as it should be; maybe it's better not to have friends weighing in with their own brand of therapy; and maybe these couples who separate will lead happier, more productive lives and be better parents because of it. Sally had said that Bill spent more time with the kids now than he had when he'd been in the same house. On the other hand, it's still a broken family, and maybe they just need a little support, which comes from a community of friends.

It seems strange to me that our inclination is to avoid that; we lock ourselves up in our houses and pull down the shades.

Betsy—from Cincinnati, five hours south of here, short light brown hair, very dark eyes, skinny, a tennis player—is a paragon of suburban domesticity, a devoted mom, a wife who's already hiding Dan's Father's Day gift in our garage weeks in advance because she's been thinking ahead. I trust her as much as I trust Donna to look out for our kids. There isn't a more thoughtful friend to me and Donna. And Dan is a great guy, a guy's guy, works his ass off all week, likes to watch Cleveland sports and futz about the house on the weekends, take naps, take the kids skiing or golfing, unless he's got to go back into the office, the honorable provider, or help his neighbor dig a patio, which he's only too happy to throw himself into. Dan and Betsy are solidity itself. Or so they appear. As do we. As do our best friends who are married. How would we know otherwise, when everyone works to appear as if nothing's the matter? Why do we perpetuate this harmful illusion that marriage is the most natural, easiest thing in world? Marriage is hard. Why should we think that it's easy? It can be beautiful and powerful, yet it's anything but safe, it's never still, and it can destroy you if you're careless. Marriage is a shark.

———

I got raw red meat over open flames on that summer afternoon of the blackout, an activity that always inspires ease and contentment, and despite the inconvenience of the power outage and the disruption in routine and work, I was particularly glad not to be, say, trapped in a subway in Greenwich Village or planning to sleep in my clothes on the pavement outside the Marriott in Times Square.

The sun went down, and we lit a fire in the living room, for its light and to pop corn. The night was warm. Dan had to return to his offices to unplug the computers, fearing that a power surge might demolish his company's files, but Betsy and the kids were over, and they'd brought over their nifty fireplace popper. We popped several batches and more or less trashed the living room—very hard to keep things tidy when you can't see. We ate and talked, and the kids played in the light of the flames, and then we all went outside.

I'd never seen such darkness here. Even during rare power outages, there's a glow above the horizon from neighboring cities. Tonight there were no lights from here to the Atlantic Ocean. It was as black as it would ever be, as black as it was when this spot of Cleveland had been rolling farmland. I put my arm around Donna, and she held me. The kids lay back in the cold grass. Betsy sat on the front steps with their littlest one. A few candles lit the walls of our living room, but that was the only light I saw. All other houses were dark. I couldn't even make out their silhouettes it was so dark, just barely the tops of trees. And so there was a timelessness to the moment. It could have been 1900. This is what I'd have seen and heard had I gone outside at 11:00 P.M., August 14, 1900. This land felt especially old tonight.

16

House Memory

"Communities without understandings of their pasts resemble people suffering from amnesia, unable to remember from where they came, how they responded to needs or challenges, from whence they drew affection and support, or opposition, and where they intended to go."

This is from *Houses and Homes: Exploring Their History* by Barbara J. Howe, and I've come to see it as a truth that goes beyond house and home. It applies to all the worlds I've explored—cooking, boatbuilding, heart surgery—and the one I practiced. Those craftsmen all knew the history of their culture well, relied on it as a fundamental wellspring of their daily work. Nothing the heart surgeon does today would be possible without the maverick work of the heart surgeons who came before him. The builders of wooden boats rely each day on the knowledge, passed down over millennia, of how to put pieces of wood together in a way that is both beautiful and watertight.

The history of my community grew important to me because without an understanding of its past, it was too easy for the people here to botch or to lose it, to give it up to the steamroller progress of the raised, limited-access freeway and the gargantuan mall. Or simply too easy to move away from.

I became a kind of Craig Bobby of my own plot of land. I joined the

Western Reserve Historical Society in order to avail myself of its library, which specialized in genealogical research services and had a big collection of Cleveland documents. A quick search of a biography of Warren G. Harding, born outside Cleveland in 1865, showed no brother named Frank; our house, alas, had not been built for a president's brother. But I had learned of a reference to Frank Harding as an executive with the Peerless Motor Car Company. I discovered a book titled *Golden Wheels,* a history of automaking in the city. Here indeed was a brief mention of Frank I. Harding, who had left the company and designed and built his own touring car in 1914, the Harding 12. A photograph accompanied the citation, but more important than the car—a standard of its era with a rectangular body, canvas top, flat windshield, running board—was its location. The car had been photographed in our driveway, our dining room bay window distinct in the background. The credit read "Courtesy of Frank I. Harding Jr."

At home I checked the phone book, and no Junior was listed (he'd have been in his nineties if alive). But Frank Harding III was listed in Cleveland Heights. I called, left a message, and a week or so later heard on our voice mail the voice of Frank III, with an offer to give him a call if I wished and his hope that "you are enjoying my grandfather's house."

The Western Reserve library held census information for the entire United States up to the 1930 census. I began with the 1910 census, some of it illegible from sloppy handwriting and age, but I found that I could read our address and learn that Frank Harding, age thirty-eight, lived in the house that year, with his wife Grace, age twenty-nine. Included after Grace's vital info was "1-1." Other women on the sheet had "3-3" or "3-2" or "4-2"—this was the infant-mortality rate on a house-to-house basis, the number of births followed by children surviving. The 1920 census would no longer record this information. Also in the house in 1910 was Frank Jr., three, and two servants, Augusta from Germany, age twenty-one, and Wilhelmina, a twenty-five-year-old Scot. These girls certainly would have lived in the rooms my children now occupied. Donna and I slept in the room once occupied by Frank and Grace. The 1920 census recorded that a son, John, had been born in 1911 and a daughter, Jane, in 1917; also that Grace's mom, named Jenny, lived with them along with a maid, a nineteen-year-old Russian girl who'd been in the country for eleven years.

In the 1930 census, a new family is listed at the address, Charles Dyer, age forty-five; wife, Mabel; and three children: Charles, Marshall, and a four-year-old girl named Margaret. I felt grateful for the names of the people who'd trod the same stairways and floorboards that we did today.

During renovation of the house, John had pulled the master bedroom's mantelpiece away from the wall so that we could rebuild the disintegrating fireplace. Behind the mantel he found an old photograph, a portrait of a man perhaps in his thirties, austere, somewhat fey-looking, balding, wearing spectacles and a rounded collar—dress of the early part of the twentieth century. The photograph, on heavy board, had been beautifully preserved between mantel and plaster wall, another of those house objects disinterred like the bones. This surely, given the style of the portrait and the clothes, was Frank Harding, the original owner of the house. I kept it in a folder and looked at it every now and then, thinking of this man inventing an automobile in our garage, which of course had been built after the house (no one in Cleveland needed a car garage in 1901). He looked a little petite to be such an executive and engineer, but there it was.

I continued to lean on Craig Bobby for information during our conversations and correspondences about the house, particularly about the eight years between its construction and the date the Hardings bought it. I was sure no one lived here before the Hardings. There were no records, no sign that anyone had. But how, I wondered, had the house been used during the first ten years of the century?

"I don't know," Craig said. "As I've told you before, I'm not interested in neighborhoods or people. But I can say that it is highly *unlikely* that no one was living there. *Highly* unlikely." I'd suggested that the Euclid Heights Realty Company had built it as a spec house in its attempt to lure Clevelanders out of the city.

"I'd be very surprised if your house was unoccupied at that time," Craig said emphatically.

I'd meant to contact Craig again. He'd sent an e-mail to say when I could find him at home, but I'd gotten busy and never called. I received a phone call from Kara O'Donnell at City Hall saying Craig had been at their offices. "I think he has some information for you, and he's a little upset that you haven't called him back," she told me.

I immediately e-mailed an apology and promised to call. Later that night an e-mail dropped into my in-box from Mr. Bobby: "Your house *MAY* have been occupied during those years by Edwin L. Thurston."

When I reached Craig, he explained he'd been at the library and, curious about my question, had checked a 1904 Cleveland blue book. The social registry often listed names not only alphabetically but also by street. Here on our street, he saw names he knew—Comey, Lamprecht, and York—but also a Mr. and Mrs. E. L. Thurston. Moving then to a 1904 city directory, he found Edwin Thurston listed, but at the time houses were not numbered.

"Which is why I put 'may' in all capital letters," he said. It was likely that everyone who lived on the street would be listed in the blue book because it would have been a fashionable address, he continued, and as there were few structures on the street at the time, and we know where the Yorks and Lamprechts and Comeys lived, it's likely that "this Thurston character," as Craig called him, lived in our house, but we couldn't be certain.

The following day, I returned to the library of the Western Reserve Historical Society and found from the city directory that this Thurston character had been a patent lawyer with a downtown office in the Society for Savings Building across from the Old Stone Church. He was listed on our street in city directories from 1903 until 1908. Also, he was living on 107th Street in 1909, the year the Hardings purchased the house. I then found a book, several volumes down from the blue books in the library stacks, titled *Prominent Clevelanders,* and here were not only the names of these people but, in the back, head shots as well. Thurston was named—born in 1857 in Rhode Island; arrived in Cleveland in 1887; belonged to four different clubs; hobby, golf. I flipped to the back, and there was the image of Edwin Thurston, almost identical to the man from the photograph we'd found behind the mantel, though clearly

older. The image I'd held in my mind as Frank Harding was in fact Edwin
Thurston. Here was evidence, then, that Craig Bobby was right—
Thurston had been the first resident of the house.

I looked up his name in the necrology index on the Internet and discovered that he'd died in 1921 "suddenly" and that at the time of his
death, in a pleasing twist of synchronicity, he lived on Hampshire Road,
almost directly across the street from the house we'd recently left.

I now had the names of all the families who'd lived in this structure.
The house seemed to demand that I know it. We were its legacy. It had
offered up the Thurston portrait in the same way it had gotten the
porch floor fixed and, soon, the unplanned work of tearing out and
rebuilding a new hearth for the living room fireplace. It's dangerous to
anthropomorphize a structure, as some have noted, but this is the feeling of what was happening as we began to use the house as a family. We
were connected to Thurston by virtue of the structure, and to the Hardings and the Dyers. I wanted to know, what did the street look like when
Thurston left it each morning for his office at the Society for Savings
Building, the city's first large bank building, where he practiced patent
law? He surely took the streetcar to and from work in 1903, when auto-
mobiles were strange contraptions. There was something to be learned
from knowing this—don't ask me what!—and the house was, in some
way, the anchor of all the information and history, its center of gravity,
pulling me toward it.

I sensed that our brick house—this dark, stately tank on a broad,
leafy street—was not simply the beginning of the wash of suburban
sprawl, spreading scarily out across our county and beyond, suburban
pavement and suburban lawns and Home Depot–Wal-Mart malls
rolling over Ohio farmland into Illinois and West Virginia and Kentucky
and beyond, connecting to all the other spreading stains on the map of
America, gated communities and office parks, expanding as surely and
unstoppably as the universe itself. Our house was a still and contained
center, and we were permanent extensions of those who had lived here.

———

I guess I shouldn't have been surprised by the notion of visits. Either ours is that kind of house or, more likely, houses are generally like that.

When I reached Frank III, he had suggested I call his aunt Jane, who was three at the time of the 1920 census and who now lived in St. Louis. A couple years back, she'd returned to the city to see Frank III's daughter married and had asked to pass by her old house—the house where she'd been a girl. She was drawn to it. Like Kley, she'd sat in the car and gazed. She'd been so happy here.

Charles Dyer bought the house from the Hardings and moved his family into it in 1927, and he would live here for thirty-five years, selling it shortly after his wife, Mabel, died in 1962.

His grandson, John Dyer, knocked on our door one day, in the middle of the afternoon on a lovely spring day. Donna answered. John introduced himself, and Donna said, "You're one of the Dyers!" It made John feel welcome in his old house. John and his wife were on their way by car from Oregon to their home in Vermont, he explained, and he had an urge to see the house where he'd lived as a boy in the late forties and early fifties, when his mom and dad had moved back in with Charles and Mabel—three generations living here.

Though he'd moved out of the house when he was eight, he'd been pulled back by the structure as if it were a magnet. Donna gave him a tour of the house. He said he and his brother had been pretty reckless. It had probably been they who'd shot at the windows from within the house, he laughed. Donna wrote down his e-mail address and phone number.

Later, when I reached him, he sent a slew of memory snapshots—the rolltop desk in my office, hiding in the bench in the alcove beneath the stairs, the "train room" on the third floor, his grandfather's workshop in a basement John remembered as spooky. "I think the fireplace in the rear of the kitchen worked," he wrote. So there *had* been one after all! When the room had been the kitchen where the maid and cook ate, when the narrow room between had been a pantry that led to the dining room. The house was all very *Driving Miss Daisy*–ish, he said. And he told me about his aunt Margie, who had moved into Jane Harding's bedroom in 1927, an infant, and spent her entire youth here. She now lived in Rye, New York, and was a vigorous seventy-seven years old. She confirmed that her nephew John and his brother were very reckless, had once sawn the legs off the dining room table for fun, she said.

Jane Harding and John Dyer were drawn to a house they hadn't lived in for decades. I could call up these people and speak to them, people who remembered the iceman driving his horse and wagon up this street, his leather straps and enormous tongs, the tinker and the bread man, the hungry men eating a meal on the patio in back in the thirties because there was no work.

I doubt that our house was unique. A lot of these dwellings had a similar draw, had different lives in their orbit. Across the street, Heather and Thomas's house, however, could be assured that no strangers would appear seeking their lost time. Not a single person alive who'd ever lived there was unknown or unwelcome—they were all family. Betty, Heather's grandmother, lived down the hill just off Cedar Glen; she had been a girl there in the house built by J. G. W. Cowles, Rockefeller's real estate liaison. Betty had been a wife and mother in that house, and a grandmother to Heather, to whom she sold the house and who now raised three, soon to be four, great-grandchildren there.

Betty remembers when a fruit truck tipped over rounding a corner too fast. Her mother, Harriet, ran to the driver, carrying whiskey for him. But usually the street was so quiet you could read in the middle of it and not have to move all day. If you heard an airplane approaching, you'd rush outside to watch it and say hi to your neighbors who'd done the same thing. When Betty was a girl, one of the servants tied a bell to a string, the string to the drawer where she kept her money in her room in the third-floor servants' quarters; the servant ran the string down through the house to where she worked on the first floor. When the bell rang, she flew up the stairs and caught the laundress, who'd been stealing her money all this time. Betty will never forget the commotion that day among all the servants.

There were plenty of kids now on the street. Often they swam at the Briggs estate up at the corner of Overlook and Coventry. Much of this land remained empty then, in the late teens and twenties, but many houses were in the process of being built. Of all the games, the roller skating and bicycle riding, Betty recalls that what she and her friends often did was to climb the scaffolding of those houses-in-progress. One friend went clear up to the top of a chimney, got scared, and couldn't descend until the fire department was called.

Betty would marry a Washington man, a member of the Office of Strategic Services during the war—the OSS, which became the CIA—and raise three daughters and a son. They lived for a time in Columbus, Ohio, and for a couple of years in Pakistan, but they always returned to this house. One of Betty's daughters, Harriet, used to play a game called "Sardines" in the basement with the kids of the neighborhood, including my friend Kley's dad, who lived down the street.

Betty now lived in a retirement home down the hill, as did Patricia Beall, called Tish, who happened to be the granddaughter of Patrick Calhoun. She has his pale blue eyes. You can see their resemblance in photographs. Tish's girlhood was spent three houses up the street from us and, after she married, just two houses up from that. She watched the whole thrilling, harrowing transformation of the country—from the Jazz Age to the Depression to World War II, the Eisenhower fifties and the cultural upheaval of the sixties, the embarrassments of the seventies—all from the window of a house on this street. Tish's mom died when she was three, in 1922. Patricia's father died six years later, and so she was raised by servants and unpredictable Aunt Mildred. The Browns in the house next door became surrogate family. Patricia's best friend, Jane Harding, lived three houses down. The neighborhood teemed with kids. Hubert Meriweather lived in the house behind hers, an older boy who could get the girls to do most any mischief. Between their houses was a garden walled by rose-covered brick, their secret garden. She and Jane Harding played in that garden and in the grassy lot between the Browns' and the Pecks'. Tish found a horseshoe in the dirt there about the year 1923. Jane informed her one must make a wish and throw it over one's shoulder for the wish to come true. Tish did so and hit Jane between the eyes with it. Blood poured down Jane's face. They were about seven at the time. My daughter was that age as she played on that same ground. I pulled the kids down the same hills in snow. Our lives were built in to the actual contours of the land. The shape of the land helped to define who we were. We lived in houses on a height.

Jane's father, Frank I. Harding, had bought this house from the Euclid Heights Realty Company and moved in during the fall of 1909. I can imagine it in part because I was about his age when we moved in, and our son was about his son's age. Jane, born in 1918, adored her childhood home. When I reached Jane by phone, she told me she'd lived in many places, but her best memories of home are around and within our house, where she lived till she was nine.

Jane's family relied on wagons to bring them milk and bread, ice for the icebox. An organ-grinder and his monkey wandered up the street weekly, sharpening scissors. Jane's mom, Grace, tall and slender with beautiful brown eyes, used the telephone to order groceries for delivery from the markets at Doan's Corners—Heinz peanut butter, meat, eggs, fruits and vegetables, and any special items for that day's meal, which she'd plan with their cook. Her father spent much of his time at the Union Club downtown, at Twelfth and Euclid.

The family ate all meals in the dining room, cereal-fruit-toast-and-juice breakfasts, meat-and-potato dinners, pies and cakes for dessert that Jane's maternal grandmother baked daily during winter months when she lived there. The cook and the upstairs maid ate in the kitchen, separated from the dining room by the pantry, where the silver was kept and where Jane's father would mix pitchers of cocktails before a dozen guests arrived for a dressy party, the booze having been delivered by the local bootlegger who came regularly to their back door and to most others' in the neighborhood. Jane would sit at the middle landing of the main staircase on those evenings, chin in her hands, to watch the adults, adoring their elegance and sophistication.

Mondays, a laundress would arrive and slave in the basement, a wretched job in those days. Coal was delivered there for the furnace that sent steam to radiators throughout the house. The basement was also where Frank, much to Grace's disgust, fermented his elderberry wine.

In the spring, when dandelions sprang up everywhere, the Italian women would hike from their neighborhood, Little Italy, up the hill beside Lake View Cemetery, and over to the Heights and ask to pick the weeds for their own potable concoction, dandelion wine. Jane was shocked yearly by the fact that these women would sit in the grass and breast-feed their babies in plain sight.

Before school began each fall—Jane went to the leading private girls' school, Laurel—Grace would drive Jane downtown in the electric car, a quiet car on quiet streets, park at the Union Club, and take her shopping at Halle's department store, presided over by Mr. Halle himself, dressed in a seersucker suit.

Jane's dad kept the radio in the library and would listen to it to relax. One May evening in 1927, when she was nine years old, her teenage brothers went crazy as the news of Lindbergh's successful transatlantic flight came over the radio, and the United States ambassador to France, Myron Herrick, whose family lived on Overlook, one street north, welcomed the celebrity aviator.

Later that year Jane finished third grade, and she would soon instruct the new owner, Mabel Dyer, not to change the wallpaper in her room, just above the library, because the floral print was perfect for a girl, especially one with two older brothers. The Hardings were headed to Florida, in consideration of Frank's health (rheumatic fever had left him with heart problems). Charles and Mabel moved in with their three kids: Margie, born the previous year, the kid sister of two brothers, John and Marshall.

Margie grew up smack in the middle of the Depression. It hit her city as it did the country, but Cleveland was still a central spot in Great Lakes industry, producing nearly half the country's coal and 85 percent of its iron ore at a time when lake shipping was the most economically efficient means of transport.

At the height of the Depression, a man would come around once a week or so selling shoelaces. Mabel Dyer always bought a pair and then instructed the man to walk around back and have something to eat. She'd tell the cook to prepare a full meal, with coffee. Margie remembers the man's shoes, tied together with string, his ragged clothes and ragged hat and how kind he was.

Her father's company, engineering consultants to manufacturing concerns in this manufacturing town, stayed the course of the Depression and surely prospered as World War II began and the city's steel industry boomed.

So the young Margie, relatively untouched by the Depression, was left to the neighborhood and all the kids here.

When she looks back on it, she thinks of it as a paradise for the children. She was best friends with Marion Peck, who lived next door. Beside the Pecks, the Browns had erected a tobogganing chute for winter games. In summer they rode bikes and roller-skated. The women of the neighborhood, her mom and especially Mrs. Oakes across the street, Betty's mom, tended extraordinary gardens. In Margie's backyard a huge viburnum grew snowball-size blossoms. And beside the house an enormous sycamore shed its bark on her father's cherished bent-grass lawn, which he tended as carefully as if it were a putting green. On Sundays before church, the Dyers would crank ice cream using dry ice, to have after the midday dinner featuring a roast chicken or a leg of lamb. Some Sunday afternoons Margie would help the Pecks pull taffy. Sunday nights the cook had off, and Mr. Dyer loved to make Spanish omelettes and elaborate soups.

The organ-grinder was still around, and Margie would rush outside to give his monkey a penny. Through the 1930s milk continued to arrive on a horse-drawn wagon, as did bread, and when the Dyers forgot to take in their bread sign, it meant bread pudding for dessert all weekend. Milk back then was something special, with the cream on top. Unless, of course, you got to it when it was almost gone and very nearly like skim. Breakfast cereals included cornflakes, oatmeal, shredded wheat, Grape Nuts, and Rice Crispies, but that was about the extent of them, long before companies thought to hammer cereal with sugar. Breakfast daily at seven-thirty was a family event in the Dyer household, and for the rest of her life, it would remain Margie's favorite meal. You could hear and smell the percolating coffee. They drank fresh orange juice, ate cereal, eggs, and bacon, and in the winter cream of wheat. After breakfast her father would walk to the streetcar and ride downtown to work at the Union Commerce Building on Euclid Avenue. The kids would be driven to school in a car pool until the war, when, due to the gas shortage, they rode the Rapid Transit to the end of the Green Road Line. On

Sunday mornings Margie's mom fixed waffles at the table, with fresh butter and hot maple syrup.

While the Hardings had been in the house, a small commercial district had gone up a few blocks away where the curving Fairmount Boulevard met Cedar Road. You could order ice cream from Miller's Drugstore on Sundays, and they'd deliver. You could have prescriptions filled there or get an ice cream soda. Damon's, a restaurant; Russo's, a grocery store; Kent's, a flower store, all named after their proprietors, prospered there with two good bakeries and Best and Company, which sold bargain clothing. Everything you needed was right here, including employment. Margie worked at Kent's from age fourteen till she left for college in 1944.

Mr. Dyer coached Margie on the ERAs of Cleveland Indians pitchers, notably the young Bob Feller, and Margie tried to be interested. She wasn't much of an athlete. Sports took place during the school day, so she was home always by three-thirty to read and do homework and play, or practice the piano. Music was a natural companion. She often gave lessons to Harriet and Luvie from across the street. Margie thought their mom, Betty, was more beautiful than Katharine Hepburn, whose movies would play at the new theater on Coventry, a short walk up Euclid Heights Boulevard.

In the summer the Dyers virtually lived on our front porch. They greeted their mailman by name, who delivered mail twice a day to the iron box that clanked shut after you retrieved the day's letters. Margie's father tended his lawn and played golf at the country club. He was an athletic, work-hard, play-hard man who wore a mustache to cover a scar he'd got playing football. Margie loved to scratch the wood matches to light his Lucky Strikes.

In the winter, after dinner, they'd build a fire in the master bedroom (Mr. and Mrs. slept in twin beds; Margie's generation would be the first to routinely enjoy queen-size beds, she said), listen to Jack Benny and Bob Hope on the radio, read and talk, and Margie would do her homework.

The places within the house became important and lasting to this girl who'd spent her entire youth here and returned regularly after marrying. That bedroom with its fireplace and lovely delft tiles, a photograph of Edwin Thurston lost behind it. Her bedroom, which looked out over a street so filled with trees they locked branches overhead to form a canopy. The main staircase that reversed direction at a midlevel landing, and the double-hung leaded windows there. Margie can still feel the tug on her arm as she grabbed the top of the newel post to swing around, careful to avoid the grandfather clock there, and descend the rest of the way. Beneath this staircase is a built-in bench between raised-panel walls. A small window here looks out to the backyard. Jane Harding used to listen from the stairs to her mom helping her brothers with their Latin homework in this alcove. Margie or John or Marshall could talk on the telephone here beneath the stairs on the built-in bench whose heavy oak seat lifted up. They kept tennis rackets in the space below. Donna called this alcove beneath the main staircase the defining space of the house. Thirty years later Marshall's son, John, would lift this seat, crawl in, and hide and never forget it; John would return to Cleveland in 2002 and ask to see it, this bench, and see as well the "Keen Cutter" shelves in the basement workroom his dad had hung, to see what he, too, called the train room on the third floor, the long narrow storage area at the top of the house's rear gable.

These places in a house are vividly recalled decades later by the people who used them because they have long been a part of the grain of their memory and their sense of time. The bay-window seat in the library, the big rolltop desk where my desk is now, the dining room table and the waffle iron, the front porch with its wood floor and ornate pillars and sandstone steps, the back patio where they cranked ice cream and fed a homeless man, the third-floor rec room with its padded floor where Margie and her friends jitterbugged with boys who would not have to go to war after all. Footfall on floorboards. The arc you make several times every day of your childhood when you hit the landing of the staircase, your hand on the newel post to change directions. A house lived in for an entire childhood is the terrain of that childhood. Terrain matters.

The final room to be completed was Donna's room of work, her darkroom. She had a lab for color and for processing and was skeptical about where digital photography was headed, at least concerning her interest in archival printing and black-and-white portraiture, but the darkroom was her critical space, the room she relied on for her work. I went out and gathered information and returned to my study to shape that stuff into story, she went out and gathered pictures and returned to her darkroom to craft them into portraits. She was an artful printer and enjoyed this work as much as, if not more than, the actual clicking.

The room we'd convert had once been a kind of storage cellar, brick like the other basement rooms, but with a wooden wall and door built up in the middle of it to make two rooms. Neither seemed to have been used much in recent years, but I imagined that long ago jars of beans and beets and pickles and elderberry wine were put up here. We chose this room because a darkroom needed plumbing and therefore convenient access to one of the two main stacks leaving the house.

I sledgehammered out the wooden wall, put up a quarter-inch-thick drywall ceiling, a headache because the room was immediately below the kitchen, so there was a network of new pipes below the floor joists to contend with. Holes in the wall needed to be patched, and dampness had eroded mortar between the bricks in the lower levels of the wall, which I scraped out and repointed. I put an exhaust fan in the window. Donna primed and painted the walls. I installed the twelve-foot stainless-steel counter and sink from the original kitchen, which we'd stored in the garage. Donna purchased some prefabricated cabinets for storage and for a second utility sink. And over the course of five weekends, it was more or less light-tight.

Her first print was, not surprisingly, of the kids, but more important than the product coming out of the room was the work itself and how it changed the house. The house felt bigger and more complex. I'd marked out my station in the kitchen at one two-by-three-foot square of the island. One of the toe-kick heaters below the cupboards pumped out warm air (the weather was getting cool now), and J. lolled contentedly in the current. That had become his spot. It was also my spot, but there was room enough for the two of us as I chopped onions and picked green beans on one chilly weekend evening. This would have been pleasure enough, but now, immediately below us, additional work went on.

Donna had called up to her daughter, who was at the time transfixed by a small TV we'd put in one of the shelves beside the fireplace, "Want to help me print?"

"Sure!" was the delighted response, and so, directly below me, Donna was now teaching our daughter the magic of putting images from negatives onto previously blank sheets of paper. The new room changed the house.

And with this particular change, the uneasy transition of our marriage took on a more defined shape. Perhaps this was a source of some of Donna's turmoil—the scary move from nurturing and all-caring mother of helpless infants and children to a mom–cum–career women. But it was not a return to who she had been; rather a transition into a new person who contained that mother and the wife she'd been to me, helping me to work. She wasn't a shell of her former self, as she'd felt; she was in fact richer and more complex than ever. But she didn't know whom she would become or the work she'd be able find, and these unknowns likely weighed on her and made her anxious. How would she make new work happen for herself, having been so long not working? And was there work for her here, in my widget city?

"I'm not saying we wouldn't have chosen Cleveland in the end— maybe we would have, I don't know," she said, acknowledging the endless practical advantages of this city, especially if you were raising children. "Anyway, I accept that we're here until the kids are out of school. But I don't like the way we arrived at the decision—it wasn't a decision, and that's always going to be a part of my feelings about this place."

She left it at that. For now. It will always be an issue.

A few months later, at the dinner table, one of us used the term "mid-life crisis" and our daughter asked what it meant. Our daughter's initiating any conversation at dinner was enough to halt our own conversation, regardless of the subject, but this question seemed especially salient coming out of the blue from an eight-year-old.

"Do you know what 'crisis' means?" I asked. She said no, and I said, "It means trouble."

"A midlife crisis is when—" Donna said, then broke off. "Oh, my

God, is that what I had?" She smiled and laughed. She'd meant it as a joke, and I laughed, too.

"But, Mom, you're only forty. I would think that midlife would be fifty."

Donna paused at the thought and didn't respond to our literal-minded girl. Donna had just gotten back from a photography seminar down in her old stomping grounds in Palm Beach County and was beginning to put together a business plan with the intent to return to work in the spring. She'd spent five days away from home, the first work time away from children, the longest she'd been away from her kids ever, and had returned invigorated. I imagine that traveling without the kids was like taking your feet out of cement buckets and walking free.

Later I looked up "crisis," sensing I'd oversimplified things, as I tend to do. Indeed, *Fowler's Modern English Usage* calls what I'd told my daughter a "SLIPSHOD EXTENSION" of the true meaning. Derived from a Greek word meaning "to separate," "crisis" describes a moment when decisive change for better or worse is imminent. The number-one Webster's definition is the turning point in a disease, for better or worse, or (b) "an intensely painful attack of a disease; paroxysm." Had I oversimplified our crisis, too?

Before completing her darkroom, Donna had painted the shelves in my office a rich, almost navy, blue, the window trim and crown molding maroon. She'd found handsome blinds for the three sections of bay window and had a cushion made for the window seat. I unloaded boxes and boxes of books, alphabetized them, and filled one wall with them. The other wall of shelves, into which my desk fitted neatly, I filled with reference books and framed photographs and mementos, old pipes, a glass owl, some bones. I packed up my books and laptop from the room in my father's house and began to work in my office. When a friend, a fellow writer (a novelist, no less) who'd also returned to Cleveland to live, saw my finished study for the first time, his jaw dropped. He actually looked pissed, said, "I am so jealous." I drew shameful pleasure from this.

Another friend, not a writer, said, "You need a tray with some single-malts here. This is where we need to sit after a good dinner, to drink and smoke cigars." It was a dark and stately room.

The final room on this floor to come together for actual use was the least-used room in the house, the living room, still a valuable room, I'm convinced, not dead yet. It was large relative to the furniture we owned. And we'd so overspent on the renovation of this house, had so burned through all of our reserves, that we weren't in the market for things like drapes and elegant furniture. Thus that final push came from my mom, whose work in Palm Beach real estate puts her in environs considerably more opulent than ours. Thanks to her blossoming acumen in that world and in her work, her love of houses, her compulsive generosity, and the rejuvenating real estate market down there, we were the recipients of surprise shipments from the UPS man. An enormous rug would be trucked up our porch steps. A couple of weeks later, a chair would arrive. These were not bargain goods. These were objects approved by someone with standards and tastes superior to ours (mine at least), an elegant sixty-something woman who still turned heads when she entered a room. These objects were the real deal, and Donna and I knew how lucky we were.

"That's it. That's all I'm doing," my mother would tell me. And then two hundred pounds of fabric would arrive. "They were given to me. I sold a house, and they were going to be thrown out, those drapes. Do you realize how good that material is? I thought it would be perfect in your living room. I hope Donna doesn't hate me."

Indeed, we couldn't have afforded one square yard of this stuff. Donna found a company capable of fitting them to our windows, and they *were* perfect.

"I got a really good deal!" my mom pleaded when the next chair arrived. "How could I not? It's perfect." I told her, please, enough, and thank you, to which she responded, "Just don't expect any money from me when I *die*. I'm spending my money now, while we can all enjoy it." She meant it. The house benefited.

It was critical to the whole situation not only that my mom had great taste but more that she and Donna shared that taste. I think I'd have put up with purple shag carpeting if these two women happened to rejoice in it. The harmony of a mother–daughter-in-law relationship of this kind, I knew, was not to be taken for granted, but rather the sort of fate for which you make live sacrifices to the gods. Indeed, the intensity of their relationship, a direct result of their like-minded teamwork on finishing the house, was almost enough to make this only child jealous. When Carole called on a Sunday morning to chat, she'd cover the bases with me in sixty seconds or less and then say, *"Where's my daughter-in-law?"* as if I were hoarding her.

Time took on a seamlessness when all the rooms here—in this brick house with four shingled gables—were engaged in their proper roles. Instead of painting rooms on the weekend, Donna could rake leaves while I could take the kids to a movie. Life changed when the house became a house rather than a project, returned to a normal routine as it had been for the families whose lives had played out in these same spaces, and we became a part of the continuum of the house.

When we'd rested and when the schedule allowed, we'd do those diminishing but never-ending bigger jobs on the house at our convenience. Only one for now was urgent. I'd almost left the mortar work too long; if I waited till spring, a winter freeze might do more damage than I'd be able to repair myself. In early September we'd rented a power washer and bought some restoration-grade acid to clean the sandstone lintels and sills of the windows on the two visible sides of the house, which were black with soot, about fifteen windows in all, as well as the sandstone pieces along the wall of the front porch. I scrubbed with a stiff-bristled brush, and I lost a fingernail for ignoring a hole in the rubber glove, but the blackness poured off the sandstones like sudsy ink till they shone bone white. While on a ladder at the guest room window, I'd cleaned a patch of brick in the front of the house to see if I could take some of the same soot off and make them seem less weary. I covered myself in cement and Lake Erie sand, blowing all the mortar out from between the bricks. Now a patch of bricks five feet square was loose, and the gaps had to be filled with more mortar before ice got in there and did some real damage.

It was a blockheaded move, and I'd delayed the repair as long as possible because it was painstaking work and had to be done right, or it would look as much a mess as the badly patched areas Inspector Archer had pointed out with such sadness. Finally, on a day cold and densely gray, with the kids at a friend's house for the afternoon, I mixed a three-to-one batch of sand and M-grade cement and enough dye to make the mortar as dark as the existing material. I'd borrowed Jack's ladder from across the street and tipped it *cl-clank* against the side of the house. I loaded cement onto the hawk, a handheld platform, stuck a three-eighths-inch tuck pointer in my pocket, and climbed. I began at the topmost joint, pressing coarse, charcoal gray mortar into the narrow gaps. I also filled smaller holes and gaps where a century of wind and water had eroded the mortar naturally, an issue we'd have to deal with soon, more global tuck-pointing.

I'd been dreading the work because I thought I'd make a mess of it and force my neighbors to bear the sight of my unskilled labor, but it didn't look bad, and from the ground you couldn't see a difference. I felt I was making the house more solid, and this was strangely and powerfully gratifying. I liked working with material that would last a long time, pressing it into the gaps of my house to shore it up. My cheeks were cold and my fingers stiff, but there's something about the dark November sky that is invigorating, at least when you know there's a warm house to go into and a fire to light when the work's done.

Earlier I'd salted some meaty short ribs, dredged them in flour, and placed each into sizzling-hot fat till they were golden brown and crisp on all sides, then set them in a cast-iron enamel pot with some stock, some onions, and tomatoes, to braise. The kitchen would be rich with that aroma as well when I went inside.

Strange, I thought, again, the hawk reloaded with mortar, that when I lived elsewhere, I yearned for home, and now, though back a dozen years and having fallen into this big old house, the longing continues undiminished, and yet nothing seems wrong with this. In one of the most famous dramatic scenes in Western literature, the balcony scene, Juliet says to her love, "And yet I wish but for the things I have"—here is an ecstatic sense of infinite love—"the more I give to thee, the more I have." I guess it was like that for me with home. A sense that deep gray of winter's coming on, the day's sharp wind and dense cloud cover, the grass still redolent, Thanksgiving near, made this longing poignant. I wished for the home I had.

Most of what I've written in books has focused on men who labor with their hands, all of whom are guided by the work of their predecessors. This point is especially salient for me in the work of the chef. The fundamental techniques a chef uses, those most basic tenets of his or her work, such as stock and sauce making, braising tough meats or sautéing tender ones, rely on principles of heat and cold that have existed since humankind first realized, many thousands of years ago, that heat changed the texture and flavor of food; their work is daily informed by the work of French chefs of several centuries before them, from La Varenne to Carême to Escoffier.

I was fortunate to meet, work with, and write about one of the country's lionized American chefs, Thomas Keller, as watchful a craftsman as I have met, and he liked to say that if you were a really good cook, you could travel back in time and be at home in any kitchen, because food and cooking work today as they always have. When you braise tough meat, it is today as it always has been: brown it first in hot fat, then cook gently in liquid. But what his observation meant to me was that because cooking relied on the same processes now as ever, because a cook in the seventeenth century was feeling and smelling and seeing the same things when he braised, say, oxtail, as I did when I braised oxtail, and if I paid attention to the process, enjoyed the sizzle and aroma of floured meat hitting the fat, keeping watch over the cooking of a deepening stew, I connected in a way with that seventeenth-century cook; I connected to all those people who had done exactly what I was doing. I affirmed my own humanity by making stew. This was part of the great pleasure and profound satisfaction of cooking, this connection.

If you eat a great classic dish all your life—onion soup, for instance—the experience can become almost ritualistic; part of the pleasure of eating a good bowl of onion soup, Keller asserted, is that you connect to all the onion soups you have ever eaten. He's right. The idea of onion soup is a reference point against which you measure each actual one, and all your experiences with onion soup—from the seventies sludge in a crock to the to the one you watched your wife eat in the hotel on your honeymoon to the ethereal one you found in a country inn, by yourself, on a cold fall day—those onion-soup experiences accumulate and become a part of a timeline of onion-soup experiences that grows richer with each successive one, a great big connect-the-dots picture, a mystery until the end. This is partly the reason we enjoy returning to some foods over and over again.

The point in bringing up this onion-soup business is to suggest that to be engaged in the continuum of a house is not ultimately what's so important to me—though that alone is great good fortune. It is to be in the same house for a long time in the city where I was born. For me it paves the way toward the ultimate connection, to God, or the life force, or whatever you want to call the overmastering order maker in an otherwise chaotic universe. To tread daily the same paths I did as a child, to school and then home, to friends' homes, then back to mine, this is important.

When I worked at my father's while Donna worked on the house, I ran at midday. That work in my old house, that daily run, staked me to my history, to all my former selves.

And the same connective, onion-soup powers rise out of the routines of home: mowing the lawn, the route to the grocery store, the smell of the kitchen when no one is cooking, the senses of every day, experienced without thought or reflection but powerfully absorbed. It will be the same routine my children absorb (and they may need to resent me for my routine as I needed to resent my father his). My daughter and son might even play baseball on the same fields I played on. The thought of that recalls the passion with which *I* lived for those ball games—my passion for a baseball game then exceeds in intensity most passions I feel now, in flabby middle age, for *anything*—not to mention the onrushing new and raw sensations of anguish and joy over girls, who are now moms I still know.

A love of home is ultimately a connection with the life circle, no different from the seasons. To live here is to engage in the continuum of my father's life, leading to mine, leading to my children's, and this obviates what might otherwise be our biggest fear—fear of death, ceasing to exist. A recognition of this continuum, and a deliberate effort to observe it, makes any such regret or worry, about death or the apparent lack of meaning in life—it makes *all* that *inappropriate;* it gives a sense of life integrity to each day and to each day's prosaic routines. It's important to roast a chicken once a week or make your mom's pasta that you ate throughout your childhood or braise short ribs if you pay attention. It was likewise important to me now to be scraping dark mortar into the spaces between the bricks of my house.

I was not doomed like Kley to stop in a neighborhood no longer mine, to stare through a rental-car window at a house, at his lost time. I lived here still. Kley probably wouldn't choose the word "doomed"— I'm sure he enjoys the experience of gazing. It's something we do. Not long ago, when Donna visited her dad on Long Island, he picked her up at La Guardia, and instead of heading north, he returned to gaze with his daughter and grandchildren at the house his father had built on 169th Street in Flushing, Queens, off Forty-fifth Avenue. It was happy and sad at the same time. Do we have a word that means happy and sad at the same time? "Nostalgia" is as close as we can get, I think, but that word is diminished almost beyond meaning now. "Return pain," perhaps. Maybe "home pain," since home retains its warmer connotations, ease and gladness.

These are sentiments that have always been a part of me, naturally and insistently. Kley and I would slip through the sliding screen door to the lowest floor of his grandmother's house in damp swimsuits, to steal another ice cream sandwich. It was a kind of elegant rec room, with a player piano. We ran continually the song "Those Were the Days" by Mary Hopkin. We sang and danced to it. I remember sensing the irony then. I recognized then that these were those days, and I knew then they wouldn't last. I tried to tell to Kley this, was unable to articulate it, though I knew he sensed it, too. Neither of us understood what irony was, of course. Now I found the song embarrassingly simplistic and mawkish, but the pathos was somehow immediately and richly accessible to a five-year-old, and so we danced, and I was even then happy-sad, until we returned to our imaginary games in the pool in the sun and felt infinitely happy again.

I called my first novel *A Way Home,* which were the best words of the whole unpublishable lot. I liked the double meaning you could read into it. Away, Home. The simultaneous desire to flee and to return. I could choose to be still, caught between both, or I could choose one, away home or a way home, and homeward it was. To stay home had a velocity all its own. It haunted me.

Returning to the streets that I grew up on, to be forever surrounded by the weather that was part of my sycamore heart, the smells of the leaves and the grass and the rain on its sandstone sidewalks, was not only the key to the practical comforts that made daily work fruitful and life fun, a good house in a neighborhood with a lot of kids, but was in fact fundamental to a deep, spiritual contentedness, a sense of immortality. This truly was why, I was only now coming to fully understand, I had to return to Cleveland. Like a salmon returning to spawn, like the eels of the Sargasso Sea fluttering back to the brackish waters of Maine and Brittany, I was just more wildlife acting on instinct. The intention to live where I was born was not something I ignored or explained away, but rather embraced. To return to these streets, to me, in this way, felt majestic, a fantastic victory.

"Hey, Michael!"

I pressed another line of charcoal gray mortar between two bricks, then turned. I spotted Thomas across the street on his front porch about two hundred feet away, the front porch built by John G. W. Cowles, Rockefeller's real estate man, in 1904. Thomas was perched upon a post of the porch rail. The street was otherwise silent and deserted. I gripped the top rung of the ladder as I looked.

Thomas turned his back to me, dropped his pants to his ankles and bent over, flashing a pale, hairy ass. He really hung it out there, waved it a little, a substantial moon. He stood, pulled up his pants, zipped, buckled, then headed for his front door. He saluted me and shouted, "Keep up the good work!"

Community. That's what it's all about I thought. This was a damned good neighborhood. And it was going to stay that way, I sensed. I stepped down off the ladder and cleaned up. Inside, Donna was painting. She remembered how frustrating it was to try to paint when the kids were in the house. She'd used this day to paint a hallway. She liked the meditative quality of the work, and she'd done so much of it, she'd gotten pretty skilled at it.

Donna had become deliberate. Once naturally impatient and impulsive, eager for the finishing and the getting onto the next, she had found the pleasure of process—the kids had slowed her down, forced her to stop measuring her days by accomplishments and instead enjoy the perfecting of whatever work she'd had time for. You could not have expectations of *quantity* of accomplishments when you took care of children; it wasn't simply their being demanding but also the unpredictability of those demands. You could, on the other hand, relish the *quality* of whatever small advances you might be able to make in a day. A stone path laid, a shelf hung, a room painted. But what was the point of these accomplishments, she asked, when you intended to move away?

This is an important fact to remember generally, I think. When you're not going to stay somewhere, you don't tend to take care of it—that's just the way it is. It's OK to trash a hotel room. You're not coming back, it's hardly filled with precious material, and someone else will take care of it. But what happens to a *country* where we all leave our places on an average of four years? Who will take care to build and maintain an excellent structure, a durable house, that they're going to leave pretty soon? We're going to construct houses and buildings that are increasingly like the rooms at Best Western and the Sheraton; our houses are going to have the quality and appeal of a generic hotel room.

Donna needed her own house—otherwise the time and work she

loved, almost all accomplishments, were temporary. She needed a permanent habitat to meaningfully anchor her days. The whole country needed this, as far as I was concerned. But at least Donna had it, one that we could both make fine, and I knew her work would also follow.

In the life of a house, there is no better time than the weeks between Halloween and the Christmas holidays. A house's purpose is here most fulfilled. With our house finally complete, Donna wanted to throw a party, a proper Christmas party. She often said, "It doesn't matter where we are. Home is where we're together." And that was true, but when we were together in our house, that was the best, and this year, with the place at last, if not finished, at least complete—no rooms any longer had stacked furniture beneath plastic sheets and huge boxes still taped shut from the move—we were ready to open it up. What was more, all the trimmings of Christmas filled the empty spaces beautifully. The living room especially—it went from nice but kind of bare to comfortably stuffed, elegant, rich. We put up a tree, and the star nearly touched the ceiling. A collection of stuffed bears lined the mantel, above which hung an enormous wreath. All manner of candles were laid out on tables. The house seemed meant for this treatment; the layout of the rooms, their shape, embraced the opulence of the season.

It was going to be a helluva lot of work, this party, and I was sure it was going to cost us hundreds of dollars more than the holidays normally did, and we didn't have this money to spare. But Donna wanted a Christmas party, with adults and kids in equal number, just people from the street and a couple others, a gathering of our closest neighbors and their kids.

"This is one of the *reasons* I wanted to have a house like this," she'd said. "This is part of what it's *for*. I want our kids to have great memories of Christmas." Interesting, I thought, that it's not just to enjoy the Christmas present but to enjoy the Christmas past even more. Can you plan nostalgia?

I bit my tongue about cash flow and reminded myself this was not the time to be so damned cheap, nor to worry. Not with Donna looking so good and so happy. It pleased her to make the house so beautiful. The kids walked around like it was a museum, examining all the objects that they were growing to associate with the festivity of the season—the giant nutcracker soldier, the porcelain Santa and reindeer—but it wasn't a museum. It was their home, and they could pick this stuff up. The house smelled of pine roping and the Christmas tree and fragrant candles and cinnamon steeping in cider.

The day of the party, I put in a half day's work, then repaired to the kitchen to begin cooking.

Fifty neighbors, half of them kids, were expected on what was to be a cold, clear night. That number amazed me. Excepting my mom and her boyfriend, who'd be arriving an hour before things began, and my dad and one of our closest friends, everyone lived on this street, notably new neighbors, a family who'd just moved into the old Coakley house. They'd be living in their attic this winter as we had in ours now two winters ago, while they restored their grand house, a Tudor built in 1907.

Donna had lit every candle—we scarcely needed electric lights, they were so abundant. And I had a moment to walk by myself around the first floor of the house, which happened to be deserted, the kids way upstairs, all the others in their rooms getting ready. I almost never had this kind of time before a party. The lights were dimmed, the tree lights sparkled. Fires crackled on both hearths. Candlelight flickered on the walls, the ornaments of the season casting unfamiliar shadows. It was a finished house in this form. Not only had Donna made it beautiful, but she'd somehow made it feel magical. The living room had become the kind of place where you might find a present addressed to you and never learn where it came from. The hallway glowed with candlelight. Donna had hung a candle in the foyer as well. The long expanse from dining room, whose table was laid for a large buffet, to the kitchen was the spirit of Christmas present, with food spread out on the island and a white-bean-and-sausage soup simmering on the stove.

So I strolled around in my own house, just looking at objects, feeling at peace, and the fire alarm began. I felt so calm that it hardly fazed me.

I'd never figured these things out. There were nineteen of them, about thirteen too many. They were hardwired to each other and to the main circuit breaker, so when one went off, they all went off, a piercing, echoing *beeeep-beeeep-beeeep* followed by a brief pause. Each contained a transistor battery, which meant you couldn't throw the switch to silence them, even if there wasn't a fire, which I quickly determined was the case. Then it stopped. And when the first guests arrived, my old friend Dave and his family, coming in through the back door, the alarms began again.

I didn't know what to do, but I felt surreally unconcerned. Because it was a families party, everyone arrived within a span of twenty minutes, so my peaceful, magical downstairs was now jammed with kids and adults, many of them sticking fingers in their ears and wincing.

Hoping each time the alarms stopped that *that* would be the end of it, we settled the children before Helga, who sat between fire and tree. Helga lived next to Heather and Thomas; she was a poet who'd been on the street for decades, used to raise goats in her backyard. As soon as she began to read a Christmas story to the kids, the alarms went off again.

Donna said to me, "Michael, you've got to do something."

I called the fire department for advice.

The start of the Christmas story was also the signal for Donna to call Jack across the street, and she had stuck to this plan. Jack, whose daughters were now old enough to baby-sit our kids, owned a Santa suit and liked to use it. He must have paused at his window, seeing the big red truck and flashing light outside our house. Two firemen decked out in enormous gear pounded through the house asking me complex questions about the alarm system, which I simply had never thought much about. On a table in the upstairs hallway, Donna had lit a holiday candle. The fireman stopped at it, glanced at the smoke alarm immediately above it, and blew the candle out. That was his job, I guess. We descended the stairs, and with the two firemen in their rubber coats and boots and firemen hats, it was quickly a comical party-chaos scene—spot the people who don't belong. The reading of the Christmas story never quite came off, which was fine by everyone, and Donna, shrewdly sensing an opportunity, dragged the larger of the firemen into the living room as a show-and-tell object, while the kids craned their necks in grinning wonder. Moments later bells sounded on the porch, Santa hefting several enormous sacks of really good gifts (parents had been instructed to drop one off for their kids in the days before—kids were amazed to get exactly what they wanted, and this enhanced the illusion of Santa's all-knowing nature). Santa trumped the firemen, who were eager to flee. I watched my four-year-old son leaping up and down, a half foot straight up in the air, in the spot right beside Santa, grinning like I'd never seen. *It's Santa, it's really Santa, no, really, Santa is here at our house, Santa,* he was thinking. You could see it. I had never seen him so happy, not even close. Even my eight-year-old daughter, who'd been grilling me and Donna for weeks on the veracity of this Santa character ("Come on, seriously, is Santa Claus like the tooth fairy?")—even she gave in, admitting that there really is a Santa—*I know that's Annie's dad, but there really is a Santa, isn't there?* The whole house was filled with people, sugar-crazed kids pounding through the hallways, toys, tipsy adults eating good food, and Donna completely and thoroughly happy, the perfect host, enjoying her own party along with everyone else enjoying each other and the coming of the holidays, which of course were not coming but were right here right now, in this very moment. We were right now in the center of the best moment of the year in the best possible place, a perfect house.

Acknowledgments

I would like to thank the following people for their help: Steve Charles, editor of *Wabash Magazine* at Wabash College in Crawfordsville, Indiana; Bill Barrow, special-collections librarian, Cleveland State University Library; Kara Hamley O'Donnell, historic preservation planner for Cleveland Heights; Ken Goldberg, librarian and information specialist for the Northeast Ohio Areawide Coordinating Agency; and Rick Hawley, for a helpful early read of the book.

At Viking Penguin: Clare Ferraro, Bruce Giffords, Maureen Sugden, Cliff Corcoran.

My parents, Carole Ruhlman and Richard Ruhlman.

As ever, Ray Roberts and Elizabeth Kaplan.

I'd like to acknowledge Rusty King (1954–2000), a great newspaperman, for his generosity, friendship, and care for our family.

As I hope is clear, none of the preceding story, nor so much else, would have been possible without my wife, Donna, whom I cherish more than I can say in words. She has been uncommonly generous to let me publish a story that's so personal.